A SLICE OF FRIED GOLD

NICK FROST

A SLICE OF

FRIED GOLD

TASTE MY MEMORIES

BLINK
bringing you closer

First published in the UK by Blink Publishing
An imprint of The Zaffre Publishing Group
A Bonnier Books UK company
4th Floor, Victoria House,
Bloomsbury Square,
London, WC1B 4DA

Owned by Bonnier Books
Sveavägen 56, Stockholm, Sweden

Hardback – 9781788707886
Trade Paperback – 9781788707923
Ebook – 9781788707893
Audio Digital Download – 9781788707909

A CIP catalogue of this book is available from the British Library.

Designed by Envy Design Ltd
Printed and bound by Clays Ltd, Elcograf S.p.A.

1 3 5 7 9 10 8 6 4 2

Blink Publishing is an imprint of Bonnier Books UK
www.bonnierbooks.co.uk

*To my kids ... if you can't cook at least an omelette
by the time I die, I've failed you.*

Contents

Foreword

Let me start by saying, I AM NOT A CHEF. Not. A. Chef. Not by a long way. I wouldn't ever dare pretend to be something that takes YEARS of toil and sweat and tears to become. To call yourself a chef you have to earn that shit. I'm a cook. At best. A self-taught cook. I'm proud of that. I may not know the difference between a sous vide and a Su Pollard but I can slice a mushroom faster than any muthafucka.

One of the questions I get asked a lot by people who believe the film/TV industry is just one long, Krug-soaked premiere is 'Who's the most famous person you've ever met?' I get it. For a civilian it's fun, it's exciting, the chance to meet famous people, to rub shoulders with the stars, it's glamorous. It isn't glamorous. Maybe for RiRi, not for MeMe. Having to wear a suit to go and watch a film is annoying to me. I hate it. I'd make the film for free and you'd pay me to attend the premiere.

The truth is I've met loads of incredibly famous/successful people but, for me, I'm often working with them. One has to be professional. Even if you are a fan, I've always felt it's best to just get on and knuckle down and get the work done, support where necessary, be a sounding board, a straight man, the funny one or just give my lines off camera to them with as much commitment and passion as I did when the camera was pointed at me. That's my job.

Maybe at some point down the line I'd fan boy out a bit to them, or I'd phone up Simon Pegg and squeal down the line that

I just met So and So. (I once, during the casting process of *Paul*, sat and ate a chicken Caesar salad with Sigourney Weaver. When she left I reached over and popped one of her uneaten croutons into my mouth. A tangible memory of the dream I'd just lived through.)

No. The people I always get starstruck meeting are chefs. Michelin-starred chefs. I'm awful around them. I had lunch once at Angela Hartnett's place and she came out to say hi and I couldn't talk to her. I'm terrible. When René Redzepi from Noma followed me on Instagram, I squealed and span round giddy as a prom queen.

I feel I've just always understood the commitment and graft it takes, day in day out, to become a Michelin-starred chef. I've always felt that cooking can be found hanging out on the corner of Art and Science. I love that. I'm fascinated by it. What talent, to master Art AND Science.

I have had some commercial experience though. As a 21-year-old, I began working as a waiter at Chiquito's Mexican restaurant in Staples Corner. I imagined I'd stay for three or four months in order to make some scratch and figure out 'what next'. I was there for seven-ish years. A lot of years, more years than I expected, but fuck it. The tips were good and I was a fantastic waiter, my as yet undiagnosed ADHD loved the chaos and lunacy of even the busiest shift. I could comfortably serve, often 12 tables at once.

After some time though the customers began to wear on me slightly. There are only so many times I could take people sending racks of ribs back because 'They had bones in', or once a woman complained her margarita was too cold so asked me to put more ice in it (?). Then there was the rudest man in the world who treated me like shit for three hours and then threw a 50p at me as he left. (The joke was on him though as not only had I used that 50p to scratch the fuck out of his Merc, but I had also dropped a tiny piece of meat into his Veggie Chimichanga. I figured I'd have my revenge in this life AND the next.) Don't fuck with waiters.

I moved into the kitchen, I moved away from the limelight into the dirt and sweat and shit and I LOVED it. At first, I learned how to use the massive knives. Then I spent hours and hours slicing huge bags of onions and peppers, then they taught me how to make the sauces; sometimes, when it was busy they let me on the dessert station, or garnishes. By and by I worked my way up the line until I became responsible for the broiler.

I loved to see the little B next to my name for the Saturday night shift on the schedule. It meant I was the broiler man. The broiler was a huge gas-powered griddle/barbecue thing. It was big and scary and fucking hot. It was maybe 4ft wide by 3ft tall. A ticket would roll out of the machine and someone would then shout out what was on the ticket. Anything meat was mine. Sometimes, on a busy weekend, I had the whole thing filled with hundreds of steaks and chickens all at a different point of readiness, all for different tables. It was fucking mayhem. Great, lovely mayhem.

When Saturday was over me and the other Ugandans who worked the line (I was the only non-Ugandan there) would slump against the wall outside, smoking, knackered but also oddly proud. They had all taught me little bits of Ugandan and I would keep them rolling around with laughter doing a little skit in my broken Ugandan. Essentially (and I feel this is a definite you had to be there thing), the sketch was about the Ugandan Police pulling up a poor man who had a monkey hidden in the boot of his car. Big Ugandan lolz. My Ugandan connection meant I also got to meet Idi Amin's wife at a wedding once. She seemed nice enough.

While Chiquito's was my first job in a kitchen, the truth was I had always cooked. Always had a fascination with it. Afraid of the flames and gas, the knives, but thrilled by the magical outcome. Ever since I was eight, nine, ten, my mum and dad had always let me watch and help them cook. Those memories I have of them now, and the secrets they imparted to me during these lessons, are some of the nicest memories I have of them.

Once I became a teenager, life got very complicated and difficult, and we were never really the same family again. Debt, grief and alcoholism meant the cooker was rarely turned on after that.

At the time of writing this foreword my mum has been dead for 16 years. Wow. What a fucking tragedy. Although our relationship was hard and bittersweet, she gave me things I can never truly thank her for. She started in me a fire and a desire to know how to cook.

There is very little I have left that actually belonged to my mum. I've no idea why. I often lie awake at night and think to myself, 'Where the fuck is everything?' Same with my dad. Where is the evidence of their lives? Apart from a few pictures and the odd painting my dad did, or bit of tat, I don't have anything. There is nothing.

When I look around at my house, at all the bits and trinkets and art and just bits of shit I own or secretly hoard (they call it ephemera!), I can't imagine it all just disappearing when I die. But disappear it did. All of it. In fact, apart from a big metal spoon my mum used to cook with which doubled as an item with which to hit me from time to time, there is nothing physical to mark her ever even being on Earth.

When I was ten, the same age as my oldest son is currently, the thing I liked to eat more than anything was my mum's Beef Stroganoff. It was rich, it was glossy, spicy and complicated. I loved it. Over the years, Mum started to show me how to cook this Stroganoff. I remember one day when I was maybe 12, flying solo and making it from scratch for them. I carried it into them on a big tray. They sat silently smiling at each other. I recognise that now as pride. They were proud of me. I made them dinner and it was good. I remember feeling the same way I did when René Redzepi followed me on Instagram.

That's where it started for me. I wanted to cook. Explore flavour. Unlock hidden tastes. Blah, blah, blah ... I guess all those things were true, more or less. I think, though, if you dig a little deeper, you'd find all I wanted to feel again was what I felt that day when I wobbled those plates of Stroganoff into the room. I wanted them to feel proud of me.

Now I know, 16 years in, I was actually, albeit subconsciously, gathering up the essence of my mum. The best bits. The sober/loving/funny/playful woman who cooked to feed her family, to nourish them. The woman who was savage and wicked and funny and affectionate. The woman who only appeared when she was sober.

I may not have anything physical (apart from that fucking spoon) but I have something more important. Something tangible that I can touch and smell and even taste. That Beef Stroganoff. Apart from one or two slight changes I've made over the years, improvements I'd call them, it's exactly the same.

For those few seconds when I try that rich, brown, complicated gravy, she is back with me. Or I'd say more accurately, I am back with her. It makes me feel like that little boy again. That, for me, is the power of food. Like dusty old Polaroids, it has the power to send you back in time.

One day, a couple of years ago, I was flicking through an old cookbook when out dropped a folded piece of paper. The page I opened the book at was the recipe for Beef Stroganoff. The folded piece of paper that fell out of that page was my mum's handwritten notes for that very Beef Stroganoff. Her actual handwriting. I sobbed and smelt the writing, hoping there was some of her left.

I knew immediately by the collection of caps, sprinkled randomly over the page, that it was hers. It was amazing. She was with me again, and again I had something tangible that was hers, like that big metal spoon. I knew at that point I had something much more important than the spoon. I had a time machine. I had a way back. A way my kids, who were born years and years after she'd died, could finally meet their savage, wicked, funny, affectionate and complicated grandmother. She would be so proud of me. So proud of them.

So, to honour that, I will teach them to cook. If they can do nothing else, they will be able to cook something, hopefully they will tamper with and adapt and perfect her Stroganoff, my Stroganoff, their Stroganoff, and hopefully they'll transfer on to their children the keys to our time machine. And so on and so on ... what a gift. Hopefully, after I die my kids will keep more than just a spoon I used to hit them with. I mean cook with ... not hit them. And whenever they cook with their children, when I'm 16 years gone, they can say that this was the recipe (turn to page 9) your grandfather taught us to cook, and in doing so they'll know how fucking proud I am of them.

Now & Back Then

Before we start on the cooking, I'm sorry if my measurements are annoying. Everything I make is in my head and I just kind of feel what the dish needs. Sorry, it just suits my way of thinking. (By the way, if I was lying in bed watching a cooking show and I heard the host say something like, 'I just kind of feel what the dish needs ...' I'd lose my fucking mind with rage! If there's one thing I hate about TV cooks it's them being overly earnest. Feel free to throw this book into the bin.)

People on Instagram saying 'I'd love to try and cook but I'm so afraid/don't know where to start ...' I'd say this: don't be afraid to make mistakes. I constantly make mistakes. In terms of bread making it's just flour, water and yeast. Don't be afraid. We're not constructing a fission reactor. You know?

Get a potato, slice it finely. Add slices of onion, knobs of butter, a turn of pepper and some chicken stock, then put it in a very low (140°C) oven for two hours. See what happens. Make notes. Cook longer? Cook for less time at a higher temperature? Does it need salt? Parmesan? How much stock is left? Is the potato soft and amazing? Crispy on top? Does it taste like burnt shit? Yes. Fuck it. It's just a potato and you were experimenting. Who cares? But imagine if it works ... You can do that kind of thing with loads of different foods if you can be arsed. Fried broccoli anyone? You can also just follow recipes. That's okay too. Or, like me, you can look into the techniques of how things work and apply them to lots of different dishes. If you can make a ragù, then you can make ... If you can make a tomato sauce, then you can make ... Etc, etc.

In our house growing up we'd pretty much have the same thing on the same day every week.

Monday – Cawl. (Welsh soup. We're from Pembrokeshire!)

Tuesday – Cold meat from Sunday lunch with homemade chips and baked beans.

Wednesday – Toasted cheese sandwich done in the Breville.

Thursday – Findus crispy pancakes (minced beef) and chips with baked beans/spaghetti hoops.

Friday – Fish and chips from the chip shop. Dad would bring it home with him. Sometimes he'd call before leaving the office and he'd ask what I wanted as a treat from the off-licence. I'd always say, foolishly, 'Surprise me.'

He'd always bring back a fucking Topic. I hate Topic.

Even to this day. I should've just told him what I wanted.
A FUCKING CARAMAC!

Saturday – This was a big day at the pub for Mum and Dad.
We'd probably have a crispy baguette with ham and Cheddar
with crisps and tea for lunch, and then for dinner (after the pub),
we'd have sausage sandwiches with tomato ketchup on white
bread. Dad would have English mustard, it terrified me. If I felt
brave, I'd smell it and it would tear my inner nose up. I'd hand it
back, coughing.

The good thing about them being in the Dr Johnson pub
(Barkingside) all day is that they let me hire any video I wanted
from the paper shop next door. Anything. So, after sausage
sandwiches, and while they slept, mouths agape, cacophony of
snoring, I'd lay on the floor, 12 inches from the TV, head in hands,
watching *Poltergeist*. Or *Phantasm*. Or *The Texas Chainsaw
Massacre* or *The Exorcist*. I was 11.

Sunday – Roast dinner. Delicious. I'd actually prefer it when
Dad cooked lunch. Usually a nice bit of beef (topside – bright red
with no fat), although chicken was also a major player. Dad made
the nicest gravy. His beer of choice was called McEwan's. I can
still see him dumping a whole can into the sizzling veg he'd sat
the beef on to roast. It was delicious and part of ten-year-old me
thought it was a bit naughty because I was essentially drinking
beer. (My own 11-year-old does exactly the same thing if I put
wine in a sauce. He came up to me and whispered, 'I think I feel
a bit drunk!' God bless him.)

I tried to explain to my 11-year-old about my mum's ever-
constant chip pan that sat on the hob, waiting to be used. Almost

everyone I knew had one. It seems crazy now to think of that mass of solidified, bright white lard, dormant, waiting to be activated, cooked with and once again left to go cold and solid. God I miss the 1970s.

CAWL

This is what we ate on Monday. I used to love helping Mum do this. I loved the way the chicken carcass came out clean. (I am not a psychopath.)

So, you will need ...

2 or 3 leeks, washed and halved

1 large onion

2 fat Dutchman's dicks, washed and peeled (in our house we call big carrots Dutchman's dicks. I'm not sure why. I'll always use a bad, slightly racist Dutch accent too, whenever I say it.)

3 or 4 white potatoes, peeled and cut into chunks

1 roasted chicken carcass (or use 6 large chicken thighs instead)

2 tablespoons Paxo (totally optional. I hate it. Mum swore by it.)

First things first, put a nice large stockpot full of water gently on to boil. There's no rush here. It's going to heat up in the background while you do the rest of the prep.

Slice your leeks however you want (I do rings!). I peel my onion, cut it in half and slice it.

Grasp your fat Dutchman's dicks and cut them how you want. Slices, chunks, even whole would be nice. It would look nice served like that. Big bowl of soup with a fat Dutchman's dick floating in it. Rustique!

Again, depending on size: 3 or 4 potatoes cut into chunks.

Once the water comes to the boil, turn it down so it gently plips away and put the chicken carcass in for 30 minutes. Give or take. If the carcass doesn't quite fit, turn it over midway through cooking.

Then ... Take out the chicken and pick off all the meat! Search every nook and cranny on the skeleton. Put to one side ... Bin the bones.

If you didn't roast a chicken the day before and you opted to use the chicken thighs instead, fry them in the bottom of the soup pot first, in a little butter and a little oil (this stops the butter burning) until they're golden brown. Set aside and fill a pot with water. When you add the root veg to the water, add the thighs back in too. Remember to debone and flake the meat off before serving. I'd probably flake a couple of the chicken thighs directly into the serving bowl and paddle the soup on top.

Then ... Add the potatoes and the carrots to the water you boiled the chicken in. Simmer gently until they start to soften. Then add the onion and the leeks. Simmer gently until all the veg are soft and cooked.

At this point, turn the heat off and put all the chicken meat you picked off the carcass back into the pot with the water and the veg.

(If you want to add Paxo stuffing, now is the time to stir

in the two spoonfuls. Although I don't like it.) And that's it. Done. Taste the cawl and season with salt and pepper.

When I make this at home, I serve it like my mum did, with slices of cheap white bread, buttered, and big hunks of very strong Cheddar. (Dad used to put a large spoonful of curry powder on top. Not for me though. Soz, dead dad.)

My mum's side are Welsh, millions of them, and I've been there and grown up there all my life. But I lived in London. The adventures and laughs and tragedy and tears and sheer fucking fear and joy I've had in Wales just fills my heart. I felt special when I said I was Welsh. I felt that I belonged. I know there'd be a ton of Welsh speakers who'd tell me to fuck off back to London, and I understand that too. You can't give Welsh to everyone. It's too sweet.

In my thirties I had a kind of crisis (another fucking one). Just in terms of: who was I? Where was I from? What did it mean to be English? Apart from roasted meats and pantomime (which is pretty good in my book, BTW), I couldn't find much that I identified with.

But when I was in Haverfordwest with my family I felt at home. The Welsh national anthem as sung by the crowd at a rugby international encapsulates that for me. I was watching the rugby the other evening, Argentina v Scotland, and they played 'Flower of Scotland' first and then they played the Argentinian anthem. It went on for about four or five minutes without any singing and I actually thought, 'Oh is this an anthem that has no singing? Is that a thing?' Then, judging by the faces of the players, I thought someone had put on the wrong version of it, or a remixed edition, and then, when I thought the tune was ending, the words started! And what words! Sung with such joy and gusto, pomp even. Yeah, pomp. I liked it.

My favourite anthem is that of Wales. I identify as Welsh, so my anthem is Welsh. I even went as far as learning it and I am incredibly proud of my heritage whenever I can stand and sing it, belting out 'Gwlad! Gwlad!' at full volume. It's a complicated song and piece of music to me. What it means, what it does to me. I have a file on my phone called On Set Sadness. To briefly explain On Set Sadness, it's a playlist that I'll listen to on set if I have to do a scene where crying or real emotion is needed. I play the songs in a certain order until the final song, which is always the Welsh national anthem – the version sung by the crowd at the rugby.

There's been a couple of times when I've utterly misjudged my running order and end up crying before the scene. In which case, someone runs in and they end up dabbing tiger balm into my eyeballs. Same result.

The playlist in no particular order is:

'Vapour Trail' – Ride

'Garden' – Pearl Jam

'Everyone But You' – The Young Veins

'Take Me to Church' – Hozier

'Neighbourhood #1' – Arcade Fire

'Shadows' – Warpaint

'Flakes' – Mystery Jets

'Say Hello, Wave Goodbye' – Soft Cell

'Same Love' – Macklemore & Ryan Lewis

'Seasons' – Chris Cornell

'Stardust' – Johnny Mathis
This is a heavy hitter. This song can literally fuck me up for three
or four hours. Be careful when and where you drop the Mathis
bomb. It's powerful stuff. This is my mum. In a song. This is the
pain and confusion and sadness of everything. I can literally
smell her.

But the winner, for similar reasons ...The Welsh National
Anthem – 'Hen Wlad Fy Nhadau'.
All that passion and pain and joy and pride from people I identify
as my own.
    When I die and as my coffin drifts through the curtain into
the great furnace beyond, the Welsh National Anthem will play
and it's only at that point I will be truly accepted as a Welshman.
Only through death can true acceptance be found.

I'm having a nice fantasy. As I die and leave this plain, I begin to
shuffle into a new phase of the experience. I can hear thousands
of people cheering and screaming and singing and I open my eyes
and I'm somewhere I know very well.
    I'm hanging on to the side of a scrum, heaving the mass of
meat and smells forward with all my might. I see the scrum half
funnelling the ball out the back of the scrum through the number

eight's feet. I stand up from my position as openside flanker and peel round the back of the rapidly collapsing scrum.

It's now that I really see where I am for the first time. I'm at the Millennium Stadium in Cardiff and we're playing England in the Rugby World Cup final. As I banana round the back, the number nine pops it up to me and I bag that ball, pin my ears back and I'm off for the line.

England's number ten tries to tackle me, but he gets a knee in the face and goes down like a sack of privately educated shit. I dive for the line and slide over, scoring a beautiful try. The whistle blows and the crowd go bonkers! We've won the World Cup!

What would be on your On Set Sadness playlist?

I don't have my mam any more, but when the camera scans across the people in that stadium wearing big daffodils, singing their souls out, tears often rolling down their cheeks, I see in those people my mam. My family and, to that end, my people. For me, it feels more of a bond than a shoulder of lamb and Widow Twanky. (My second favourite anthem is Italy.)

BEEF STROGANOFF

My mum always used rump steak. It was cheap and flavoursome. Traditionally fillet steak is used but the cooking time of this recipe means a cheaper, fattier cut is preferable over fillet steak. It's also expensive. So now I use rib-eye.

2 rib-eye steaks (maybe 500g in total)

Worcestershire sauce (3 seconds' worth of shakes)

2 tablespoons curry powder

3 or 4 teaspoons English mustard

Let's start with this ... Get a nice, sturdy, wooden chopping board. Not a glass chopping board or a tiny chopping board or a tiny glass chopping board, this isn't an episode of *Come Dine With Me*. If you have a tiny glass chopping board, close this book and don't open it again until Amazon have delivered a nice, sturdy, wooden chopping board. Please.

Then, using a nice sharp knife, cut the steaks into very thin slices. If you need a human object to quantify very thin slices, think of a piece of meat the size of a £1 lighter you'd buy at a market.

Put the slices into a nice large bowl. Again, this is a bugbear of mine when you watch a cooking show and see them putting a ton of ingredients into a tiny bowl. Then they stir it and it all slops over the side. Fuck that. Use a big bowl.

Now, flood the bowl with Worcestershire sauce, the curry powder and the English mustard, this may bite your nostrils a bit. Give it a good stir – I use my hands to get everything really coated well. This should not be overly wet, it should coat the beef nicely. Cover with foil or clingfilm and stick it in the fridge. Marinate this overnight if you can. It does make for a richer, deeper flavour, but if you can't be arsed, leave it in the fridge for, at the very minimum, 2 hours.

Make sure you take the beef out of the fridge at least an hour before you use it. Then, in a big, deep frying pan, add a couple of tablespoons of oil and a knob of butter and fry the beef strips in batches. DO NOT throw it all in at once. Do it little by little.

Once the pieces are brown and your kitchen smells

lovely, put the fried steak back into the bowl and leave to one side to rest a bit. As the steak sits and rests it'll release some steamy, beefy moisture that you *definitely* will want to use.

For the next stage you will need ...

butter

extra virgin olive oil

1 extra-large white/Spanish onion, halved and sliced (maybe an extra half too if you're cooking a big batch)

1 tablespoon(ish) plain flour

2 tablespoons tomato purée stirred into 200ml boiling water

beef stock – either a cube or the good stuff you get from proper butchers, or even, at a push, 2 Oxo cubes (this is what my mum used to use)

Now, in a large frying pan, melt a big knob (hehe) of butter and add a nice hit of extra virgin olive oil. Let them heat up. The butter will foam and start to colour.

Add the onions and cook them until they are translucent (a bit see-through) and they're starting to brown and catch on the bottom of the pan. This is cool, all those little bits that burn and catch and stick to the bottom give it a nice flavour.

Turn up the heat slightly and add the flour to the onions. I always feel at this point like I've fucked up a bit. Adding the flour to the buttery, brown onions makes them go all congealed and stick to the bottom, and it looks awful. Even now there's a moment when I think, 'I've fucked it.'

I haven't. We haven't. Turn the temperature down a bit and then, bit by bit, add the tomato purée and boiling water. And then the stock too. Scrape the bottom of the pan with a wooden spoon to get all the bits off. Adjust the heat so the liquid is gently rolling.

Now, take the bowl with the beef in and tip the lot into the oniony liquid. Even that lovely juice that's oozed out of the resting steak. Give it a stir and now we wait. I'm not sure how long this is going to take. We want the liquid to reduce down until it's a rich, thick gravy. The beef should be not quite fall-apart-tender but really, really close. We're almost finished.

This is the point where I say goodbye to my mum's original recipe. This is my little adaptation. Bye, Mum.

You will need ...

butter

1 whole punnet of mushrooms – any kind (I use either
chestnut, little button, or portobellos chopped up.
Don't use enoki or chanterelle or cep. You could, I guess,
I just haven't.)

1 bunch of flat-leaf parsley the size of a tangerine,
ball it tight and chop it finely

soured cream

Melt a large knob of butter in a frying pan. Add all the mushrooms. Fry until golden brown. Stir in the parsley.

You can do this at any point during the cooking process and leave them in a bowl until you're ready to use them.

Once the beef is tender, and the gravy is rich and spicy and complex, stir in the cooked mushrooms. At this point I'll stir in a tablespoon of soured cream, a big mill of black pepper and I'll taste it to see if it needs salt. If yes, salt.

That's it. We've always served it with white rice. Mum used to put the rice around the outside of the plate and put the steamy beefy stew in the centre. So that's what I do too. Unlike Mum, I always serve it with roasted sweet potato. I wonder how my kids will adapt it?

Thanks, Mum! Enjoy.

TUNA PASTA

I spent a lot of time as a kid at my Auntie Linda's down in Haverfordwest, escaping from my own parents. I was angsty, what can I say? My Auntie Linda is very Welsh but she married an Italian beefcake (Uncle Giuliano) in the 1970s and immediately became Italian. She's an amazing woman. I watched her cook this once when I was, like, 13 or 14. God I was angsty, endlessly riding a bus listening to the Smiths or Spacemen 3 on my tape Walkman and wishing my parents were dead. Tracing the path of a lonely raindrop as it trickled down the outside of a steamy window. When Auntie Linda served it up to me, I didn't know what to make of it. I wasn't used to proper, non-processed food really (apart from the Findus crispy pancakes), but I was brave and it tasted amazing. I loved it and made a point of remembering how she did it.

This is the version that I make my kids. They LOVE IT. (And they're fussy fuckers sometimes.)

Here goes ...

Gently fry two cloves of chopped garlic and half a finely chopped white onion. Don't let it burn. Be gentle. Use a fair bit of nice extra-virgin olive oil.

While this is happening. Chop up, like, six big, ripe, deep-red tomatoes that smell like summer. (Me and the boys are often stood in a grocery shop while I make them smell endless different tomatoes. I love it.) Don't deseed or skin. Once they're chopped, add them to the frying pan. You may want to turn the heat up slightly. (Just a little.)

If the green vine (stalk) the tomatoes came attached to smells nice too, stick it in the pan. It'll impart a nice summery, Mediterranean vibe. (Obviously take it out at the end.)

In terms of cooking and the heat on the pan, I find that I'm constantly bumping the flame up and down when I cook. Over the years I often judge how something's getting on by the sound it makes. You get to know the difference between a rolling boil and little plips. This needs to be something in between. Brips.

Once the tomatoes are in and the heat goes up, give them a stir/toss and then turn the heat down. I'd say slowly cook for at least 30 minutes. Plips. After about ten minutes, I add about 300ml water. I always have a little cup of water nearby when I cook. If something looks a bit dry, sprinkle in a few splashes of water.

And that's it. That'll be the tomato sauce. You can use it for loads of things. On its own tossed over a bit of penne or spaghetti for the kids. They love it. You can also poach meatballs in it. Or poach a nice piece of firm white fish in it (with white beans and parsley) or spicy sausages.

This sauce is a staple. It's one of those things that once you can cook it well, you never forget it. It's cheap, it's easy, and it can be adapted to be used in loads of other things. It opens doors in terms of things you can use it for. Learn the technique, not the recipe.

However, here, what we use it for is Tuna Pasta. Once the sauce is cooked, taste it and add salt and pepper if it needs it.

Then ... Open up a can of tuna (or two depending how many are eating) and chop it/stir it into the sauce. Distribute well.

Big pot of water. Salt. Olive oil. Boil hard and add the spaghetti. When it's cooked, I'd like to say, in keeping with some age-old Italian culinary heritage, that the pasta should be served al dente, but my kids moan that it's raw and it winds me up, so I wait the extra three minutes and serve it like a pensioner's hard-on.

Drain the pasta, retaining a little of the hot water and then transfer the tomato and tuna sauce into the spaghetti pan and stir well.

Sometimes I cook the sauce in the morning and leave it covered in the pan until we eat later that day. It doesn't need to be hot. Mixing it with the freshly boiled spaghetti instantly reheats it.

Serve up a bowl each with a glug of nice olive oil and a turn of black pepper. I also suggest heavily grating Parmesan all over this mutha, but maybe that's just me.

BREAD

For a long time, I never made bread. Actually, I made bread once, a small, white loaf. It turned out nice, crispy and brown. It filled my kitchen with memories and hope. (Whenever you read a sentence like that in this book, please realise a Japanese wind ghost who lives inside one of my teeth has briefly taken control of my hands. I'll keep it in though, as I think it adds a wistful melancholy to the prose. Arigato, Tooth ghost-san.)

Like 66,000,000 other Brits, I didn't care about bread or where it came from as long as it was in my bread bin, relatively free from mould and I could lightly butter a piece and put some strawberry jam on it. That was enough for me. I never thought about making my own. It seemed so complicated and full of chemistry and none of my business, except it was my business. I made it my business, and I'm glad I did.

Every now and then my partner Hayley and the ladies gather at the house for a lunch or a light supper, and I love it! I love to cater for them, I love feeding the girls. I always make a fresh bread, and it always disappears. Now I know a bit about yeast and its ways, it makes me want to broaden my knowledge and make brioche or a chocolate babka, or a panettone! When I read the recipes on the page I can hear my muscular sofa-dweller shouting from the front room 'Fuck off!!!' But why? It's a recipe. What have I got to lose? How many people do you know who can make brioche? Or panettone? I know NONE. If the world collapsed and humans needed to start again, I'd be the baker. That said, I've no idea where I'd purchase wheat. Maybe I should learn to grow wheat. Yeah, that's what I'll do. Wheat. Wheat and 3D-printed weapons.

Anyway ... When I decided I wanted to make bread, I read so

many different bits of recipes for bread. There's literally millions to learn, and it's in a completely different language. From the hours of scanning and looking at nice pictures, my brain decided we'd make focaccia. It seemed super simple, and it was only flour, yeast, water, salt and olive oil. Easy.

There is a movement, it seems, to overly complicate something people have done for thousands of years, instinctively. Not just bread either. I got so confused reading the language of bread. What percentage hydration am I doing? How warm should my Ramgalp be? What is a Ramgalp? What flour should I use? I don't want to use a thermometer. I really want it to be easy. Surely people made focaccia in Italy 2,000 years ago without using battery-powered Bluetooth temperature probes, right? I honestly don't think temperature probes had been invented then.

I used regular plain flour. I bought a sachet of dried bread yeast, which since that first time I've bought many different times and got a lot of different results. Yeast is very interesting. A live fungus that will eat the sugar in your flour and guff out little bubbles as you ferment it and let it rise. Thanks yeast.

So, the recipe tells me to get a big bowl. I like. Flour goes in. Then, on one half of the flour, sprinkle the salt. On the other half, sprinkle the yeast. Never the twain shall meet. The salt will kill the yeast: keep it separate. Okay. Now I stir it all together and slowly add about 200ml warm water, and also a big glug of good extra virgin olive oil. I use a wooden spatula and bring it all together.

Unusually for me, I completely follow the recipe's instructions. I'm beginning to see magic happen in the bowl, strands are forming, it's warm and it smells like bread. It smells so yeasty, it's quite something. Once it's all come together, I keep reading down and it says to leave it in the bowl in the fridge for 48 hours. Balls. Okay, whatever.

For me, having to wait 48 hours for anything is a complete killer. Re-reading the theory it should slow down the pace of the ferment and put a lot of great flavour into my focaccia. Great. Okay, I'll wait. Two days later my phone's alarm goes off and I know it's time. It's 2:30am and I nervously remove the bread dough from the fridge and remove the clingfilm. Peering inside it doesn't look like the dough in the book. Not at all. I instinctively know it's kind of fucked.

Nothing has risen. It's beige and flat, watery, there's no bubbles in it at all. It seems completely dead. Usually, I'd put this in the oven just to see what happens but with this 'matter' it seems disrespectful. Fuck. The dough looks like something a science teacher makes in class to show children the method they use when a factory produces slime. Or how BFGoodrich vulcanises rubber. It's a total fail. I'm not giving up.

I read loads of different recipes. Loads. It's so confusing. I'm not sure what to do next. Why didn't I have to knead that one? I thought bread had to be kneaded. Through the research I find out that yeast and salt hate each other. Lots of recipes tell me to keep them apart completely. Separate for as long as possible. Okay. I think my salt killed the yeast. Sonofabitch.

I find a recipe which says I should have a plastic jug with warm water in and add the yeast to that, let it bubble and bloom, a sure sign it's alive, and then combine it with the flour and salt. This is the one. This makes sense to me. Lots of recipes that use this method say I need to measure the water temperature precisely with a probe. Again, this is a new thing. I can't imagine old Nonna Focaccia had a probe. I find recipes written by people who describe their warm water as being lukewarm. Too cold and the yeast stays dead. Too hot and you scald it to death. It needs to be just right. One lady I ask says if you can put your fingers in, that's fine. So that's how I test it. Easy.

I pour 300ml lukewarm tap water into a plastic jug and stir a couple of heaped teaspoons of yeast into it. I feel it's too much, but last time was shit, so let's go the opposite way and dial it back if I need to. I make a subconscious point of remembering this difference between loaf two and loaf zero. I've got ten minutes to wait while it hopefully comes back to life. I peruse further recipes. Oh. It says never use tap water, it should be filtered. Balls. Why? Nonna Focaccia didn't have a water filter.

The alarm on my phone goes off and I remove the tea towel I had laid over the jug. I felt like if it were dark it might be better. I peer into the jug and something has/is actually happening. First of all, the smell – super yeasty and deep bready notes. There's a raft of bubbles and foam now on the surface of the water. Okay. Let's do this ... Quick ...

I briefly stir the flour and salt mixture and I pour in half of the liquid at first. Using a clean spatula, I begin to bring it all together. It's coalesced into a pleasing strand ball. I glug three seconds' worth of olive oil into the dough and a bit more water. As I'm still using a no-knead method, I just keep bringing it all into the bowl until it's now a lovely doughy ball. Wow. What a nice thing to do. I feel so relaxed I sleep, right there, standing up for 11 minutes.

I have a nice big, clean, silver bowl. I lay Doughball into bed and slap it. I then drizzle over more olive oil and leave it to prove for 30 minutes. There's so much chemistry involved in this. I like the fact there's old breads and you don't have to be a scientist to make them. I don't want to filter my water, or use ice, or have to buy a digital thermometer. Would the finished loaf be better? Maybe. Maybe not. I'm not sure I'd be qualified to know.

After 30 minutes my alarm sounds and I look into the bowl. It's risen a bit. I gently take strands from the ends of Doughball and pull them into the centre and stick it to the main body. I turn it a bit, loosen it from the bowl. I don't know if this is going to work but I'm really enjoying the process. I do the same process five times in all over the space of two and a half hours.

It's not as huge as I expected. After maybe two or three hours of proving it reached its zenith and then didn't get much bigger. Hmmm. Note added to brain. I use my implement and turn the ball out onto an olive oil-lined baking tray. After perusing many of the ancient manuscripts, I decide to leave it for another 30 minutes to chill in the tray and rise into the corners ready for when we get to do the good bit with focaccia ... You make holes all over its surface with your fingers! What?! Yeah, you jab your stiff fingers into the dough and then you cover the whole lot with an oily, watery, salty brine. Yes, brine. Some of the books say the amount of liquid that goes on here is fairly alarming. They promise, though, that the dough and the heat from the oven just absorb all the water, it also makes for a super crispy loaf. I'm jumping ahead of myself ...

Turn the oven on to *hot* hot. 220°C at least. It should be plenty hot for when it's needed. My phone trills again. This is it ... I pull the tea towel off and there it is. The dough has spread out and has filled the tray. Wow. I love how vibrant and active it is. I could take a leaf out of Dough's book, I could learn a thing or two from Dough.

Here comes the good bit ... I get to stick my stiff fingers all up in Dough's shit. It should leave big, thick holes all over the dough. It's focaccia's trademark, the dimples. Oh, and the brine. The dimples and the brine. I remove my fingers from their individual shrouds and I stiffly jab them deep into Dough's guts. It does not go well. I've never been so close to victory only to fuck it up. Something awful has happened. It just sinks flat.

All the yeast farts the dough had been storing have just gone. It's flat and the holes don't hold their shape. Now what? Maybe the dough will prove once more and it will rise as it cooks. Yes! Of course! I think I read that in book 2,006. I have perhaps 200ml tap water and oil in a cup, I pour it over the dough and sprinkle salt all over the top. Here we go, into the oven for 22 minutes at first. Let's see how that does. I'm nervous, I'm excited, I'm hungry, not just for the thing in my shit oven, I'm hungry for life. This dough that puffs and crackles and expands and lives in my oven is actually feeding me spiritually, I can feel it.

I breathe and nervously open the oven and what I see, essentially, is a blackened, rectangular tortilla. It's flat as fuck. I pull it out of the oven and look at it. I watch in horror as it creaks and flattens by about half again. I've no idea what it is I've made but I honestly doubt a human could recreate whatever this is if they tried, and part of me is really proud of that.

I guess I should try it after it eventually cools. It cracks like a teenager's duvet cover. The 'bread' doesn't actually smell bad. It smells nice. It smells like a big, flat breadstick. It's not what I wanted, but it's something. I taste it. It's nice, salty but nice. Is it focaccia? No. Could this 'loaf' be eaten? Yeah, it could. By llamas. Llamas would eat it, or you could use it in a Lebanese salad. If you stuck the loaf in a bag and smashed it into pieces, you could put it in a salad. Lovely texture for a salad, dry and crispy, ready to take on juice and flavour.

Again, let's discuss what went right, let's look at how we got to where we got. What did I do wrong? I Google these words: my focaccia lost all its air when I fingered it ... I spin up file after file, baker after baker, scientist upon scientist, and what I'm learning is very interesting. From what I can garner, the dough and the yeast and their guffs need time to develop strength. Gluten. My dough has not developed strength. Everyone tells me the same thing: knead the dough!

I've never kneaded a dough before, so knead it I will. I essentially do everything the same as I did in D2 (dough two), but this time I'm going to turn the dough out on to a floured surface and knead it for ten minutes. I get on YouTube and check my technique is up to scratch: it is. I bring all the dough together and turn it out on to my work surface. A tip here ... It was super sticky for me. I added a lot of flour as I want to keep it from sticking to me/the work surface. Apparently this is a symptom of a wet dough. Which is meant to be a good thing.

My phone alarm goes off and I stop kneading. It's really tactile and beautiful. It's totally different from the others. It actually feels strong. Kneading it, for me, completely worked. I now leave it to prove as before and turn it over every 30 minutes before I cook it. Every 30 minutes the conditions improve. The dough is big and puffy and it smells lush. When the time is right, I take the shroud off and carefully jab my fingers into it. It works. The dimples stay. I brine it and salt it and gently plop her into the oven, slightly cooler this time, for 22 minutes ...

I pull the loaf out and lo and behold, it's a loaf of focaccia. It's an actual loaf of bread. Obviously last week my ADHD bought three or four different, brand-new focaccia loaf tins for today. The loaf slides out easily. The bottom is brown and crisp, it's a bit bubbly like a really nice Detroit/Chicago deep dish-style pizza base. It smells amazing. I leave it to cool and for 15 minutes then I slice it open. Okay, hmm. It's dense. There are little bubbles here and there but it is dense. But it's also nice and thick and risen.

I find an article online and it's pictures of ten well-known chefs' own versions of focaccia. Fuck me, some of them are absolutely pitiful. It gives me a great deal of hope. Already mine looks better than two of theirs. One is flat and yellow. No bubbles, just horrible. It looks like Lembas bread. If I was served that in a restaurant I'd think it was to be used to secure a table wobble. I try mine. It's lovely. It's crisp and soft inside. I pour a little oil into a saucer and sprinkle some salt on top of it, then I push the bread hard into the salty oil and feed. It's pretty bloody good. It's also 4:15am.

I had terrible problems with sleeping at the time. I've had insomnia for years and years. I'd fall asleep with the aid of a pill I take for other 'issues' (no, not erectile disfunction, brain disfunction). I'd fall asleep fine but I'd be awake by midnight. I was then compelled to get up. As soon as my eyes opened, my brain would scream awake. I was then bombarded with hundreds of tunes, thoughts, ideas for films, doing a stunt, soup recipes, friends' faces from the 1980s. Mum, Dad, sounds, music, lines from films ... OH A BEE! It's fucking tiring and it's relentless. Rather than just lay there, I go downstairs and cook.

I decided to teach myself bread to help fill the dark, lonely hours I find the most difficult to be in. I paint too, only watercolours in the house. I paint people. Faces. The Nightfolk

I call them. The people who were with me when everyone else was sleeping. The bread and insomnia worked well eventually. It means my kids have good, healthy, fresh bread every morning. They love it.

Again, I look at what didn't work, what did work, what was different. Was it warm? Cold? What time was it? Was it humid? Everything affected the bread in some way, shape or form. Every little thing made it react a little differently. Sometimes I felt like I'd really cracked it, and then a loaf would emerge and it had completely failed. Balls. Now what? What can I try? Hayley would often tell me to stop fiddling, leave it alone. I couldn't though. I wanted to make it perfect. So, my brain made me buy a hand-held mixer with dough hooks.

Two things: it's a lot of fun, and the kids love this bit. I started to mix the dough for ten minutes using dough hooks. So sweet. The bread that came out from this method was really good. When I cut it in half, the crust was really open and bubbly, the bottom was firm and crisp, and the top was golden and salty and crackled when you pressed it. I can honestly say, hand on heart, it was better than all ten of those chefs' focaccia photographs. It looked like something you'd find in a bakery in Rome. It was incredible. I was so proud. But ... that loaf was two years of trial and error. That's a lot of work. Sometimes I'd make two or three a day!

Still today I search for perfection. Every time I do it, it changes a bit. Again, perhaps the process is the important bit for me, the hunt for that bubbly inside, those oily, salted crackles. Sure, using it to mop up a sloppy ragù is a rare treat, but having the knowledge it took to magic that up from absolutely nowhere is another joy. It's also something I add to my list, my proud list of things I taught myself to do. That list includes EVERYFUCKINGTHING! (except driving).

If I can allow myself to climb up my own arse a moment (my brain has taken that literally and I've had to stop writing and sit back while Brain flashes images of my clambering into my own anus, oh God), I never stop and enjoy what I've done or my accomplishments. I'm embarrassed and shy when it comes to accepting any kind of compliment. You should've seen me at my fiftieth birthday when people gathered round to sing 'Happy Birthday'. I put a napkin on my head and made this noise (buuuuuuurrrrrrrrrrbbbbbbbb) until everyone had sat back down. It's not meant to be rude, although I understand it is a bit, or that I don't appreciate it. I do. It just shuts me down. I just find it hard to believe these amazing people love me.

I had a shit time at school, I had a shit time with my parents and I ran away essentially with no exams, no future and no idea what to do. Not once did I ever think or feel, 'Fuck, what are you going to do about your future? What career are you going to choose?' NOT ONCE. I just had faith that it would be alright. Where the fuck did that confidence come from? I wish I had that faith now. I try and leave a lot of that shit fear-based thinking out of my brain but it's so hard. It hurts me so much. 'How am I going to keep enough work flowing through the books to keep us all going?' Don't for a second believe because I did *Shaun of the Dead* 20 years ago that I'm so minted, I don't ever have to worry. A few years ago, my accountant called me and said, 'Hey, you don't have very much money left. Let me know what you want to do.' Writing this has made my heart beat faster.

If you, as a fan of me or a fan of my film, or comedy or TV work had thought, 'Surely everything you did for 20 years means you never have to worry again? Right?' No. Wrong. It cripples me, it terrifies me, it compels me. Fear. Try and think about the shows and films you watched as a 15-year-old human. Now tot up how many of those actors are still around. What about the other ones? Yeah. Exactly. My average pay cheque would last me 40 days before I needed to borrow or sell shit or sit down and for the first time in many years drink a litre of vodka in the shed. I may smoke 40 fags too. Fuck it, right?

It's a constant crushing fear that the work dries up and then what ...? What would you do? How would you find money to pay for your whole life and the lives of all your children and family? Seriously. How would you do it?

This pressure and the ability to find a solution, hopefully long term, are also things I've taught myself. I never knew how to act before *Spaced*. I taught myself, and it's a job I continue to learn, even today. I've never felt like 'Yes, acting has been completed.' The good thing about teaching myself is that I don't know when to stop. I shouldn't stop. Which feels right. Also, as I age, my characters age too, which is great. I now get to teach myself how 50-year-old men act.

I've figured out that the one way I can be fairly sure of having a smooth future is to have faith in myself. I've taught myself, over the last 35 years, to cook. I started posting food on my Instagram, which led to a DM from Sara, who later became my literary agent. We got this book deal. I did that. I also wrote this book. (My third.) I wrote a book! I left school the first chance I could get because I hated it, and had no qualifications, ADHD and was dyslexic and blah, blah, blah ... I couldn't do school but had no idea why. Everyone thought I was lazy and careless and didn't give a shit. It wasn't true. But, even with all those disadvantages, I wrote some books! I did that. I had issues with anxiety, and depression and fear, and basically living in the darkest, most desperate place a human should ever dwell. I met an art teacher, Tamsyn, and she made me start painting. IT WAS AMAZING! Two years later, three of my paintings were included in an exhibition! I did that! Good focaccia, I DID THAT!

What's the point of this? I guess I just need you to tell me that it will be okay. It's really hard once you've spent the majority of your life desperately trying to control not just every aspect of your life, but every aspect of the lives of everyone around you too. (So tiring.) To disengage from that and tell yourself, 'Relax, you'll be fine.' You should know that as I write this, a voice in my head is screaming 'But how do you know that?!!!' I don't. I guess that's the point. My life didn't work the way I was doing it before. In fact, the harder I squeezed, in a desperate attempt to hang on, the more wormed out between my fingers.

So, this new way is all I have. I make things happen. I have to believe this and have faith. You know what? For the last eight weeks or so, I've slept all night. I haven't baked any bread but I've dreamed about baking it. I think my attempts at teaching myself things, bread in particular, are a way my subconscious grabs that steering column and pulls it back as hard as it fucking can to avoid smashing into a mountain. If teaching yourself how to make bread, or buns, or cake, or sewing, or swimming or gardening means you can be happier as a person, get busy. Do it. Do anything you have to.

There's a very muscular, well-developed part of my brain that fully believes in the healing effect of just lying under a big towel for three months, but that guy is an arsehole. He's wrong. He's completely wrong. Don't listen to him. (I did, for many years, and it almost killed me.) If you need a couple of days on the couch, yes, please go for it. More than that, nope. Get up, do something. Make a focaccia. It's easy essentially, and if, by trial and error, you can serve up something that Nonna Focaccia would be proud as fuck to serve, what an achievement. You'll also have that skill forever.

GARLIC BREAD

This is one of those things that is cheap and if done right, i.e. don't skimp on the butter or the garlic, it's amazing. It can be made very quickly, is really easy and it goes with lots of things. It's a staple.

This version, and I guess there are lots out there, comes from an ex-girlfriend. We kind of lived together (we didn't, I just moved into her room, much to the annoyance of her actual flatmate). It felt very grown-up and part of that was about her cooking for me. Not much, just little bits. It was sweet.

She made a scrambled egg thing with chilli flakes and slices of frankfurter, it was lovely. And she also did this grill bread, which I still use. As a side note, the house she and I shared became the house me and Simon Pegg shared. She and I didn't work, so she left. I was so sad and hurt I made a point of saying as I left for work, 'Just go. Take everything but my books and leave.'

When I got back from my shift, the flat was completely empty. Except for my books. The only thing left was a big wardrobe lying on its back. Sometimes I'd get inside it while Simon stuffed lit matches through a hole in the side.

Eventually we got a TV and a DVD player and we'd lay around

on a mattress watching endless episode of *The X-Files*. It was nice. (After I got over her cheating on me.)

That aside, her flat was the one I sat in day after day at an ironing board desperately trying to write a novel that would impress her enough to let me sleep with her. It worked. If you want to impress a girl, write her a novel. It works. Anyway, as part of our lovely, innocent, gentle, fun, essentially pointless courtship, was this garlic bread. It's beautiful. Thanks, C!

(Other things that happened in this house ... Pies in a bowl. Ask Simon! And a lady ghost kissed me on the forehead.)

1 baguette

1 whole salted butter (maybe not the whole thing)

1 whole bulb of garlic (the whole thing)

parsley (the leafy kind, not the tougher, curly, pubic-style parsley)

black pepper

optional cheeses – I've used Parmesan and Cheddar, separately. Mozzarella might also be pretty nice.

So ... Slice the baguette, but not all the way through. It should be joined at the bottom. I've seen people do that thing where they put two wooden spoons either side of the bread so it stops the knife cutting right through, but fuck that, what a faff, just don't cut all the way through. Even if you do a bit, who cares! It's garlic bread, not the trigger wires on a suicide vest.

Leave the bread to one side. Get your oven on and heating to 200ºC.

Now leave the butter out for ages until it's super soft. Peel all the garlic cloves and either use a Microplane to grate/slice them or smash and slice with a knife. Add the smashed/grated/sliced garlic into the butter.

Chop the parsley and add it to the butter and the garlic. Now use a nice wooden spoon to mix the three ingredients together. It should smell lovely! Big turn of black pepper. If you're using Parmesan, I'd add it to the butter, parsley and garlic mixture. That would work real nice.

Now, with a butter knife, carefully open up the slits you put into the baguette and spread the garlic butter on to both sides of the cut, then push them together. I always feel like a bricklayer when I do this bit, nice oozy garlic mortar leaching out the top when you squeeze the slices together.

Once you've buttered the whole loaf, wrap it in foil. The method I use is I pull a long sheet out, sit the loaf in the middle and then gather the foil around it, sealing at the top. (Sorry to be obvious, but some people are really fucking stupid.)

If you want to use Cheddar and/or mozzarella, I'd put it on top now before you seal it up.

This is one of those things you can make and just leave to stick in the oven at the very end once you've made the other components of the meal. Also, if you've got a small oven, break the loaf in two and do a couple of little ones.

Cook in a hot oven of around 200ºC for at least 20 minutes. You can open it and have a little butcher's after 20 minutes. Be warned, hot steam will burn your retinas off.

If the butter and cheese and garlic is all melted and the bread is crispy, it's done. Either serve it in the foil, straight out of the fire, or slice it and serve it in a big bowl. Lovely. This also would work on a hot BBQ, maybe sat on that little shelf on the back that no one uses. Enjoy.

This goes great with any kind of pasta or ragù-style sauce. Anything a bit saucy actually – lasagne, Bolognese, etc.

TOMATO SOUP

My favourite soup is from a small, local, family-run business called Heinz. I think they even do beans. Baked beans. It's quite popular I hear.

The tomato soup they do is, for me, I think, my favourite soup of all. Yes, it's canned and people might say, 'Surely you should use your own soup recipe in your own book.' And they'd be right, and I'm going to, and the recipe is good and delicious and easy, and it's cheap and really fucking good for you ... but it's not Heinz. I'm alright with that. They're different things. Same but different. One is wheeled out with, perhaps with a homemade Focaccia, when the in-laws pop over for a light lunch, and the other is Heinz.

If it's cold and I'm sad and anxious or a bit fluey, it's always going to be a tin of Heinz Tommy soup. Maybe even a lentil soup at a push, with loads of white pepper. My mum used to serve it with slices of white bread, thickly buttered, folded in half and ready to be dunked. Heinz tomato soup is, for me, time-machine cuisine. I can be back on the sofa, snuggled under a quilt, pretending to be sick to get off school so I could be with my mum. I can taste that.

I don't think a page in a recipe book, if this is what this is, would be good if I just wrote, take one can of Heinz soup, open it, heat and eat with white bread and butter, or a ham sandwich, or a toastie. So, here's a recipe I've cobbled together over the years for not-as-good-as-Heinz Tomato Soup ...

1kg ripe tomatoes

First of all, go to the Mediterranean shop and buy a kilo of great, wonderfully smelly, juicy, ripe, smashing Tommy-Artos. I happen to have an amazing shop just around the corner from me in Twickenham and it's simply called the Mediterranean shop. It's absolutely amazing. It has EVERYTHING. I love it in there. It's run by a lovely Turkish family. The dad pulled me aside one day and winked at me and said, 'You are the reason I learned to speak English!' I was thrilled. He said he watched *Shaun of the Dead* so much and he loved Ed so much it made him want to speak English. How cool is that?

My sons love the shop too. I totally let them wander around on their own while I'm at the back smelling tomatoes. Every now and then one of them finds me, holding some kind of biscuit or huge Toblerone used for jousting. 'Nope,' I say, and they trudge off, dejected. I'm rambling, but the Mediterranean shop has the best produce I've seen anywhere.

Sometimes if the weather is hot and sunny I like to buy tomatoes that aren't quite ripe. I enjoy leaving them out in the garden, in the sun, to ripen. I know it's not much, but for me even that little thing shared with my babies is a niceness. We're popping out every few hours to smell them and see the colour deepen. It's a nice memory for the kids. Most of my childhood memories involve my tortured mother trying to bludgeon my father to death with a heavy crystal ashtray. You see now how even tomatoes on a table outside is, for me, a lovely kind of memory. No one gets killed ... and because of that I'm going to use our sun-kissed tomatoes, along with ...

olive oil

1 big white onion

1 stalk of celery

1 small carrot

1 whole bulb of garlic

*1 small bunch of thyme, leaves removed
from the stalks*

Turn the oven on to 180°C. Slice the tomatoes in half and arrange them, cut-side down, on a baking tray. Do NOT throw the stalks away. Leave them attached, or if you've had to remove them, then put them in the baking tray too – there's so much flavour in the stalks. I'll be friggin' fuming if I find out you threw them away. Remember, I have teams of people who trace the buyers of this book and go through your bins at night. They have wolves.

Halve the onion, put with the toms, same with the celery. Chop the tomato stalk into four bits. Peel and halve the carrot. Stick in the tray and then cut the garlic in half and that can join all the other veg. Sprinkle with salt and grind in a fair bit of pepper. Glug some nice olive oil over the top. Not too much, and then stick in the preheated oven for about 45 minutes.

When it comes out it should all be starting to melt and brown a bit and char. At this point, add the thyme into the roasting tray too.

Sometimes I take the tray out with all the veg in and cover with foil and leave it until it cools down.

Once cool, scrape everything into a saucepan and add about 750ml vegetable stock, or you can also just use water. If using the stock, make sure it's not too salty.

Take out any tomato stalks now and remove the skin from the onion and garlic.

Take a hand blender and blitz it all up. I'm feeling a vibe here where I'd let this just sit too. For at least one hour, you could even leave in the fridge overnight.

Finally, take a nice clean saucepan. Stick a fine mesh sieve on top (chinois) and, using a ladle, pass spoonfuls of the liquid through the sieve. You may need to add a little more water at this point if it's too thick. If you want to make this richer, you could add some double cream too.

Slowly warm this delicious soup up in the pan. Serve hot, in bowls, with a sandwich or bread and crisps.

Or ... make a cheese toastie in the Breville.

GOLDEN PEPPER STEW

A few years ago, my then father-in-law, Vernon, who's sadly no longer with us, while running for a bus with heavy shopping bags, tripped and badly broke – no shattered – his shoulder. Poor fella, he was in a lot of pain for a long time. In the direct aftermath of his injury, he found it difficult to eat and to move. His beloved Trudy had arranged to travel to India with her sister and they decided together that she would still go. It meant that the rest of us would rally round and take care of Vernon. To cheer him up I decided to cook for him and go and sit with him for the afternoon. This Golden Pepper Stew is what I made, with spicy merguez sausages.

Vernon hadn't been eating very well and was in pain and generally miserable without Trudles. I wanted him to eat something fulfilling and nourishing and tasty. He proclaimed that he wasn't hungry, and he didn't want any lunch, but I served it up anyway and sat at a distance and watched. I took so much joy, peering at him over a newspaper, seeing him at first just put a tiny forkful of peppers into his mouth, then sit and gradually DEMOLISH a big bowl with a couple of pieces of crusty ciabatta to mop up the sauce. I was thrilled and proud that afternoon. What an amazing thing it is to cook for someone. What a delicious responsibility. I love it. As someone who has the defect of character of being a people pleaser, cooking is the ultimate symbol of that for me. To spend all day, and possibly some of the day before, planning and then shopping and then cooking and then serving food to my family is the greatest gift I can give them. (Or maybe cash? Maybe cash is the greatest gift one can give, or organs. Not like synthesiser organs, I mean liver, heart, eyes.)

This stew does not take a day and a half to plan, or shop or cook. It takes maybe an hour, top to bottom. That said, it can totally be prepared the day before and left to mature and develop. Although I would cook the sausages on the day you eat them. This is simple, and very tasty. Although I'm sure there's a million different versions, I made this one up. I figured it out. I thought about it and I went and cooked what I thought about, and it tasted exactly as my thoughts said it would. Thanks Brain.

olive oil

handful of flat-leaf parsley

2 nuggets of garlic

½ red onion, thinly sliced

2 yellow peppers

1 red pepper

1 tin chopped tomatoes or 3 big ripe tomatoes that smell like Sardinia, chopped

8 Merguez sausages

Chop up the parsley. Set it aside.

Take a nice deep-ish frying pan, maybe like a 7.5cm sauté pan, from base to lip, not across ... that would be a really tiny frying pan. Maybe there's a specialist hummingbird egg pan that's that size. (How utterly confusing from me. Sorry.)

Use a nice big glug of a good olive oil. Don't overheat it. This does not have to be cooked rapidly. Put the garlic in to gently fry. Don't burn it. Be gentle, imagine your frying a slice of delicate lace. (What?)

Add the onion. Softly fry but don't colour it too much. Then slice your peppers. I generally do that thing where you hold the pepper and slice one of the faces off at a time. Unless you want rings, then you'd do it differently. Throw them into the pan. Watch the heat. Toss the pan and cook until the peppers start to wilt. Then toss in the tomatoes. I'd say watch the amount of toms. It is a pepper stew after all.

Toss everything over and turn the heat down. Before lidding this, take a big spoon of smoked paprika and a smaller spoon of ground cumin and toss them in. Continue cooking for a couple of minutes, then lid up and let it cook down for about 30 minutes. If you need a splash of water as it cooks, go for it, but remember it's a stew. Not a soup.

Now I use a spicy French/Moroccan/Algerian sausage called merguez. It's spicy and made with lamb. It's lovely. I guess, thinking about it, you could also use chorizo for this recipe. Not a Richmond sausage though, that's reserved for full English breakfasts and crusty sandwiches served at lower-division rugby clubs.

So, here's just a little note on the method to this recipe. The way that I've written it, you cook your stew, then you either drop your sausages into the stew and let them cook out, poach in the liquid I guess, or you can separately fry the sausages and drop them into the cooked peppers.

There's also a third way ... Take the sausages and fry them in butter. Set aside under foil like a dead marathon runner. Then ... glug of oil ... and cook from above ... garlic, then onions ...That would taste great. You'd use the onions and peppers to deglaze the pan of all that lovely sausage juice. (*heave)

Once the peppers and onions and tomatoes are cooked and melted into each other to make a really delicious, summery, life-giving stew, that's kind of it. Here's a thing: if you now make dents in the stew and crack eggs into them, lidding up and letting the heat and steam from the peppers set the eggs, you've just made Shakshuka, a Middle Eastern breakfast dish. It's delicious. Mopped up with a fresh pita bread. Yes, please. I digress ...

At this point I take a tablespoon of crème fraîche and stir it into the sauce. I taste it, season it and then put the sausages into the stew. You can then, at this point, serve it with a handful of parsley and a squeeze of lemon or stick it in the fridge and let it mature.

Despite my demented ramblings and my hummingbird style of writing, this is such an easy recipe and really fucking tasty. It also leaves a lot of nice juice/sauce behind. Juice/sauce I believe should be mopped up with something soft and crispy.

In terms of the whole 'learn techniques' kind of thinking, I've already talked about adding eggs and making Shakshuka but you could also put fat prawns in this stew. Or a big cod fillet. Or salmon. Or lamb chops. Or a big rectangle of sharp Feta. It would be such a delicious counterpoint to the sweet peppers. You see what I'm saying? It's a really good base sauce to have in your locker!

I don't have Vernon in my life any more, sadly, but I do have the memory of him silently eating that stew and it's a nice memory. (One of many, I might add.)

CHICKEN PAPRIKA

8 chicken thighs (skin on)

butter

olive oil

1 tbsp flour

350ml white wine

punnet of mushrooms

splash of double cream

1 litre chicken stock

2 nuggets of garlic

2 white onions

1 red pepper

1 green pepper

1 tbsp smoked paprika

tin of chopped tomatoes

150ml soured cream

This is for four people (a lot like the Golden Pepper Stew), but instead of sausages it's made with chicken. It's easy and delicious.

Let me just pull my neck in a second ... It's all very good me saying this is easy and that food is easy, and this prep technique is easy and using a mandoline is easy ... It's easy for me because I've been cooking for 30 years. If you hate cooking and food, and you have no clue about the kitchen or the utensils that dwell deep inside its dark places, it won't be easy. It'll be weird and difficult and the language will be totally foreign to you. And that's fine. You sit back, pop the telly on and let me take care of it. I've got you.

I use chicken thighs and wings with the skin on. I take a casserole dish, my favourite is a yellow rectangular one from the 1960s, a Le Creuset. Feed it a knob of butter and a splash of oil, then once it's hot, fry off the chicken until it's lovely and caramel tinted. Always be ready to turn the heat down or up or even just move the pan off the heat, even for five seconds. Cooking for me is, I imagine, what flying a helicopter must be like – tiny but constant corrections and getting feedback from every sense I have. Smell, touch, hearing, knives ...

Take the chicken out of the pan and put it on a plate and cover with foil.

What you're left with in that casserole pan is a lot of chicken fat, crispy bits and brown grease, and pieces of burnt chicken. Lovely. You could at this point turn the heat up and add a little flour, cook it out and then deglaze that hot pan with half a bottle of good, white wine. That's the basis of a bunch of very tasty dishes. Add some nice fried mushrooms and a touch of cream and stock, pop the chicken back in and there's a nice Chasseur-style dish. But this is chicken paprika, so shut the fuck up. Okay. Sorry.

I love you. I love you too. Don't ever leave me. I can't promise that. Oh.

As the chicken rests, put two smashed up garlic nuggets into the chicken fatty pan, cook for a bit, then add two medium sliced white onions. (Why white and not red? I'm not sure. White works nicely for this kind of food.) Lid up at this point and let the steam from the covered onions deglaze that pan for you.

I've been lucky enough (and I've also worked my fucking hole off) to be in a position to eat in some of the best places in the world. Not necessarily the most expensive, I might add. There's something about sitting in a car on a cold afternoon eating fresh cod and chips and the windows steam up and no one can see in. That's priceless. Sharing a little lolly with my daughter in the garden, it costs virtually nothing but again, is priceless. The flip side to this is telling a series of huge lies so I could come to be in Copenhagen, alone, on a Saturday night with a reservation for a table for one at Noma. At the time the best restaurant in the world ... It was, and excuse the swearing, fucking amazing. Amazing! My mouth has a signed picture of René Redzepi hanging in it.

I'm rambling, but the point I was trying to make is this: the point of cooking is to take some things, and do things to those things and then sweet, sweet magic falls out the other end. Tasty, incredible magic. It's about getting as much flavour and taste into every stage of the cooking process. That's the skill. That's where that sweet buttery magic lives.

Once the onions have melted and browned slightly, lid off and stir to get all the bits off the pan. Add one sliced red pepper and one green pepper (diced though, not sliced). Leave the lid off and sauté all the ingredients down gently. Add a big spoon of smoked paprika into the mix and a tin of chopped tomatoes and about a pint of water. Bring it up to a nice slow simmer and put the chicken pieces and any juice that came out back into the pan. Cover with the same foil you used to house the waiting hen bits. Don't be wasteful. Cook for about 45 minutes–one hour.

Don't overcook the chicken. If the sauce is too watery, take out the chicken, keep warm under the foil and turn up the heat to reduce the sauce a bit. Taste it. Does it need salt? Yes, I think it does. Then season it, motherfucker. Add a twist of black pepper, too. A tablespoon of soured cream and Romeo Dunn. Add the chicken back into the pot and serve with either rice (use one of the bags you stick in the microwave – fuck making rice in a pan with water) or little crunchy potatoes.

STUFFED PEPPERS

These are really, really delicious and always taste nicer fresh and made at home than the ones in Greece they make in the mornings and warm in a microwave. I'm sorry if that hurts, Greece, but in my experience it's true.

Find some big ripe red or orange peppers. Really big ones. Big as you can find. No, bigger, that's it. Perfect.

Can the peppers stand by themselves when you let go of them? No! Okay, okay, relax, relax, please, relax. What I need you to do next is both technical and stress-inducing and, well, it's not for everyone. Let me clarify my position ... Take a small knife and trim the bottom of each pepper so it's not only flat but I don't want you to have breached the peppers' cargo bay so to speak. If you puncture the pepper, juice will fall out of it and that's not fucking cool. It's not cool.

I'm assuming it just worked. Let's crack on. Oven on to 180°C. Grab your lovely big peppers. Cut the tops off. This is easier said than done. If it screams and bleeds when you slice the head off, assume the pepper is haunted. Put it into a bag with a cross and a pound of salt. Tip in a shot of vodka and a bar of Wright's coal-tar soap. On the outside of the bag, in sadly your own blood, according to the writings of Salvador Pepperasmus, the Pimentonicus, write the word: NO. The pepper should stop screaming immediately. Toss the bag into a tidal river. It has to be tidal. And that's it. Now it's someone else's problem.

If it didn't scream and it's a regular pepper, great. Cut the top off so it's a lid. You need a lid. Then, using a nice, small, controllable veg knife, do that thing where you trim all the seeds and bits of white pith out of the pepper. It needs to be a big round hole, ripe, sweet and ready to accept the filling.

If the peppers are big, serve one as a portion, if they're medium, serve two. Take the peppers, pour a little olive oil inside and a little 'hey, presto' of salt and pepper. Roast in the oven for about 45 minutes. Maybe less. The pepper needs to be nice and soft when it's eaten. This means it needs a little pre-cook first. The balance here is making sure you don't overcook and then it won't stand up. If that happens, cut it in half lengthways and stuff it lying down ... You feel me, ladies? It's not the end of the world, it's only a pepper.

Let's continue ... Take a frying pan, lots of olive oil, loads of chopped-up garlic and onion, sauté slightly, then add a load of chopped tomatoes. A can would work fine too if you don't have fresh. Stir in a little water and cook gently for a bit. Now, here's my favourite pasta: orzo. Yum, yum, yum. Stick a cup or a handful or hell, even measure it out properly, don't listen to my ADHD ass. This will cook and suck all the flavour and the taste into the orzo. Salt and pepper it. Taste. It should be amazing. To make it more Mediterranean, please add some dried oregano at this point as well as some wet parsley. (Leaf, not pube.) This is now the heart of the dish. It's a stuffing. If it can be stuffed, stuff it with this. Tomatoes, stuff them with this. Marrows, stuff them with this. Or eat it exactly as is. It's good and good for you. But we're stuffing ...

The peppers are cooked nicely and timed just right, so in 45 minutes it'll be exactly where you need it to be. It'll be perfect and tanned and juicy and slumped to one side like a chubby, sunburnt swimming instructor leaning on a pool table. Yum.

Fill the peppers up to the top with the pasta sauce mix. Squash down a bit and fill again. Place the lid back on. Roast in the oven for 35–45 minutes. Then take out, plate, drizzle with good olive oil, salt, pepper and serve ... With what? Here's what ... nice, fresh, crisp, green salad and chips. Yamas!

Stuffed tomatoes are great too. With this you can use

the guts of the tomato as part of the stuffing. Learn this shit. Stick Stuffed Peppers on your 'I can cook that list' and take the rest of the day off.

BUBBLE & SQUEAK

I've asked a lot of people over the years what their family recipe is and none has ever been the same ... remarkable. Honestly, I will only ever make this on Boxing Day but it's amazing and so easy and should be made once a week in all truth, and it's super economical. If you have a Sunday lunch, then you can defo have a Bubble & Squeak. In fact, if you have any leftovers at any point, Bubble & Squeak can be produced.

I'm going to use the leftover roast potatoes from Sunday. It's 3:30pm on a Monday afternoon, I open the fridge, pull out, crack and gulp a very cold Coke Zero. Done. I then begin going through silver foil-wrapped parcels: ten roasties, some sliced cheesy leeks, cabbage, roast carrots. Yes, we can do this. I take the carrots and slice them into little bits. I chop up the cabbage and the leeks. I then smash up and roughly chop the potatoes into bits.

Big frying pan. Oil. Get it hot. Dump in the potato, fry for a bit. Then put all the other ingredients in. Fry and chop it all up as you go. Once it's all hot and brown and fried, that's it. Bring it all together, salt and pepper. Plate up and away we go. Everyone can eat this. I'd serve it with a big fried Burford Brown egg on top. Also, if you've got any leftover meat, then a nice big slice of cold belly pork would go great with the B & S.

Q & A ... 'Isn't it more like a hash?'

'Yeah, this version is very hash-like. So fucking what. Anyone else? No one?'

Cool. I've made Bubble & Squeak out of old mash too and chopped in the veg like in the hash one but instead of just loosely frying the mix, I've made it into cakes and fried them in butter. Also, really nice. Egg and pork slice also likes it this way. Slice of cold ham. Nice. That kind of cake would also go great with a fried/roasted piece of salmon, skin on, crispy and maybe a little butter and chive sauce. That sounds nice. Big glass of ice-cold cider. Delicious. I don't even drink and that sounds so nice.

I cook a lot of salmon for Hayley. For me too, actually. I love it. The fillets you can get in supermarkets are soooooooo smalllll, probably though that's the deistic amount one should eat. I say, nah. Go into a proper fish place and let them know what you want: two fillets, skin on, 300g each. Cheers.

If I cook salmon, we either have it Mexican style with salsa and guac and rice and beans, or with roasted sweet potato and salad and stuff, or sometimes in a burrito. However you'd serve a sirloin steak, salmon works too. I love cooking fillets of salmon. They end up looking so beautiful. The colour is amazing.

I've got about six or seven different frying pans. It sounds like a humble brag but you'd be wrong. It's not humble at all. I OWN SIX OR SEVEN DIFFERENT FRYING PANS. DO YOU ALL HEAR, HUH?! DO YOU?!!!! THANK YOU, *SHAUN OF THE DEAD*.

Take a nice little non-stick pan, little oil, knob of butter and heat it up gently until it's nice and hot. Now place the salmon fillet skin-side down and fry kind of gently for a few minutes.

Turn it over. The skin should be caramelised and crisp. Now I fry on each side for four to five minutes until it's really nice and tanned on every side. Things to watch: the butter and oil kind of burn. Lift out the salmon. Tip the fat into a cup. Wipe the pan and go again. A little oil, little butter and maybe turn down your heat. Don't forget to drink the fat you tipped out. Collapse trembling.

I think the point of my screamed megalomaniacal pan nonsense was this: have a couple of good pans in a couple of different sizes. 'Good' may mean expensive. I have expensive pans. I also have these little frying pans with a stone/copper Teflon base thing, non-stick like mad, not even air can stick to it. I buy them in Homebase for £7.75. They work great for six months, then you've got to bin them. Buy cheap, you buy twice. I'm alright with that, in the case of these cheap pans. Sometimes, just like raising a child, having a very big, celebrity chef-endorsed pan is not just a ton of work, it's expensive and it's tricky to clean and if you do it wrong they turn into pricks.

Back to Bubble & Squeak a minute, if I may. Making little fried Bubble & Squeak cakes using all the leftover veg is a real treat for me. After the day or two prepping for Christmas Day lunch, and the sometimes days of finding and sourcing the best ingredients I can (the bird itself is ordered in early November – maybe this year was exceptional in as much as there was talk of not getting one at all due to driver shortage and fuel shortage and Covid and ...), the ease of Boxing Day feels like a little treat. It'll never be a cooked lunch. It'll be a table full of cold meats and cheeses, slices of cold turkey, hams, cheeses, nuts, fruit and, of course, the only cooked element is a bunch of little Squeaky Cakes.

My Homage To Curry

I love curry. Period. But is it curry if I cook it? I mean do I need to hail from India, Bangladesh or Pakistan for it to be able to be called 'curry'? I don't think so. I like to think food from everywhere is for everyone but just in case, this section is called 'My Homage to Curry', a food I've known and loved as long as I've known and loved food.

My first memory of eating out in a restaurant was in a curry house. Me and my mum and my dad. I can remember how thoroughly exotic it smelled, and the music, that high-pitched twang of the sitar, the wistful howl of the lyric. How happy and attentive and beautiful the waiters all seemed to me. Their white smiles and crisply ironed shirts, rushing sizzling-hot platters every which way but loose.

I was in a different world. I had omelette and chips. I was too nervous to eat what Mum and Dad had. I got braver though. Eventually.

When my Son Number 1 was four or five, me and him would

sometimes slip off on a Thursday to Green Spice on Twickenham High Street for a little cuzzer. I'd have a Madras and I'd get him Korma or something else mild and sweet. He never really ate much. He picked and enjoyed crispy, buttery naan dipped in sauce and some rice here and there, but that was it. It doesn't matter what we ate. What matters is a dad and a little boy hanging out. Having a laugh. Having a cuddle. When we finished our food, I'd slide round his side of the booth and we'd split a dessert. Lemon sorbet served in a frozen, hollowed-out lemon. What a great thing. After dinner I'd take him back to his mum's and I'd wave and blow kisses before driving off, parking up and crying my fucking heart out for 30 minutes.

Hopefully this curry will make you cry with joy, or maybe if you're from India/Bangladesh/Pakistan, you'll be laughing with embarrassment. If that's the case, I'm sorry, I don't know any better, teach me. Tell me where I've gone wrong. Here goes ...

MY CHICKEN CURRY

Take one jar of masala cook-in sauce ... KIDDING!!! I'm kidding. Sorry.

I use chicken thighs here. I can't say how many you should use, I don't know how many are in your family. Let's all be on the same page. Let's say a kilo of boned and skinned chicken thighs cut into bite-sized pieces.

Grab a lovely big bowl. In the bowl, put the chicken and then some good Greek yoghurt and finely sliced stalks of coriander. (Save the leaves for the curry later. Use the stalks for this part. The Marinade.) An onion, finely sliced. A lime, squeezed. Dump the lime into the bowl, too. Then, two or three big spoons of a very decent garam masala. One of the mums from school saw my effort on Insta to make a 'curry' and sorted me out with a big jar of her mum's garam masala. It made all the difference. Take your hands and stir and squeeze and mulch all that together. Also salt and pepper. Cover with foil, or clingfilm, and leave it in the fridge for at least four hours. Overnight, if possible.

The next part I do in stages. Fry the chicken pieces. Don't overcrowd the pan, fry a few and then leave the chicken aside in a big bowl. Build it all up with onions and deglazing and layering flavour upon muthafunking flavour. Use a combination of oil and butter and fry the chicken in batches. I try to remove a lot of the yoghurt at this point because it can burn. If the yoghurt burns at all, wipe it away with kitchen paper. Easy. Remember, as this sits, a lot of nice juice will run out of the chicken, adding to the overall flavour.

In the same pan, add two finely sliced red onions, smashed-up/grated thumb-sized ginger (the thumb of a powerful athlete) and garlic too, also a sweet, phat red chilli, finely sliced, four cardamom seeds, two curry leaves, a teaspoon of ground turmeric, a teaspoon of cumin seeds and then more oil and butter, and fry until beginning to bubble and brown. Take your garam masala and sprinkle two or three heaped teaspoons on to the oily, buttery onion mix. Fry hard and stir.

Now take a pint of cold water and tip half of it into the onions and masala mix. It'll hiss and sizzle and foam, turn up the heat, stir, add a little more water, hiss, stir ... you see what's happening ... you're making a sauce and using the water and steam to deglaze the pan. The sauce may split slightly during this process and that's fine.

Once enough water has been put in so it's now a bubbling, dark brown sauce, turn the heat down and put the chicken and any cheeky curry gravy juice back into the pan. Turn the heat down and cook very plippy, very slowly and controlled for a while. How long is that? I can't tell you. I won't tell you, figure it out. What I will say is this: have a container of water at the ready and if it dries out, then add more water. You've all eaten curry, you know how it should look.

After maybe one to one and a half hours, it'll be done. You now have a choice. Who's eating? Just adults? Or are the kids eating too? Let's say just adults.

Cook a couple of bags of microwavable basmati rice and serve. Rice in one bowl. Curry in another. I cover mine with loads of coriander and slices of red onion. Also season it. Taste it. It shouldn't be hot; it should be complex and tasty and just absolutely moreish. When you put the garam masala in earlier, if you want this hot, you could add cayenne pepper, hot chilli powder and chilli flakes at this time.

Bring to the table with loads of roti or naan or chapatti and bits and bobs, sauces, poppadoms, slices of onion, rice, big jug of cold water ... Enjoy.

If the kids are eating it, don't put any chilli in it and then, at the end, mix the curry with two or three big spoonfuls of yoghurt. It's amazing. The kids mostly like it, even if it's just dipping crispy bread into sauce and eating the rice. The point isn't the food. The point is the connection. The point is the memory. It's indelible. It's permanent. You and your friends and your kids and their kids all sat around a table, bowls of this and that are being passed around, people are chatting and laughing, kids are being funny idiots, some like it, others won't touch it.

That chaos is the thing. That's the memory. Chaos can be hard for me to sit inside. Chaos I haven't caused anyway. It can be too loud. It can leave me twitchy and BUGGURK!!!! But this is something I need to learn too. Sometimes the chaos is theirs and kids like it just as it is. The chaos is their memory not mine. It's not always about me.

I've made this curry with prawns. Lovely. I've made this curry with little cubes of lamb, lovely also. It's a good base sauce to have in your locker. At some point in the making of the sauce, there's also a chance to use coconut cream in here. It makes it gentle and sweet and ready for not only meat but huge cubes of seasoned monkfish. You see what's happening here ... You've just made like five different 'curry'-style, gravy-laden dishes.

Once you get the hang of making the gravy, you can mix it up a bit. You'll become able to improvise, this is very important and you'll take a great deal of joy from being able to do this. Here's an adaptation of the curry sauce based on an improvisation ...

Fry off the onions and the garlic and the ginger paste, add ground turmeric, ground cardamom, cayenne pepper, mild chilli powder, ground cumin, coriander seeds and a big load of garam masala and 100g salted butter. Let that bubble and foam and deglaze the pan with a kilogram of very juicy, very sweet, chopped tomatoes. The heat will cause steam, which will deglaze the pan, and the tomatoes will wilt and die and release their juices so that it will all begin to fit together and create something truly delicious, right in your own home. (You may need to add water as I said, so always keep a little container handy near the hob.) But this sauce can be used for a kind of Rogan Josh.

Blend this sauce and add a load of cold butter, some yoghurt and a fistful of coriander, hey presto, another type of curry.

That feels like a really early, largely unseen Clint Eastwood film. A *Fistful of Coriander*. Maybe Clint's only Bollywood film, *A Fistful of Garam Masala*. A powerful spice merchant and his cruel, rowdy men turn up in a small village known for its production of a kind of sweet, coconut-covered doughnut ball mainly enjoyed during Diwali. Maybe a guy oversteps the mark and feeds a dog one of the balls. All the men laugh. Except one. Clint.

Clint ends up sticking a big bunch of coriander in the prick's face. Fearful, all the other bad men jump on their mopeds and ride off. The village, thrilled by what Clint did, come out and do a huge dance. Clint too, although he insists it's shot in a wide so his double does all the dancing. He just comes in for tight shots and reactions.

I grew up watching Clint. When I was a little boy, I was allowed to watch whatever I wanted. Clint was on that list. *The Good, the Bad and the Ugly*. Yes, please. It's funny to think in a different part of the country Simon Pegg and Edgar Wright probably also watched it and loved it. Also, *Every Which Way but Loose*, right turn Clyde!

This was the film that eventually led to me doing an impression of Clyde the Orangutan in *Shaun of the Dead*. I used to joke with Simon how despite what the critics thought of Clyde's performance, the orangutan was actually very limited in what he could provide in front of the camera. (Clyde was sadly beaten to death by his keeper later in life with a broom handle. Again, proof that the film industry is far from glamorous.)

I met Clint Eastwood once. Back in 2011 outside the sound stage we were shooting *The Adventures of Tintin* on. Steven ... Steven Spielberg, Uncle Steven, whatever (mic drop ... KLANG!) had a really nice trailer set up right outside the door. It even had a little picket fence and an area of astroturf so it felt like a front garden.

Lunch was called and I ran out in my horrible black, skintight suit we used so the computer could track my movements straight into Steven, who was sat in his garden smoking a lovely big cigar. He nodded and said, 'Nick, this is Clint ...' I panned across and the Clint he mentioned was Clint Eastwood. Just sat there having a cigar. Steven Spielberg and Clint Eastwood just sat together smoking cigars. There I was in my skintight black suit. I hated it. I looked like a dinosaur egg. One of those naughty dinosaur eggs where only the legs have hatched and it's running all over the place and being naughty. Simon looked good in his. Bond looked amazing. His seemed bespoke but whatever, he's Daniel Craig.

This is a food book(ish), so I should try to tie the story into food ... I'd already set up that bumping into Clint took place at lunchtime ... Boom. Easy. Maybe I should talk about food on set. In my experience, it's either good, bad, or ugly. (Author takes rest of day off.)

For a lot of the cast and crew, lunch can be something either to look forward to or to dread. I've even, fairly recently, seen whole departments walk off a job because the catering is shit. Here in England the catering is pretty shit most of the time. With the massive US TV shows shooting here, with their big saucy budgets, they obviously snag the best on-set caterers, for years in some cases. It means the rest of us are left with the Bad and the Ugly.

On a set you arrive to, generally, a full English breakfast. Everything that's in a full English is available as separate items. Then there's always a big table and on that you have yoghurts and a toaster and cereal and pastries, croissants, etc. Fruit. I look forward to breakfast on a set. Many is the time I've spent my drive in thinking about what I'll have, pretending I'll have something different this time. I always have the same thing, near enough. Toasted bacon sandwich, heavily buttered!!! (Yeah no wonder you're so fucking fat. BREXIT! My kid could paint that. You're shit. ENGLAND, ENGLAND, ENGLAND!!!!) And lashings of coffee.

Then you're on set working. Sometimes people come through set with a tray of fruit or biscuits 10:30/11am-ish. There's also constant tea and coffee. There you'll find a box of cheap as shit smashed-up biscuits. After six hours, I think the producers have a legal obligation to feed the crew a lunch of some kind. Lunch is always the talk of the set. People either like it or loathe it. You can tell by looking in the bin and seeing how much food is in it. As a producer, bad catering is the bane of my life. I hate it, the crew hate it. If the crew hate it, they hate the job. As a crew, they literally jump from job to job. For me, being the writer or the producer or in some way responsible for the film, I want to food to be great. When I see a ton of food in a bin, I see money we could've used on screen.

You know the food is not being enjoyed when at 12:20pm the camera team says something like, 'Nick, we're getting fish and chips delivered. Fancy it?' After lunch, generally there's a lot of talk for a couple of hours about what was good and what was awful about the food. 'What did you think of lunch?' is a question one hears a lot on set. It's either answered with a warm nod, yes, or the nose curls and you'll see a 'Nah' kind of face.

You'll also hear someone saying something like, 'The caterers we had last week were great. Can't we have them back?' Electricians should always be fed good, crispy, salty chips. I've seen sparks fuck off a job because they were sick of not having chips. I hate shit food. There's no need. Usually, the job is being catered for by an older cook who's stopped giving a fuck trying to do something magic with a tiny budget. It's not their fault. If the production's budget for catering is a tiny amount, you still have to take the caterer's budget and profit out of that figure too.

Then at 5:30pm-ish, you'll start to see people wandering round with sandwiches: 'The sandwiches are out!!!' Being an actor and in a very privileged position, sandwiches of all kinds are saved for me, usually under a plate, so if I'm in front of the lens when they come out I don't end up with the shit ones. Also, cakes. Mr Kipling style. There'll always be great chat around the sandwiches. What's in them? Noses crinkled up in confusion. 'Is this egg? Tuna?' Often groups of people just stand around, silently looking at the trays of sandwiches, not sure what to do. Every now and then a person silently leans in and lifts up a corner of bread to see what it is. Maybe then the silence is broken with the utterance of the word 'ham'. Someone usually deploys a powerful Maglite so the make-up team can see what the sandwiches are.

In Ireland, when we shot *Into the Badlands*, it was a little different. The sandwiches came individually wrapped in clingfilm. Here in England, they're all laid out cut into quarters and wrapped as a whole tray, like the sandwiches you'd get if a pub catered a funeral.

Things change on set depending on what time you shoot. If you're not shooting regular days, starting 8am and wrap at 7pm, you get to shoot what's called French hours. I much prefer French hours because you get to wrap at 6pm. But ... you don't get a break. I find the whole stopping for an hour at lunch very disruptive. Then, after lunch, it seems to take ages to get back up to speed.

French hours means no one gets a lunch break, you just push on but in natural breaks in the actual filming process, lighting a shot, moving equipment, setting up for a different scene, etc., people eat then. Lots of polystyrene boxes handed out and people grabbing a little something on the go.

The other kind of day you get is called a split day. You usually start shooting at 2pm and go into the early hours. This kind of day is used if you need to shoot exterior scenes both night and day. They can also be used to transition a unit into full night shoots or out of full nights, although usually productions are cheeky because you'll do a full night – 5/6pm until dawn – and then they'll use the Saturday and Sunday as the break. Even though you'd have to probably sleep all day Saturday. It's not really a day off, it's more like a recovery day.

Anyway, a split day is slightly different because breakfast is served at lunchtime. It's usually all the breakfast items but you have the option to have them with Chippy Chips. Which is fun. Sometimes a chicken burger is offered. Nice. Then you'll have lunch at 7pm-ish and sandwiches are replaced with perhaps a warm element. A toastie or a pasty or a sausage roll, etc. What a treat.

The thing about set food is the caterers will ask the assistant directors when they want lunch served or ready. It can only be an estimate. If we're in the middle of something juicy and emotional or fun, or it's overrunning or the first needs to finish a scene to stay on track, then food waits. We get what we need and once that scene is finished, we break. I've rarely seen us stop mid-scene to eat.

The only exception to this is if we've just started a scene and to finish it will take at least two hours. We break. So, the problem is when do you get the food ready for? This isn't like a dinner party. The food that's designed by the catering staff needs to be flexible enough to taste okay sat for 40 minutes in a box wrapped in clingfilm. No pastry here. As a result, it can be just cold shit. Crews look, poke with a sustainable fork, and then bin it.

I saw a very famous actor get so tired with getting shit food, he ended up throwing a box with a wet burger in it at an assistant director. Not cool behaviour, but it might highlight how important food is to everyone on a set. On that film, the next day a space was cleared in the middle of a massive forest, two easy-ups were installed and tables put inside, and then takeaway food from every single culture was put inside to ensure that actor got hot food he'd like.

I always knew how I'd do set food. Part of me still wants to set up a set-food business ... It always seemed so simple to me and then shooting *The Adventures of Tintin* dressed as a big egg, speechless because I'd run into Clyde's dad, I ran straight into the queue for lunch there in LA, and there was exactly how I'd do set food ... exactly as I'd dreamed. Every day in LA the wonderful Mexican chefs and caterers did BBQ.

I know the knee-jerk reactions from European jerks will be to say, 'But weather is raining here. It's different across the pond in the American country.' Bullshit. They can cook outside as it's sunny, sure, but over here you do it either under easy-ups or kit out a food truck to be able to do BBQ.

The food never sits in a box. It's totally moveable should lunch be pushed and you stagger putting your meat and fish on the grill to ensure latecomers' food is still as good and fresh as the first guys in the line. There it was. Chicken and thin minute steaks, BBQed to perfection. Cheeseburgers. Check. Salmon. Yes, please. There were then two tables and on them were salads and tortillas and loads of sauces and desserts. It was perfect. That's how you do set food. It's simple and really clever.

A few years ago, I got a call to say I'd been cast as one of the main characters in the big Christmas episode of *Doctor Who*. I was going to be Santa! In a

Christmas *Doctor Who*! With bloody Peter Capaldi!!!
(Lovely, kind, funny.) I was thrilled and honoured,
and it turned out to be a great episode. Every now
and then I'll go around the world to do signings and
comic-cons and Santa is always a firm fan favourite.

Anyway, I turn up at basecamp in Cardiff to shoot
the episode and the lovely runners and assistant
directors show me to my trailer. I begin what's known
to actors as 'the Transformation' and a runner knocks
and asks if I want some breakfast. I do. I order and
continue transforming. When he returns he's greeted
by a shirtless Santa smoking a fag. He drops down
the food and I thank him and he hands me a receipt
and then stands around waiting. I'm confused and
I'm like, 'You okay?' And he's all like, 'Do you have
the money?' I'm like, 'Money for what?' He says,
'Breakfast.'

'What do you mean?'

'Sorry, did no one tell you?'

'Tell me what?'

'On *Doctor Who,* you have to pay for your own
breakfast.'

I couldn't believe it. The most popular TV show in
the world and Santa has to pay for his own toasted
bacon. Ho, ho, no! Santa has no money. He's a
Time Lord!

SUNDAY ROAST

In our house, rain or shine, on a Sunday we usually have a roast. That said, after like ten on the trot, I'll get moody that no one else cooks and I'll go on strike. For a week. Before I realise I'm also doing the roast for me too. I love a Sunday when I'm going to cook. As far as I'm concerned, I can't start early enough. Get as much of the prep work done and just relax into it. No matter how much pre-prep you do, there'll come a bonkers ten minutes when everything is ready at the same time. People come to sit down, kids screaming and running around, the gravy boils a tiny bit too hard for a moment, I'm playing with instrument dials trying to work out which oven I'm using for what. It's a tricky ten minutes but, once all that food is on the table, my day is done. If you cook a big lunch for ten people, you don't wash up. Them's the rules. No sir. You're done. Sit back and enjoy the silence of your hungry friends and family enjoying the delicious fruits of your hard labour. A Sunday lunch is long-winded and time-consuming and stressful, but do it right, no, do it at all, and people love it. It's a big part of my culture as a British person; I'm proud that I can make a nice roast. It's showing off a bit.

Timing is everything. Write it all down – it makes it a lot easier. Work out what time you want it on the table and work backwards. Let's work to a 3pm table time.

What meat are we going to use? God help me, I almost wrote what protein. Sorry, a bit of America crept in. It's meat. Call it meat, not protein. 'And what protein would you like with that?' Stop!

Obviously, these timings are from my own personal experience and down to the size of the piece of meat I'd be using for the size of my family. So ...

Big chicken – one and a half hours

Leg of lamb – one and a half hours plus (although there is a long version which takes six hours, at least)

Single bone-in rib of beef – one hour (+/-) for medium rare

Belly pork – four hours at least

These are my cooking times. I always remove the meat and give it at least 30 minutes to rest. You could even give all the above meats an hour to rest if you need some wiggle room. Wrapped in heavy foil, these proteins will just sit there and rest and cook a bit more and stay warm. The meats still cook after you take them out once you've wrapped them in a heavy foil. A medium rare piece of beef can actually become a medium while it rests and cooks a little more. Bear that in mind; if you want it to rest for more than 40 minutes, then cut the cooking time slightly. Or cook for slightly hotter for slightly less time.

All this takes time and comes with experience. Don't beat yourself up. It's daunting. I have two ovens on my cooker, I'm lucky. I could use just one but it takes a real dance to do it. As you can see though, if you're resting the meat for an hour, you can do all the trimmings in that time. It's totally doable. Also ... I've had my current cooker now for six years, it's totally shit. One oven is hot as fuck, while the other, main oven, is rubbish. Sometimes the door just wafts open, I lose a shitload of heat this way, the seal is also gone, sometimes mid-cook I'll have to try and re-attach it. It really burns. But they're mine. I know them inside out. It's important. So, for a big chicken to sit and rest nicely for 30 minutes, you have to get it out at 2:25pm. Which means you have to put it into the oven at 1pm.

If I've done my prep correctly, the cooking of this roast is now just putting things into and taking things out of the oven. You'll have your cheesy leeks cooked (see pages 153–4) and sat under foil, waiting to be heated in the oven. When do they go in? I figure they need 45–50 minutes in a medium hot oven. So, we're eating at 3pm, they go into the bottom of the oven to warm through from 2:10pm. If they brown too much, you can always stick a foil lid on the dish.

Earlier I mentioned Dutchman's dicks. I get up early and they can be prepped first thing. Big saucepan. Big jar of very nice chicken stock from the nice butcher up the road. I'd also point out, I use different stocks for different roasts: chicken, use chicken stock. Beef, use beef stock; same with lamb, use dark beef, and then pork, I'd use chicken stock too.

Poach the carrots until they're nicely soft all the way through. Take them out of the water. Keep the water though, it's important. Now the carrots I leave to cool smothered in butter and pepper, wrapped in foil in the dish that they'll eventually roast in. This makes it super easy, like the cheesy leeks – they're cooked and only need heating up essentially. It makes a complicated roast super easy. Well not super easy, vaguely less complex.

I've also done the carrots this way too, which works nicely and frees up oven space. You poach them in the morning so they're soft and when you're 30 minutes out, fry them in butter on the hob until caramelised and delicious. Both ways I glug some bright olive oil on top and sprinkle a little parsley to serve. Salt, too.

I'm going to try, in a page or so, to capture the magic of the roast potato. I'm fully aware there are whole books devoted to the spud and its ways. I hope I don't disrespect these ancient artists and their spud magic.

I hate peeling potatoes. But if you want roast potatoes, you have to. So, peel potatoes – I peel them all. A kilo, for four of us. It's never enough. Then I chop them into nice chunks, usually quarters, and I put them into the pan I used to poach the carrots. Boiling liquor and all. We're going to reuse the stock from the carrots to parboil the spuds and then combine that liquid with the chicken stock I bought and together it will make lovely gravy.

I use olive oil usually, although I know people swear by lard and duck fat and goose fat and engine grease and blah, blah, blah ... They all work in my opinion. In theory, if you can get it hot enough, it'll roast a spud. I'll use goose fat at Christmas, as it makes them extra special, but for me, olive oil works just great. Once the spuds have parboiled, they're ready to go. If you can push a slim blade all the way through the spud, they're ready. I transfer these using a slotted spoon and put them into a colander.

I get the roasting tin I'm using for the spuds and I'll drizzle oil into it. I always think not too much; I've seen spuds floating in oil and it works, but it's not what I do. The oil should barely cover the bottom. Turn up the heat in the oven to 220°C and put the roasting tray on the top drawer for at least ten minutes. At least. In that time, take the spuds in the colander and gently toss them over and over in the colander. The colander is nice because the little holes act like a grate and you're left with fluffy spuds with lots of nice gentle, soft edges. Roasties love soft and gentle edges ... If the oil is hot enough, they all get turned into crisp, crunchy facets of the roastie – it becomes like a pomegranate but with spuds. Does that make sense?

So, you have your spuds ready, and then remove the fiery hot tin from the oven. Please be careful as the oil becomes super runny when it's very hot. It can often take people by surprise just how quickly it moves in the tin. Now I have a big central gas-burner on my hob, so when the oil comes out I stick it directly on to the flame, and there it sits ... super heating. When it's close to summoning the undergod Pyrus, I take my colander-puffed potatoes and, very carefully, empty them all out in one swift motion into the roasting tin.

They will scream and shout and sizzle. Ignore them. No matter how much they plead, do not turn the heat down. Lift the tin up and slam it into the top shelf of the oven. Keep it at 220°C for at least five to ten minutes. Turn it down to 180°C after this first bit of hot, hot roasting. I find I have lovely potatoes after an hour. I get them out of the oven and turn them over every 20 minutes or so. That way you can always turn it up if needed too. There are a lot of ways to roast a potato. This is a version of mine. Find what works for you.

So, the potatoes need to be ready just before 3pm. An hour to roast, plus ten minutes faff time in the middle getting them out of the water, plus, I'd say 30 minutes to parboil them ... Okay, so you need to put the potatoes into the boiling salted water at about 1:30pm.

Yorkshire puddings ... this is going to destroy a lot of you. It's going to pull the rug out from underneath you. It's going to force some of you to reassess everything you thought you knew. Once I was going to LA to do some press for a film and someone happened to DM me to say 'Hey dude, you should check your Wikipedia entry.' So, I did. It said that I was murdered, assassinated, shot in LA the following day. The day I was due to arrive. I feel maybe that happened as a result of someone finding out that I DON'T MAKE MY OWN YORKSHIRE PUDDINGS. Never have. I use Aunt Bessie's. I'm so sorry if this has come as a terrible shock.

Yorkies always come at such a delicate part of the timeline, kind of near the end. My ovens have never really been hot enough either, and it always seems like a terrible faff. I found a note on my phone which said simply, 'learn to make Yorkshires'. I hadn't. Yet. Whenever I say to my partner, 'I was going to attempt to make homemade puds,' she always lifts her glasses and says, 'Really?' She doesn't wear glasses. I wish she did. Cute.

I've tried probably ten times and it's never worked.
I get these waxed leathery stadium-shaped biscuits.
At best. I know in theory what I need to do, but I
just can't do it. I felt a really lovely, warm, caring
hand on my shoulder. I scrunched my eyes closed,
wishing more than anything it was Mum. I swivelled
around on my heels, tears pouring down my face
expecting to see her fried gold hair, Clairol, light ash
blonde number 102. Looking at her fake nails and
remembering the time she'd woken me up, drunk,
at midnight, she showed me her hands, her huge
red swollen hands. Mum had glued on her fake nails
with Super Glue as she'd lost the regular adhesive
and her hands had reacted terribly, awfully, painfully.
She cried and drank and begged me to pull them off.
So, I did. I made the decision to do it. I found a long
needle and a steak knife and I sat her down beneath
a lamp. While she swigged her drink and sobbed I
took that needle and I slid it between her real nail
and the fake. I levered each nail up slightly. I got a
little gap between each and it enabled me to get the
knife in there and make a tiny gap bigger and bigger
until I could pull it off by hand.

I did it nine more times before I could go back to
bed. I was ten. She slurred and reminded me that
'Mummy loves you'. Then I had to go and have a
cuddle and a horrible kiss on the lips. But then I
could go.

As soon as I saw the nails I knew it wasn't Mum.
I was disappointed but also a little appointed. Even

though it wasn't my mum, it was someone even better ... Aunt Bessie. She put her mixing bowl down and opened her arms and smiled the warmest smile. I fell into her arms and she held me like I'd never been held before. She smelt like buns and perfume and kindness. I never wanted her to let me go. I pulled free and she held me a moment, drying the tears from my eyes with a lump of home-style mash. I notice something in her other hand. She offers it to me, smiling. I take it, it's a noisy blue plastic bag. I read from the front, Yorkshire Puddings ready in just 5 minutes. Fuck yeah. Foolproof. She starts to disappear, to drift off back to her big kitchen in the sky. 'What's your first name?' I ask. She smiles. 'No one has ever asked me that before.' 'Tell me then.' 'I can't. It's a secret Birds Eye Ltd don't want anyone to know.' She winks. I smile. 'Fair enough.' She drifts off into the smoke. Was that a flirt? Did I just flirt with Aunt Bessie? I get a text from Birds Eye asking if the smoke element of the fantasy can actually be rewritten to be steam produced from a vat of boiled spinach? Birds Eye feel the connection between their Yorkshire Puddings and the word smoke has a negative connotation. Like house fires where folk perish. But steam means kettles for tea, boiling water for rich suet puddings to cook, parboiling spuds for roasties, etc. These images are all seen as positive by the Birds Eye Ltd Public Relations team. I agree to change one. I look at the bag of Yorkshires in my hand. I can't wait to try them. Then out of the steam I hear a name drift out: 'It's Alison ... Alison Bessie.' Alison Bessie. Beautiful.

Me and my ex-wife Christina went to have Sunday lunch with some relatives of mine in Kent a long time ago, maybe ten years ago. They're from there so we drove down and met them in a local pub for a roast. It was lovely to see my relatives. My ADHD is such that sadly if I don't see you for a while, it's as if you don't exist to me. Not being moody though, you're just not there. It's terrible. My family must think I hate them.

Anyway, the roast turned up and it looked amazing. I couldn't wait to start. The only thing missing was the Yorkies. We all looked expectantly, none of us really being able to commit until they arrived. Now something happened here that left me and C mouths agape, it really underlined for me why I don't see them very much. Something so foreign happened and it just left me speechless. You know how when you spend Christmas with your new girlfriend's family and discover that their Christmas Day routine was written by a high-ranking Nazi cunt. 'You don't have any presents until after Bubble & Squeak on Boxing Day?' 'Yeah, fuck off.'

Seeing no one had Yorkshires, a relative of mine decided as it was her local she'd take charge, so she went round the table asking everyone individually, 'Have you got your Batters?' She then assaulted a waiter and a low-ranking supervisor, badgering them for immediate, hot, fresh Batters. In the next five minutes I think I heard the word Batters 20 times. I looked at Chris. 'Batters'? What the fuck are Batters? 'Nick, d'you get your Batters?' I don't fucking know.

Hang on. Does she mean, do you mean, Yorkshire puddings? And she did. She's calling Yorkshire puddings, Batters. Batters.

We ate and left. It wasn't until we were back on the M25 that either of us brought up 'Batters'. When we got back home and started making Sunday roasts again, we'd jokingly call Yorkshires 'Batters' to make each other lol. Now, sadly, sometimes we call them Batters without a hint of snide irony. Batters made it into our family's lexicon. (Three more names for Yorkshire puddings – Fried Mousehat, Gravy Chalice, Stadium Biscuit.)

Once the potatoes are out and you're spooning them into a nice bowl to go on to the table, turn the oven heat to super-hot, 220°C+! Put all the frozen Batters on to a tray and straight into the heat. The only other thing you'd be cooking this late in the day is something like white cabbage. I love cabbage with a roast. A nice green element which isn't a cheese-drenched leek. It's fresh and buttery and crisp. It's a completely different mouthfeel too. Slice the cabbage and cook it for three minutes in the same water you cooked the carrots and potatoes. Now take it out. What I usually do is refresh it all in a sink of very cold water. It immediately stops the cabbage from cooking too much. Set aside in a bowl or Ziplock bag.

At the very end of the roasting procedure, heat some butter in a frying pan and sauté the parboiled cabbage until it's starting to brown a bit in places. Into a nice dish, butter on top and a turn of pepper. Serve. Lovely. You could do those first thing and refrigerate them all day.

The meat and gravy for me are always the last guests to arrive. Bowl the Batters and send them to the table. My kids love the responsibility of taking bowls of food to the table. I like seeing them panic a bit but then triumph. It's good for them to feel a bit of pressure. Even if it's only a bowl of Batters.

I used to try and be like my parents in the 1970s and get amazing cookbook slices of medium rare meat on everyone's plates. It goes cold. Everything gets cold while they wait for you to slice meat. So, a long time ago, I shifted across to the hunks in a bowl paradigm. I just slice and cut the joints and put it all into a bowl to go to the table. I always salt the meat at this point. You can put the foil back on top while it sits on the table too, then whip it off at the last minute when the gravy arrives.

At this point, if you were a Tour de France rider, you might be forgiven for taking your hands off the bars and raising a gravy boat in the air as you cross the finish line atop the Alpe d'Huez. You've literally done it. The kitchen, although not spotless, is totally in a good shape. Your family and friends are now sitting down and they're passing dishes around full of delicious food you've spent the day happily producing. The only thing left is the gravy. It should be in a saucepan with a gentle heat beneath, either keeping it hot or reducing it slightly to compound the flavour. Remember to take all the juice that has run out of the meat while it rests and slurp it into the gravy. More flavour. Amazing.

The reason gravy comes last for me is that it's something that's very hot that can help reheat elements of the lunch that may have gone a bit cold sitting in a bowl. The hot fresh gravy brings everything back to life. I always say these words ... 'Be careful, the gravy is very hot and there's plenty more!' People tend to do a bit of a 'Hooray!' Sometimes, and it doesn't happen that often, my warning is starker ... 'Chaps, be careful, this is all there is.' Shit tends to get a bit real then. I find what happens is the children get their gravy wielding right revoked. Kids are pricks with gravy; they'll pour a litre of it on to their plate to juice up half a roastie, then they'll want to get down from the table eating neither. When gravy is scarce, the parents decide.

That's the shape of Sunday roast. I'll sit down after bringing the gravy and Hayley usually takes charge and makes sure Daddy Bear gets a nice plate. I heavily gravy mine because fuckyouImadeit! It's nice knowing you're done for the day. Other people will clear the table and wash up and put away. It seems fair. I also think there's always an element of sport of some kind on a Sunday too, whether that be listening to football on the radio or taping the F1 for me to watch later. Sometimes West Ham will be on. If that's the case, I finish my lunch and quietly drift into the front room to see how much of the game I can watch before the kids realise I'm missing.

BRAISED MEATS

If this was a proper cookbook, these recipes would be in a chapter called something like Winter Warmers, or One-Pot Magic. And that's fine, I think it's a good name to call them. If I had to offer a different name I'd call it ...

Meat sleep inside Wet-hot.

Make a mirepoix ... We're there now! We did it! I don't need to tell you. Sadly, I have to tell some of the others, so go and blow a cheeky zoot out of the window. Take:

3 stalks of celery

2 fat carrots

1 large white onion

Chop your veg, not finely, but kind of coarse – rustique. Take a good, big, Brian Blessed-style glug of olive oil and splash it into a thick, cast-iron casserole dish, bring it up to temperature.

This is a recipe which, again, I've never written down before but it's technique rather than my actual recipe, you know? I've made it with lamb shanks, ox cheek, pig cheek, it would also be a good base for Osso Bucco. (Never made it, though. Let's concentrate on lamb shanks. I love the taste of a nice shank; they love to be cooked like this and go great with a buttery mash or rice or even a cheesy Pommes Dauphinoise (see pages 230–3). The sauce/gravy is also so nice.

To business. Look through your messy drawers and

cupboards until you find a nice big Ziplock bag. Into it tip 30g plain flour. Salt. Pepper. Throw into this bag four shanks and shake. Gently toss it all around to coat the shanks with a thin layer of seasoned flour. You'd also do this with ox cheek and pork cheek. Throw the shanks into the hot oil and fry them to get brown for however long it takes. Five minutes a side? Try not to move them when they're cooking. We want some colour. Do this for all the meat. If there's four meat-eaters, you get a shank each.

In between each shank you may need to add a little more oil to the pan. Once the last shank is brown, take it out, stick it on a plate with the others, cover with foil and leave to rest. Now ... Take the veg that you chopped earlier and toss it into the pan. Toss in a good size sprig of thyme. Stir briefly and then turn the heat down and lid up. We want that veg to steam all the crispy, crusty bits off the bottom of the pan.

Lid off the pan. What do you see? Yes, me too. Take your tomato purée, squeeze it on to a wooden spoon and pop it in the pan. Turn up the heat and fry the purée, stir and let it all sizzle. Hopefully you've listened to my skill and boiled a kettle before you chipped out to zoot. In a nice jug – metal, Pyrex or plastic – measure out 500ml boiling water/beef stock. You can also use just water or just stock but make sure it's a good one with low sodium. If you have a good butcher like I do, he usually has a great bag of jellied stock.

Pour the stock into the pan of cooked veggies/tomato purée and stir. It should sizzle and instantly deglaze the pan. Add two tins of plum tomatoes. If you want to spend five minutes with a wooden spoon stabbing the toms, go for it. It's fun, I get it, honestly I do, but they can stay whole too. We'll probably blitz this sauce down later, so they can stay as big red testes if you'd rather. Or ladies may prefer to smash them down now. Maybe get some long, sharp scissors, imagine a horrible man you despise and then use your scissors to snip his balls to fuck. Wow, this got so dark, so quick. Fun though. Fun and dark. Like life should be.

Take the resting shanks, or cheeks, and now nestle them into the sauce. Ideally the meat should be covered with liquid. With the cheeks it's easier because they're smaller and not on a bone. With the shanks you can add a little more water to get the stock level up or lay them on their sides and cook that way.

I cover the whole top of the now-bubbling sauce with a thick layer of foil. This helps to keep moisture in and the meat below the surface. With the shanks I'd get them out of the oven and baste every 30 minutes.

Tip alert ... If you want the bone from the shank to be white after you cook it, wrap heavily in foil.

Turn the heat down. Plippies. Gently, listen to it. Turn the heat up and listen to that, it sounds hot. Too hot. Turn it down. You should use every sense while cooking. Cover with foil and then the lid and cook, very low, for three hours. Plippies sounds like a nickname for a tasty little bivalve enjoyed in a beachside shack somewhere near Cape Town, washed down with lashings of cold white from a vineyard called Umbithi or something. I can imagine my best friend Tony's wife, Jacqui, shouting something about plippies ... Say these next few sentences in a thick South African accent ...

'Hey doll, why don't we head out for some nice, fresh plippies?'

'You must try the plippies babe, they're divine.'

Or 'These plippies are nature's gift to man, fresh from the ocean, babe.'

Take the lid off the shanks and prepare for a lovely smell. The meat, be it lamb shank, or ox cheek, or pork in some form, should be really soft and wobbly. In theory you could take a spoon and gently cut the meat with it, such is its softness. Take the meat out gently and pop it on a plate wrapped in foil to rest and breathe. Try to keep it whole, try not to let it break up. The lamb shank, if cooked enough, should want to fall off the bone – try to convince it to resist this temptation. I like serving it with the bone. It looks cool.

Wrapped in foil, the meat will sit there for ages without getting cold. Trust. Head back over to your hob to get a noseful of the wonderful sauce cooking that meat for three hours+ has produced. It will have reduced; it will be brown-ish with a deep red under hue. Floating in it will be tasty little vegetable bombs of sweetness. Also, you may see beads of meat fat on top, there may be strands of meat floating around. A mouse? No, there shouldn't be a mouse floating in your pan, get rid of it. Quick. Before he sees. I want you to get in there and, with a spoon, taste it. Let that big, beautiful tongue of yours do its work. I like to call the tongue the detective of the mouth. Let it sleuth. Let. It. Sleuth! For God's sake.

Dip the spoon in. Taste the sauce. And? Nice? It's okay. Just okay? That's fine, do this ... Put sauce on your spoon ... take a couple of little salt flakes, add it to the sauce, drink ... It's much better, you say ... Thank you. The salt has given you a better indication of what the finished gravy will taste like. So, without further ado ... Let's finish it.

I think there are a couple of ways to go about this. I'm not sure which is the right one. My ADHD is swamping my thought process with notions of people mugging me off because I did it wrong, which may actually be true. That said, I did tell you all I wasn't a chef right at the start. I'm just going to say everything and hopefully there'll be a nice sauce at the end of it.

Leave the sauce as it is with nice little pieces of visible veg. Reduce slightly so it's thicker. This is it. Done. Once it's as thick as you want, add salt and pepper, a few chopped leaves of parsley and that's that. You may think about gently lowering the meat back into the pot to warm up. You don't have to, I think splashing hot gravy over it should be enough.

That was method one. Method two is this: take your trusty stick blender/hand mixer and buzz up all the veg until it's a thick, rich sauce. Reduce and season, taste, then keep warm until needed.

Method three feels the most Michelin ... Lol, what a cunt. Take a big jug, take a strainer and pour the liquid that you used to cook the meat through the strainer into the big jug. Use a ladle to get all the flavour out of the pan and into the jug. What you're left with is, relatively, a smooth, rich, spicy gravy. Pour the gravy back into a saucepan and then reduce it, take your time. I want it at least halved. Right, Michelin Fatty-Tyre? 'Oui, Maestro!'

Keep tasting, notice what's happening. Look at the colour. With this much reduction of a sauce I often find you won't need to salt the sauce. I'd still pepper. Remember this process of reduction will make any salt that's got into the sauce before much saltier. This is why we taste what we cook. It's so important.

I'd have my meat on the plate, still warm from being tucked up in foil. I'd have my accompaniments ready, in this case trimmed French beans. (Let's go through this real quick ... Take a packet of French beans, use a little knife to top and tail them. Pan of boiling, salted water on and cook the beans for an amount of time that works for your taste. I like mine bright green and a bit crunchy still, maybe five minutes. Remove from water, put in a little plastic box. Add a knob of butter, let the butter melt and shake the box like Bez with a maraca until all the beans have been coated with warm butter.)

The other accompaniment that I always seem to combine with this dish are Pommes Dauphinoise (see pages 230–3). I make these with lamb a lot. I remember the first time I made these and served them I felt so amazing. They looked incredible and the kitchen smelled nice, and the cheesy sauce that comes from a Dauphinoise combining with the reduced gravy that comes from the lamb shanks was super tasty.

Things I Hate But Actually Aren't Bad

Having been diagnosed with a bunch of brain disorders at 47, highlights include ADHD, OCD, PTSD, dyslexia, anxiety disorders and a healthy slug of hypervigilance, meant for me lots of time looking back through my life and saying out loud in many cases, 'Oh, that's why I did that?' The reason I hate custard was one of those memories that flashed through my head. I can't tell you the number of times I heard the words 'could do better' or 'needs to concentrate', 'amazing imagination but little application', 'talks too much', 'class clown', blah, blah, blah. Looking back these were all red flags that something was wrong, but it was the early 1980s and people just thought I didn't care about school or I was naughty. I was a bit naughty but I just couldn't do it. I couldn't read well, I had no compunction to be sat, I couldn't listen for more than a couple of minutes and keeping ideas fresh in a head that was full of sounds and noises seemed absolutely impossible. I found a friend and a teacher in TV. I watched TV all the time. I loved it. I often think TV was my school.

I can make custard and I would totally say yes if you want to add it to your golf bag. People love it and you can use the process to make lots of different things, crème pâtissière is one I use a lot when I'm making a tart. It's the same process, but ... I hate custard. Even writing this, I can feel my mouth watering, my boke response has been triggered. I can smell it inside my brain-nose. Heave. When I was ten I was at a junior school called St Peter and St Paul's in Ilford. I was quite the swinging dick, let me tell you. Vincent Heggarty was my best friend and we liked The Jam and we dressed like mods. Loafers, stay-pressed trousers or Farahs or waffle trousers, then on top we'd have button-down shirts and Gabicci V-necks. It was the fashion.

During lunch one day, I decided to make the guys laugh by loading three or four portions of jam roly-poly and custard. I just loaded them on to my tray and the guys were laughing and we sat down and ate and I picked at one dessert but the joke was now done. Our laughter and the dinner ladies grassed me up. When I got up with the gang to leave, I was stopped at the rubbish food bin by a teacher.

'Sit down.'

Once again I was super cheeky and was showing off to the guys, but in the end I had to sit down and the guys had to leave.

'I'm going to be late for class, Sir.'

'That's fine. I'll speak to your teachers.'

'Why?'

'Because you're going to sit here until you finish all of those puddings.'

The hall was empty now, the cleaners swept and the food was

packed away and the big bain-maries were wheeled back into the kitchen. It was me and the teacher who caught me. I tried to eat one but the cold custard and the smell just made me heave really badly. The teacher kept saying, 'Eat it please.' I kept gagging and gagging until the fighter in me stood up and said, 'Fuck you!'

I pushed the tray away, crossed my arms and sat back. 'I'm not eating another bite.'

'Then we'll sit here until you do. Until leaving time if we have to.'

It was about 1pm. I sat there until 4pm, when my mum essentially kicked her way into the hall. By this time, I was just terribly sad and crying and frightened. What a way to treat a child. Mum was FUCKING FURIOUS. She and I left, while she cursed at the faculty. She was always so strong and protective of me. I always felt so safe with my mum, nothing could hurt me when she was around. (Except for her.) Maybe this was part of the reason I was so hurt and lost and lonely when she decided to choose alcohol and addiction over me. My hero became the thing I was afraid of and finally the thing I hated more than anything else. It was only after I'd been diagnosed with all my neuro-fuckery that I came to understand not only how but why she could've done what she did. And in doing that, I myself found not only a peace but a way to forgive her, after 40 years.

What I couldn't/wouldn't forgive was custard. Custard wasn't an alcoholic and for that I was grateful at least. What it was though was disgusting and I never forgave it. That is why I hate custard. And as a little PS ... If one of my children was ever treated like that by a teacher, I would literally get that teacher in a headlock in front of the school and guff into their mouth until they slumped unconscious in a puddle of their own piss and the kids were all pointing and laughing and chanting, 'We hate Mr Guffmouth!'

It's not cool. Shit stays with kids forever. Shit that happened to me has stayed with me forever. It has hurt me and sadly I admit, with a great deal of shame, that I'm sure things I've done, the people I became during times of dark madness, will stay with my children forever.

To make amends, all I can do is love them as much as I can, support them, encourage them, never deflate them or make them feel less than. I can help this by not being a horrible, frightened, aggressive, resentful, no self-esteem, why-would-anyone-ever-love-me Dickhead. Thankfully that me has gone. Not dead, it never dies, but it does lay dormant. The fear of a return keeps me working hard every single day to not do to them what my poor, weak, hurt, broken mum did to me. Fucking custard.

I also hate porridge. There's a consistency thing happening which means it can make me heave. Same as custard or Congee or the aspic I found the Japanese suspended everything in. I loved Japan but weirdly did not like the food. Or the hotels. Me and Joe Cornish went with *Attack the Block* to do press and when I got there they'd put me in a room on the 50th floor. I'm not a diva but I am terrified of earthquakes. The thought of being so high and then a big eight or a nine hits, and you're right up there and the whole building is moving back and forth ten feet. FUCK THAT. My heart would burst.

I asked very politely to be moved to a hotel whose windows one could jump out of to safety should push come to shove. Which they did. It was lovely. I took full advantage of the treatments on offer and ordered a masseur to come to my room. I showered and prepared myself for the geisha I believed was en route. The door knocked and I sprang up and opened it. The hotel manager led a 90-year-old man into my room who spoke no English. He shoved him inside and left.

I think they thought I was a foreign sumo athlete and got a man whose speciality was power lifters. I thought he had nodded off slightly but as I approached, his eyebrows twitched to life and he pointed to the bed. I took my robe off and lay down.

I watched him for the whole 20-minute walk across the room. He took off his shoes and prepared. He spent a long time just rubbing his face in my chest hair. He had a grip like an iron fastener, and every time he tried to massage me it hurt so much I squealed and every time I squealed he hit me. Then he got on to the bed with me to really get going. In my mind I was cursing myself for choosing the 90-minute full body. Fuck, why did I have to be so greedy? I'm greedy.

Because the bed was really soft and I'm really heavy, every time the old man let go of the headboard he fell into the hole made by me and on to me. It was tiring for us both. After three attempts we left it and he dozed in a chair until the door rang and the manager, and I'm assuming his great-grandson, came in once again to remove him. It was confusing. I was so fucking stressed. I thought, dinner will cure that I'm sure. At that point, I think Tokyo had more Michelin-starred restaurants than anywhere else. We didn't go to one of those though. We went to a tiny black door in a wall under a railway arch. We knocked and were led into a small curtained-off antechamber. At some point the lady pushed back the curtains and there in front of us was a very impressive old-fashioned village. Each little house or shop was a table and ninja-like waiters whizzed this way and that.

There used to be a big restaurant in Redbridge near the

station, it was like, I want to say a Harvester. It was a real treat to go to a Harvester and that one in particular as, like the Japanese restaurant, it was set up like a higgledy-piggledy village. Cute.

The Japanese place was cute and the food that wasn't jelly was nice, but the whole magic/ninja element was too much for me. The restaurant had been built with lots of secret holes and panels and passageways, which would open up without warning and a shrieking ninja would leap out to serve another ball of prawn phlegm suspended in aspic.

I didn't eat much. I was awake at 5am, wandering about looking for breakfast. I found my hero there ... McDonald's. It was delish. The McDonald's in Japan was different from London as it has loads of businesspeople sleeping in it. Later, I found out that because of the size of Tokyo and the fact that these people work until 10/11pm at night it's not worth them trying to go home so they sleep in Maccy D's. It's a bit sad.

Sometimes in the mornings my vile/amazing kids will scream at me the words 'APPLE PIE!!!' Nothing else, just that.

It means they want Apple Pie Porridge. Now you can have it. Heal your souls ... Let's go. I'd also point out, sometimes I make the porridge and the children either refuse to come to the table, or they burst into tears when they see it or there's another ludicrous reaction. Choose your battles. Also ... It's their loss. It's amazing.

KID'S PORRIDGE

I use either Braeburn or FGD. Peel. FML. Cut into quarters and then slice out the core bit. Cut the apple piece in half lengthways, then cut across into chunks. Set them all aside into a little bowl. You could also peel these and use a corer if you'd prefer.

Big knob of butter. Unsalted. Melt the butter and then into it empty two tablespoons of brown muscovado sugar, also brown demerara would taste nice. That said, if all you have is white, use white. I'm sure some of you will be shaking your heads about using sugar in kids' porridge but it's not much and they love it, so fuck off, you judgey prick. They get a great start to the day.

Pour the sugar into the foamy butter and shake around until the sucre begins to melt. Into this young caramel (good rapper's name), toss the apples. It may crackle and foam slightly. If you're nervous, take off the heat for a few seconds. Shake the pan round and round to ensure all the apple pieces get turned and covered in the sauce. Turn down and cook the apples until you can slide a thin blade between its ribs. (Wait. What?) Nothing. Shake the pan almost constantly, don't let the caramel catch. Now add in enough oats for three people. I don't know how much that would be. A cup?

Stir the oats into the caramel and apple mix. It'll be dry dry, but this is your chance to smash the apple caramel directly into the DNA of the porridge oats. After a bit, stir in 200ml milk. Stir with a wooden spoon or heatproof spatula. This is like a breakfast risotto. I don't stop stirring this during cooking. By the way, I don't know if this is technically correct. It just feels nice and right, so that's how I do it.

Taste the oats as you go until they're cooked how you like them. At this point, I'll generally add half a teaspoon of ground cinnamon into the pan and stir to add that genuine apple pie vibe. Of course, leave it out if you hate cinnamon.

Here's a hack for the kids. I hate myself for genuinely using the word 'hack'. Once the milk goes into the pan, I take the bowls I'll be serving the porridge in and I'll leave them in the fridge. When I get them out to serve, they're really nice and cold and it cools down the porridge really quickly. The apple chunks covered and cooked in molten sugar can be not only tasty but downright molten. Take precautions. Employ the fridge-bowl system. Also, my kids love it when they see an adult do something they know seems ludicrous for an 'adult' to do. Putting bowls into the fridge is one of those things. Daddy snoring loudly while pretending to sleep in their bed with a potty on his head would be another one.

My kids hate garnish, they're super suspicious of it, and basically just move it and throw it on to the floor. But for the adults, thin slices of raw, crisp, fresh apple go well with this porridge. Enjoy.

The banana version of this is basically the same, except this ... There are two ways to do the first bit: you can either take three whole, ripe bananas and stick them on a roasting tray at 160°C for 20 minutes. When they come out they should be dark and sweet and have a tang of West Indian molasses. You'd then scoop all the banana-y flesh out into the pan and add the oats and then it's the same ... (But no cinnamon.)

Or do it the same as the apples. Cut the bananas down and fry in butter and then add sugar to caramelise the bananas. Then cook it like the apples (But no cinnamon.)

The kids eat it or they don't. The parents don't seem to mind if the kids refuse this breakfast and it seems to all get finished by someone. It's a real winner. You could also use the butter sugar apple or the banana version for things other than porridge topper. (Sorry.) They go great in pancakes. On yoghurt, on ice cream. (To name but three ...)

Other fruits that could be cooked this way and added on to yoghurt, cereal, ice cream, porridge, etc. are:

Nectarine

Peach

Berry medley

Pineapple

Pear

Plums

Apricot

Fig

And no other fruit. That's it, the comprehensive list. Don't bother looking for more. It's pointless. Please don't look.

Parenting

Our morning drill almost every morning is the kids get up at 7am and then we all come down. Baby gets changed, Middle Dreamboat screams at us for oat milk and TV and I check my phone to find 30 messages from Big Boy asking if he can buy a skin on Fortnite for £20. (On this occasion I'd gone to bed and he had bought it anyway. Not cool. Sadly, it was a boundary and it came with a ramification. Four weeks no pocket money. When I broke the news to him, he burst out crying. He was so sad. I'm always the soft touch, so I think it hurt all the more. I left the room and went into the toilet and had a little cry myself.)

It's odd for me, wanting my kids to be as happy as possible all the time, then having to punish them doesn't come easy. But as we often remind ourselves in our house: 'Children are allowed and absolutely encouraged to feel and to sit comfortably in every emotional state.' They're completely allowed to be sad. Human existence becomes invalid if a child is only happy, right? Yes, it would be nice, but it's completely not possible to carry that into adulthood. Then what do you have? An adult human who is not used to being disappointed or sad or afraid. It then becomes difficult to deal with these things. Sadness is just as valid an emotion as joy.

Son Number 1 recently got a phone and sent me a text saying sorry. I texted him back saying I was in the kitchen if he fancied a cuddle. You know what he said? 'I'll come and have one in a minute when I've stopped crying.' My fucking heart broke again. I was making veggie Shepherd's Pie for lunch and he lolloped in and buried his face in my armpit. We had a nice cuddle. He tried to smile a bit. Eventually we had a kiss and he lolloped off again. It felt nice. For me anyway.

I find it really hard being a parent. It's so much responsibility. It's especially hard being a parent who is also neurodiverse and suffers from anxiety and has lived a life in trauma and grief and has a TON of life experience both good and extremely bad and a world-class imagination. I know what can happen to human beings when they get fucked over during their childhood. It's not good.

I guess the constant hum in my brain asks, 'Are you fucking them up now?' 'Did you just fuck them up a bit?' It's impossible to tell. It's like the time-travel paradigm. You go back in time and as you leave the time machine you stand on and kill a filthy bug, and when you get back to your current timeline all your children are violent heroin addicts!

What do you do? As a father with people-pleasing tendencies the notion of doing nothing is a difficult one to get my head around. Maybe that's what cooking is for me too? Possibly? The way to give them something, to drip feed them something without making them feel like they're in trouble or this is a life lesson they must learn. Take it or leave it but know it will always be there. It will always be a constant that you can rely on. That feels like a good kind of parenting. It beats being lifted in the air and hit with brushes and spoons. Being screamed at or grabbed. I remind the kids often that that is always a method of parenting we could try at some point. We laugh. Them not so much. (Maybe we should do nothing but love intensely and support and guide and be gentle and honest? Feels nice, right?)

BEANS/SPAGHETTI ON TOAST

I know you might think I'm taking the piss a bit, but beans/ spaghetti on toast is not only relatively healthy but to me it's absolutely delicious, a food of my childhood and it also feels like a British culinary tradition – like the Bubble & Squeak I mentioned earlier. I love the taste of a nice tradition.

Keep it simple. Use white bread. Use salted butter. Use a saucepan, NOT the microwave.

While the beans/spaghetti is coming to temperature on the hob, toast two pieces of bread. Don't worry about the fact they'll be cold when they're on the plate, you're going to cover them with magma-hot B/S. The cold base-toast also stays firmer and crisper for longer too.

Take the two pieces of toast. Butter heavily. Put on plate. Keep the B/S warm while you're waiting for secondary toast.

Toast two more slices. When they are done, tip the B/S on to the base-toast. Then heavily butter and halve the other toast. Et voilà! You're done. I often grate a vintage

Cheddar on top and let it melt a bit. Also ... white pepper ... yes, please. It's completely alright, in fact I'd recommend eating this with a hot cup of tea or a very cold pint of milk. How easy is that? Also, cheap as fuck. My dad used to splash a bit of Lea & Perrins on top. He's sadly no longer with us and I've, personally, always blamed that culinary choice he made. That and lung cancer.

I paint a bit. My dad was a fantastic watercolourist, just amazing, really precise and although not photo-real, pretty close to it. I can't do what he did, but then I'm not sure I want that. I want to paint large, chaotic, abstract canvasses. Or so I thought. I could never paint faces because I'm not an artist and then a couple of years ago, during a particularly brutal bout of months of insomnia, I sat up and filled pad after pad with faces. I looked at faces, I looked at shapes, what was there, what wasn't, what mattered, what didn't. Over the course of the winter, I filled 12 A3 pads with hundreds of faces. Eight hundred or more. The Nightfolk.

Ever since that winter I've moved away from wanting to be an abstract artist. What I want to paint now are people. Someone who came to the studio suggested I painted people because I'm lonely. I crave company. Sometimes I sit back and see all those faces looking at me and I think perhaps they were right. What I like about art is that I can't get it wrong. There is no wrong answer. I can't make a mistake. I have a portrait by a young artist called Michael Sydney Moore, it is completely photo realistic. It's of an old man who is clearly an alcoholic. Whenever I carry my babies from the bath to bed, as we pass the painting on the way, we always say, 'Goodnight Grandpa.'

It's an incredible painting. I have stood, probably for hours all told, and studied individual brush marks, it's remarkable. What a skill. I looked at that painting and others like it and tried to draw a face like his and everything I did was so shit it made me furious. I'd actually get so frustrated and cross I'd snap my pencils in half and petulantly toss my pad down the garden. Why? I never had an art lesson, so why was I so mad at myself for not immediately being perfect at something that's actually really fucking hard?

Still, I started looking at other artists and portraits generally, and by and by, my focus moved from the photo real paintings of actual people to the faces that people like Picasso and Giacometti painted. Yes, of course, they are incredible artists but their choices when it came to portraits were incredibly simple. So simple, in fact, that these paintings and many others besides must overhear these words thousands of times a year: 'My fucking kid could paint that.' (Probably the same dick who thinks I'm a billionaire.)

Picasso would draw a triangle for a nose. Giacometti's faces were literally three ovals and a circle. Eyes left black. Frank Auerbach's faces were just mounds of thick paint with a few black marks for features. All of them, though, worked as portraits. I was hooked. Paint emotion. We all know what a fucking nose looks like, but what does grief look like? What does fear look like? What does a mouth look like when it says, 'I don't love you any more?' or 'Goodbye, Dad'? That's what's important. Who cares about what features look like? There are what, 7 billion people on the Earth, give or take. And apart from the odd set of twins, triplets, etc., we all look different. All 7,000,000,000 of us look different. I find that completely amazing but, no matter who you are, or what you do, what house you live in, what city, if you're trans or Black or an Australian Aborigine or a car dealer from Houston or a man who fishes for tiny lake perch in Kenya or a Dutch underwear model, no matter who you are, or who you think you are, the one thing we all share is our emotions. (Or lack of in some cases.) We all share the same emotions. Joy, pain, fear, anger, guilt, jealousy, etc. Maybe this is why we don't give a fuck about what Picasso's noses looks like. When humans look at those simple abstract paintings that we allow ourselves to perceive as human, what we're reacting to is the emotion the artist has imbued in those simple abstract shapes.

I was sat in my front room once, which looks out on to a main road, and a huge lorry parked up outside and blocked the sun out. I sat up, 'Who the fuck's this now?' A man knocks on the door. I get up and answer.

'Hello.'

'Where do you want them, mate?'

'Want what?'

He hands over his delivery note, but being dyslexic as fuck, a delivery note is like a funfair for my eyeballs – they roam across the sheet eating sugar clouds, not seeing anything until my left eye focuses on the word 'canvas' ... oh. Are these the canvasses I ordered? But the canvasses were only 12 inches by 6 inches.

I watch this man struggle with a huge packing case I've seen in documentaries about Damien Hirst. Bernard Cribbins!!! Eyes and brain, what have you done?

'Hey mate, how big is that canvas?'

'Canvases. Two of them. 12 feet by 6 feet.'

Oh fuck. I need to get them round the back before Hayley sees them.

When we were shooting *Hot Fuzz* in Wells it coincided with my ex-wife Chris's 40th birthday. She was coming down to hang out and celebrate her birthday. There was this classic old traditional jeweller in Ealing, and I knew they did what I wanted to get her as a gift, those silver necklaces with a name on. During scenes I called up and gave them the order, they used my card and I paid. It was actually a lot more than I thought it would be but I thought fuck it, it's a nice pressie.

Once it was ready, it was shipped to me down in Wells where we were shooting, and it arrived the morning Chris was due to get there. I was on set so the necklace was dropped off in my trailer. Chris arrived at 5pm just as I wrapped. We met in my trailer and there were cards and nice 'Happy Birthdays' when she got there. I hadn't had a chance to look at my gift so I handed it over. 'Happy Birthday, love.' Chris eagerly unwrapped the gift and opened the box. Her eyes widened, not in a good way – it was a mixture of joy and disbelief I think ...

'Is it okay? Do you like it? Let's have a look.'

'Um ... okay.'

She lifted out of the box something I can only describe as a sterling silver number plate. It was enormous. It was like something Flavor Flav might've worn. I'd gotten the numbers all mixed up. Centimetres and inches is tricky.

PIES IN A BOWL

This was an invention of mine about 25 years ago. I ate it a lot and then Simon moved in with me and he too fell into Pies in a Bowl in a big way. It's really simple and it's hearty and cheap as fuck, and naughty and bloody lovely. Here's how you do it.

You will need ...

2 individual Findus chicken and vegetable pies (a note here on pies ... use whatever pies you want – I've done minced beef and onion, steak and kidney too)

egg cup with some milk in

boiling water

Bisto chicken gravy granules

ketchup

white pepper

You can also traditionally serve it with two slices of thickly buttered white, sliced bread. In fact, I've even eaten Pies in a Bowl as a fucking sandwich. A sandwich. Pies, in a sandwich. Get the fuck out of here.

'Okay I will.'

'Bye.'

'Bye.'

'Can you leave your keys?'

'Seriously?'

'Yeah.'

'Okay. Who is it? Can I ask?'

'It's the guy who was on our plane coming back from Greece.'

'Papa Ricky??!!'

'Yeah. Papa Ricky.'

Mind. Blown.

Follow the instructions on the box. From memory it's like, cook from frozen. Use a double finger dab of that milk on top of the pie and pop 'em in the oven for 20 minutes at 220°C. Something like that.

Timing is the important thing here. You need the kettle to boil just as the pies come out. Use the gravy granules (chicken) to make a thick gravy.

Turn the two pies out of their foil underpants into a bowl, lid-side down, stab a couple of times as a way the gravy can enter its pastry host, squirt with ketchup and lash on a drift of white pepper. Job done. Dig in. I've drunk a pint of very cold milk with this and it was Mintox!

Quick note here on ketchup ... Whenever one mentions ketchup on social media you invariably get a bunch of idiots saying shit like ... 'What, no brown?!' And other shit like, 'Sorry, ketchup?! Please, unfollow sir!' What I'd say to those people is: 'Your flaccid opinions are not facts. Stick whatever you want on top of a pie. I literally couldn't give less of a shit. I prefer ketchup. So, ketchup it is.'

There's another reason PIAB made the cut in the book ... When Simon and I first started living together, our place was small and shit. You had to walk partly through another person's hallway to get to our front door. He was a very angry Irish alcoholic and I hated coming home late after work. His telly would be blaring and the only thing that illuminated the room in which he sat and waited. His lair. If you were lucky, you'd get to the door and he'd stay asleep/passed out and that would be that. If you were unlucky, he'd be awake and waiting for you. The sound of my key in the front door would bring him out and he'd shout and spit and wave his huge fists, swollen with rage and alcoholism. I was constantly afraid living in that place. It was my ex-girlfriend's place. She lived with another girl called Morag.

I put in a lot of graft trying to get Cheryl to fall in love with me but I think she did fall in love with me. I did with her. She asked me to move in. Or I just didn't want to leave. Morag hated it. It drove us closer and them further apart. Morag moved out. I wrote a whole novel in that flat trying to get Cheryl to fall ever deeper in love with me. Man, I had it bad. The book was absolutely shit.

Me and Cheryl didn't last that long. A few months. I had stopped drinking at about the same time. I think I stopped for three years. It wasn't compatible with my love affair. I think, and rightly so, Cheryl wanted us to go and drink and hang out and spend long weekends drunk and horny. She ended up having an affair and she left me. She moved out of her own flat. The last time I saw her I was sad, alone. I loved her a lot, but we weren't right. Like a lot of my relationships with women growing up, I didn't love Cheryl because we made a great couple, because we were right for one another. I made her fall in love with me because people said it couldn't happen. She was so beautiful; she was way out of my league. 'I'll show you ...' In the end she showed me. I knew it would end like this but I liked it, deep down. What do the French call it? Ennui?

We kissed for the last time. I can still taste my tears on her lips. Warm, salty (like the gravy on the pies). Simon's relationship had ended as well, so we decided to move in together.

Pies in a Bowl was a step closer to this. One evening, stoned to fuck, I stood up, I gasped, dramatically ... 'Oh my God ...'

I got him. 'What? What the fuck?!'

'I've got pies in the freezer.'

We actually stood up and did a dance and high-fived. I opened the door and stood back. Let him through. Watched him as he danced down the dark hallway past the bathroom where I was kissed by a ghost. As I followed him into the kitchen, my smile had dropped now, my face serious.

'Go on. Open the freezer. They're in there. The Pies.'

'I can't wait!'

Nor could I. I couldn't wait. Weeks earlier, Simon had ended up getting off with Lovely Lucy Miller. The porcelain-skinned ginger Australian waitress I fancied the arse off. Man, I liked her. She liked Kippy though (and Simon, evidently). Kippy's real name was John. John was actually one of the inspirations behind Mike Watt TA from *Spaced*. Lucy was smart but Kippy was in the military, so I never really stood a chance. Still one evening I'd invited her over for a roast chicken. We never ended up roasting it, instead we lay in bed doing dabs of super-strong pink-champagne speed. Nothing happened. Still, I liked her a lot and Simon knew that and still he got off with her ... Well, now I'd get my own back ...

Simon opened the freezer.

'Where are they? I can't see them.'

'Get right in there. They're right at the back.'

I watched him poke around in there for an age. He knew at this point. He had to know. He turned round, his brow furrowed, knowing the truth but not wanting to believe the truth.

'Where are they?'

I smiled. It went better than I could ever have imagined. Too well. His face was so hurt. I pulled the triggers and let him have it. This is for Lucy ...

'There are no pies, Simon.'

'What do you mean? No pies, you said ...'

I nodded. I knew what I said. I smiled. I knew what I'd done, the fuse I'd lit, the blast I now stood amongst.

His face fell, his heart broken. He hummed, head shook, no pies. No fucking pies ...

I started to laugh maniacally. He stepped back, afraid. What was happening?

I grabbed the V-neck of my T-shirt and with all my might ripped my shirt into two pieces. I screamed to the sky. Simon was confused but laughing too at this point.

That was for Lovely Lucy Miller. No poontang. No pie.

If you've gotten older and you've forgiven your best mate for getting off with Lovely Lucy Miller, then perhaps you've also reached a point in your existence when you've started to make your own pies, from scratch. It's a long process to make your own pies, lots of things need to be done. You can also do lots of these steps a day or two before. The last thing you do in that case is make your pastry, or roll out your store-bought one, stick it in and on your pie dish and cook it.

The pies I make the most are ...

Chicken & Leek
Chicken & Mushroom
Steak & Mushroom
Mince Beef & Onion

And then fish, but that's a different animal altogether. I'll come to that monstrosity at the end. Homemade fish pie is a ton of work but if you get it right, you'll burst with pride. It's amazing and I like to use the back of a spoon to cover the mash with 'scales'. Sensational.

CHICKEN & LEEK

Whenever I use chicken in a pie, I start with a load of chicken thighs, skin on. I slash the skin, sprinkle with olive oil, salt and pepper and then I roast it in a low oven (150°C) for about an hour. When it comes out the skin should be crispy and a little treat if you fancy a bit, the meat will be soft and the bone (if there is a bone) should just slip out. Leave it all in a bowl covered in clingfilm, lots of juice and fat and flavour will leach out of these thighs as they cool. This will make a delicious addition to the finished gravy.

Get a nice big steel bowl. You can probably guess by now that I absolutely love big steel bowls. They're cool and fun to own and if you have one in every size you'll use them all the time. I have one that I use when I make cakes has a rubber base so you can whip butter and sugar together and the bowl doesn't wobble.

A word about the crispy chicken skin ... It's absolutely delicious, but I'm not sure technically/traditionally if you'd put it in the pie. I have but it felt weird. From six thighs, I chopped three skins and put it into the mix. With hindsight, you could probably chop it to fuck and put it all in. My only concern is the crispy skin becomes wet and flabby. I'd love to know what a proper chef would do with them. Guys? I've mentioned before, from watching Michelin-starred chefs prep food, the game seems to be about getting as much taste and flavour into every stage of a recipe. So, maybe with that in mind, once you've pulled the crispy skins off, leave them on a roasting tray in a warm oven to completely dry. Then, using the spice grinder your in-laws got you last year for St Jacob's Dagan, drop the brittle, fragile sheets of the skin in and blitz until it becomes a fine powder. Transfer the powder into either a small plastic bag or a little homemade envelope made from perhaps a glossy magazine or ironically, a lottery ticket. When you serve the pie make sure every guest has their own envelope of what street dealers are calling 'Bird' or 'TurboHen' or simply 'Cluck'.

Just before everyone digs into your delicious pie,

encourage your guests to rack out a big line of Chickaine and, using a dry slice of rolled-up iceberg lettuce, snort the powdered crackling deep into your brain. This will quickly seek out and latch on to your brain's taste and pleasure centres. The user will usually fall to the floor and immediately fire out a huge magmatic gush of rich, meaty gravy all over the kitchen ceiling. Bon appétit! (Don't ask me to tell you in what gland gravy is produced. For argument's sake let's say, testes in men and the, um, thymus in women. Also, if you're seriously going to ask me this, you should probs close the book now and use it to prop up a wonky Chesterfield.)

I wish there was a food that made a human react in this way. Imagine that. It would be amazing and so terrifying. A food stuff that was so tasty and amazing that it caused the human body to spontaneously erupt litres of delicious chicken gravy. I definitely see it becoming a new avenue of as yet unearthed gastronomy ...

You can't get a table at the restaurant for love nor money. The waitlist is huge. The *Evening Standard* did a huge article about it and then *London Tonight* sent Giles Coren and Monica Galetti to try it, live, on the Friday show. The country and then the world falls for the exquisite naughtiness of Heston's La Maison de Squirt. Soon after, in June 2028, Michelin gives it an unprecedented fourth star.

Imagine having to wait 13 months to get a table for

your parents' 31st wedding anniversary! This is what they want. They saw *London Tonight* too.

It would be so nerve-racking I bet. Those things always are. You never quite feel like you fit it. You have to dress up too. It's so formal. I went to Pétrus once and it was nice but so formal. I couldn't relax. I was looking through the wine list and the most expensive bottle of red was £79,000!!! You could buy a house for that. Does that really sound any more ridiculous than a place that offers lines of 'Cluck'?

The guys on the front desk are super nice and not snooty at all, and they make a fuss of Mum and take our coats. We're led to the bar and we have a bottle of champagne! (I called from work on Monday and pre-paid using my card, Mum hates the price of this sort of thing. I thought rather than have an annoying to and fro about how expensive champagne is, just ring and pay beforehand.)

We're led through to the dining room and it's really warm and welcoming. Really Spanish, you know? Me and my Melanie flew to Zaragoza for her 30th and we did the whole 'Pig Anus' tour with another couple. All the little bars we went into then were like this, bright white tiles and lovely warm Moorish-inspired fabrics. And served pigs' anuses.

They've done a really clever thing, and it really made us feel at home – they immediately brought the freshest, crispiest, loaf of sourdough for the table. The butter is also incredible. So rich and salty. It's made using tortoise milk.

Apart from three different starters and three different desserts, the main course is set. It's Cluck. We order the Cluck. Melanie and Mum both have scallops to start. Dad has a Trompette du Porc. It's incredible, as the waiter plays it as he brings it to the table. If other guests have it at the same time, the restaurant fills with a delicious melody. I have soup.

Then it's time ... Marcelo our waiter comes round with a huge tray covered by a shiny cloche. When he lifts the lid, a huge pillow of smoke wafts out filling the air around the table with the aroma of an old Chicken Cottage. Under the bell there's probably a kilo of pure, crystallised Cluck.

Another waiter comes round and you're each given your own unique drilled-out hen rib to snort your meal through. (We got to keep ours! Mel was thrilled.) More well-dressed waiters arrive and they politely slip Mum's skirt off and begin to wrap her bottom in a conical skirt of medical-grade plastic. It's a bit like what a dog wears when it's had stitches in an ear wound, but it goes around the waist. The cone has a little silver jug attached at the back, which swings and clatters against the table as they secure it. The silver jug and, in fact, the whole design of the HenHood was created for one purpose, to capture the rich gravy as it involuntarily fires out of Mum's body.

Having dished the four of us out a huge line of Cluck, the waiter nods, sagely, 'It's time.' He takes out a wallet and hands us what looks to be a £25 note. Upon closer inspection though, instead of King William's face, it's Heston's! And it's not a banknote, they're actually wafer-thin, dried, compressed flamingo embryos. Apparently, Marcelo tells us proudly, Heston began the processing procedure in 1978. We all agree that's why we love Heston, he's ever so playful. He's a cheeky one. He thumbs his nose at the establishment and their outdated ideas on, so-called, 'fine' dining.

We're all now wrapped in the plastic. I hear Mum whisper to Dad as she rolls up her flamingo embryo.

'I'm a bit nervous.'

Dad takes her hand and says, 'You were like this in Cambodia, remember, before we ate live mice.'

'Yeah, I was.'

Mum leans in and they try and have a tiny kiss but their lips barely reach now the bulky, semi-rigid, broth-traps are in place. They laugh. We all laugh.

'Bottoms up!' says Mum, as she and Dad reach down to schnarf their rails.

They pop the rolled-up 'Heston note' into their mouths and almost immediately Mum's eyes roll back, she grips the table, shuddering, groaning loudly. (It's the kind of groan you only hear when you're on YouTube and you've fallen down a rabbit hole entitled 'Horrible Old Men who Bully Animals Getting Their Dicks Kicked Off By Powerful Shire Horses'.) We watch as Mum leans back and gracefully fires off an incredible PFFFFTTTTTT of the rich amber nectar into her gravy cloak! It fills the air with the most amazing smell. Imagine a Sunday lunch x10. What a magical way to spend an anniversary.

Mum briefly wakes and giggles just as Dad is uncontrollably firing an arc of clean, fresh, hen-amber into his Tabard du Consommé.

Mel looks at me and says, 'Let's eat!' She bangs her line.

I smile and snort my Cluck; Marcelo helps me with my Stockshroud and I've done it. I've hoofed it, my first line of ba-gaaaaawk!!! There's an intense rush of pleasure, but pleasure that tastes like roast chicken. My arms shoot out and stiffen like a boxer reset by a crisp right hook. I can actually feel my gland begin to produce huge amounts of liquid, then I shudder and slump into Marcelo's arms. That's all I remember. (That said, I have a vague shadow of a memory of waking slightly and seeing Dad pumping pints of his hot gravy into Mel's hungry, eager mouth.)

I awaken, full, fresh and thrilled to see my family now fully dressed and cheerily sipping wine. It's so nice to see Dad smile again after his diagnosis. He's had a tough year. God knows he deserved a treat. All of our sauce shrouds are gone. They've been replaced by four of THE MOST incredible-looking pies. With a sharp tug, Marcelo finally slips my catheter out and hands me the silver gravy jug full of the most delicious, richest and biblically tasty sauce ever produced by human glands. We dig in, greedily pouring the hot gravy on to our pies. The huge bowl it sits in is so deep and voluminous as to accept a lot of gravy. ('Probs from Scandinavia,' says Mel. She's usually right about flatware provenance, too!) Yum! The only two items on the menu available as sides are chips cooked 60 times (which have to be ordered when you book to give them the time to prepare) or Birds Eye potato waffles.

At the end we're all stuffed and everyone gets a bit carried away and tipsy and eventually we all begin to hand our gravy jugs around so we can taste each other's merry emissions. I must say they were all remarkably similar, except for Dad's, which was a bit bitter and 'almondy'. Marcelo suggested we could probably taste Dad's prostate cancer. So interesting. Marcelo told us in confidence that Heston's next big venture was to open an eatery in Antarctica next year called Tümøur: 'All it serves are benign growths cooked directly on lava.' The guy's a genius, make no mistake. What's next?, I hear you cry. Tiny poached owls that fly directly into your mouth? (Actually, that's a pretty good idea.)

I GUARANTEE you that there will be a branch of Cafe Squirt on Mars by 2050. I GUARANTEE it. I also think Salt Bae will definitely want to get involved somewhere along the line. How can he not? You're looking at least $350 per head. (And that's just for our gear.) I can definitely see him turning up at your table and doing a huge line of Cluck off the blade of an ancient scimitar. Wearing his trademark sunglasses, he opens a hatch in his suit and begins to fire litres of nutstock over you and your numerous guests that have gathered to celebrate Sarah's bat mitzvah.

Squirt Bae's is not only fucking expensive, it's also a bit corny. Squirt Bae goes on to open 1,500 restaurants in Dubai alone. In one year!!! Eventually the public's desire for Cluck cools. It essentially marks the downfall and hegemonising of a once-revered culinary trend. The following year the rights to Cluck are bought by the Nottinghamshire-based brewhouse that runs the successful Irish-themed chain outlet, Brendan McRacists. That is kind of that. The death knell has sounded. What a shame. I guess that's what fine dining is like essentially. One day they're squirting hot, rich gravy out of a gland. The next, they're not. C'est la vie and bon appétit!

Get your lovely big, silvery bowl ready for action. I like it when you open the cupboard door and you can hear their little tails clanking against one another, wagging, eager to be used. I chose the one with the rubber base, but shush, don't tell cloths.

Once the roasted chicken thighs are cool enough to be handled, and that can take a hell of a long time to happen, you'll want to try and safely flake the soft white meat into rubberbowl.

At this point could I just draw your attention to a TED Talk I gave in Trømso in 2017. I argue that the energy released during bone-heat retention, or BHR, could realistically heat and light Bangladesh, cleanly, economically for many, many years to come. I was laughed off stage, but they'll see, they'll all see.

Once the value of your BHR drops beneath the safety ceiling mandated by Bugenhaagen's 1987 'Stockholm Address' (886ppmmc, parts per million microclucks), you're then safe to break the soft meat away from the bone, by hand. Peel off the delicious, juicy chicken thigh meat and pop it all into your smashing bowl, your lovely shiny, whale's eye of a bowl. Remember to encase the bin bag you use to toss the remaining bones in 50,000kg cement and make sure Veolia sink deep into the Mariana Trench.

Get a nice big, clean, Teflon-rich frying pan and into it pump a big knob of butter, let it foam up and start to sizzle. While the butter is coming to temperature, clean three delicious leeks. Listen closely, take one leek and cut it in half, cut that half lengthways and then slice down the leek, turn it 90 degrees and chop finely. Set aside. If there's a more complex explanation on how to chop a leek, I've yet to see it.

The other leeks should be sliced across the grain and turned into discs – imagine the seat on a stool made for a mouse. Toss these leeks into your hot, butter-filled frying pan and gently sauté them until they are sweet and a super light brown. Add these leeks into the bowl where the chicken thighs dwell.

Take a medium Dutchman's dick (carrot) and peel, then chop it finely. Now add a couple of mushrooms, just normal bog standard, farmhouse mushrooms – 'Log-dwellers', as we used to call them in the Army. (As a guide in terms of sizing, I always imagine the mushroom a pale, Japanese lady mouse would use as a parasol to protect her delicate pink ears on a blazing hot Tokyo afternoon.) Fairly large. Chop them finely. You should now have three little bowls with carrots, mushrooms and chopped leeks. In cuisine this trilogy is known as the 'traffic light of flavour'. They also go by the names mirepoix or soffrito, depending on whether you live in France or Italy. We shall now go on and use this traffic light of flavour as the basis of a super gravy that will cuddle and protect our leeks, protect our chicken in their hour of need, all wrapped up in a pie.

For this next section you'll need a big glass of nice white wine. Go into the toilet with it, lock the door, turn the light off and silently down it. Silently scream into a towel and then return to the kitchen.

When your wife asks, 'Are you okay?', mumble the automated response, 'Everything's fine, darling.' Give a really big thumbs up. Smile with your mouth alone.

Pour another glass of white wine and leave it to one side. You'll also need a litre of really nice chicken stock. (You may not need it all.) Also, a couple of big tablespoons of flour to make the roux. I'm never bothered what kind of flour I use. It would be good to know, professionally, if there's an opinion.

So, butter, into the same pan we've used throughout, little glug of olive oil, temperature up and now toss in the diced leeks, the carrots and the mushrooms. Fry them off, nice and slowly, if you need to add a bit more butter, do it. Once all the veg is fried and brown, add a couple of tablespoons of flour into the buttery veg. Turn up the heat.

Caution! This can be a tricky balancing act getting

the temperature just right. As I've said before, if you're panicking or it's smoking or catching, just turn the heat down or simply lift the pan off the hob. Don't panic, it's cool. Trust me, hey, stop a second, trust me, okay? (A tiny smile begins to erupt, a cheeky wink, he turns and walks straight into the relentless mouth of an industrial threshing machine.)

Once that flour is 'cooked out' – let me explain this term, when you're making a sauce or a gravy or a béchamel using flour, you need to cook it, in this case you're frying it in the butter and mirepoix mixture. If you don't cook it out enough your end product will taste a bit like flour, it's not a nice taste either. I'm not sure how you'd come back from this, maybe you'd need to start again? You idiot.

The frying pan is now hot and the flour and veg and butter are all mixed together and frankly it looks weird, a horrible brown powder with lumps in, but it'll be fine. Trust me. If it isn't, fuck it. Bin it. We'll go again on Wednesday, get a Deliveroo. That new Turkish place that's just opened up looks great.

Take another massive glass of white wine and quickly down it before the kids come back from Tumble Teddies. Clean the glass up and put it back in the cupboard. Open the fridge and take out the white wine, uncork it and smash a big glug into the hot flour. It will sizzle and bubble; stir all the while, don't be surprised if all the wine evaporates quickly.

You don't want this to dry out now. Turn the heat down and add a glug of chicken stock, stir gently, again this may evaporate a lot of the liquid, just keep adding stock and stirring. This whole process not only thickens the gravy, but it also cooks out the flour taste, too.

The amount of flour you put into the frying pan at the beginning will go a long way towards shaping how thick the gravy will be. More flour and butter can take more stock, meaning more gravy. It can also mean a thicker gravy. It's all down to personal choice or indeed what your family's 'Pie Tradition' is.

If you make a lot of thin gravy for your pie, when you open it up all the liquid will just run out, which is totally do-able – the gravy will all still be there, it's just now in the bowl, not in your pie. I like a nice thick gravy and the more the merrier as far as I'm concerned. I want that motherfucking gravy to caress that chicken and leek shit so damn good, you hear me? I want to open that sweet mumma up at the table and see her clutching my filling in a most delicious wet suspension.

Take a spoon and dip it in the sauce and taste it. Is it nice? It should taste lovely; you may need a sprinkle of salt but I'll talk about that in a second. Does it taste like flour? Yes? Shit. A lot? You've fucked it. Turn everything off, shut it all down. Go and sit at the end of the garden. When your partner comes in and shouts 'Hello! We're back', pretend you haven't heard them at first. 'Ian! Where's all that white wine gone?' she shouts. Ian's eyes close.

Stumble into the kitchen clutching your guts. Pretend to have diarrhoea, tell her you're sleeping in the spare room 'just in case'. (Point at own anus.) Head into the spare room and sit in the cupboard swigging the white wine you hid in there earlier in the day.

A word about salt. Don't put salt into anything until the very end. You get a better gauge then of what the finished dish needs. I've made this mistake a couple of times and what's worse is I can actually see myself doing it and can't/won't stop. This is me all over, issues with impulse control, making mistakes on purpose or being naughty just to see how it feels. To see what happens.

When I was 12, I was playing hide and seek with my then best friend, Brett. He was weird and cool and quite the entrepreneur.

He'd go to a cash and carry with his dad and buy boxes of sweets and chocolate at cost price, then come into school and bang it out to the kids at a vastly inflated price. Anyway, it was winter and it was dark. His folks were out and we'd finished school and I was at his hanging out. So, we started to play hide and seek and I found a great place high up on top of a cupboard. I lay there for what seemed an age. Eventually my mind wandered and I began to focus on a bulbless light fixture hanging down from the ceiling. I look at it and then I hear the words, I actually hear them, clear as a bell. It's my voice for sure but it's older, so I trust it and it says to me, 'I know there's no bulb, but I wonder if the switch is on?'

What a good question. I silently think my reply to me: 'How could I find out?'

'Put your finger inside, Silly.'

'Of course, hang on.'

I shuffle across the top of the very high cupboard and hang off the side just far enough to enable me to lean over and stick my fucking THUMB into the bulbless socket.

Lots of very interesting things happen all at the same time. Firstly, a huge arc of blue light explodes out from the socket that has a thumb inside of it. For a moment it completely illuminates the dark room. It looks lovely. I stop feeling pain. Wee comes out. I go to sleep.

When I wake up I have butterflies in my tummy and I'm now on the floor across the other side of the room, about 10 feet from where I began. It jolted me through space/time. Then Brett opens the door and says, 'Found you!'

I also leapt from a moving car once just to spite someone who was being rude. We were all tired after a busy day shooting a show I did called *Danger! 50,000 volts!* No one saw it really, but I loved making it. It felt fresh and naughty and it was me on my own and I drove the show and comedically could do what I wanted. I was thrilled to get the gig, the character I did for that show is kind of my spirit animal.

We were all tired and just wanted to finish and go back to the hotel and have a few beers. We were all sat, crammed into a two-door Ford Focus. We were all out of ideas and getting a bit angsty with one another. The producer flippantly said to me, 'Can't you just do something funny?' My immediate thought and, in hindsight, a stupid one was 'Do something funny?! Funny? Okay. Turn the camera over. I'll do something funny. You'll like this. Funny. Okay, here we go.' I opened the car door and simply rolled out. We weren't going super-fast, like 17mph? It doesn't sound a lot but it felt quite a lot.

I can actually remember, so clearly, the sensation of bouncing and rolling across the hard, unforgiving tarmac, thinking to myself, 'God, you're a dick.'

Because I added a little turn of black pepper into a sauce I find myself thinking, 'Hey, you've peppered it, you should salt it too, right?'

'No, stop I shouldn't, I'll salt at the end. Trust me.'

My ADHD laughs, 'Trust you?' ADHD brain rushes in through the double saloon doors, knocks a bunch of shit over as he barges his way in, desperate to help. He grabs at me with his titanium hooks, 'SALT IT, PRICK!!!'

I salt it. I taste it. It's good. Nice. Well done. Thanks, me. I then begin to merrily splash huge ladlefuls of salty stock into the frying pan, reducing it over and over again. What I'm actually doing is reducing and concentrating, not only the salt I put in but the salt that's in the stock.

The finished gravy is so fucking salty it's like drinking a geode. It's terrible, and I've done that more than once! Salt and pepper at the end and always try and use a stock that has little or no added salt.

Take your pan of delicious pie gravy and pour it into

your bowl. Cover all the chicken thighs and beautiful fried mushrooms and dump it all in. Take a spoon or clarinet and stir the mixture around until it's just a tasty cacophony of flavour.

Also, I've just remembered: that little dish you roasted the chicken thighs in, it's full of chicken flavour and liquid and taste. Pop this into the bowl too. The liquid, not the little dish. This is something I also do when making a Sunday gravy. Once the meat is cooked and it's resting, wrapped in foil, it gives us a lot of liquid, either into the pan or directly into the foil bag it rests in.

This juice is heavenly stuff, please keep it safe. I've fucked it before at Christmas when I probably had a litre or so of delicious turkey juice sat at the bottom of the resting turkey and in my eager transfer of bird on to the board to be carved, I ruptured the foil wrap and watched gallons of hot, greasy, tasty liquid spill out on to the floor. It's a wretched Christmas when all you have to moisten roasties is a budget piccalilli.

As an aside, if you don't get a lot of juice out when you rest meat it could indicate you've overcooked it. This juice can also be used to tell whether or not poultry is cooked. If you pierce the thickest part of the leg, or the breast, with a skewer and the juice that comes out is crystal clear and golden, you're done. It's ready. If that juice has blood in it, you should contact your GP immediately. It also means it needs longer to cook.

You now have a delicious, well-seasoned, moist, tasty fucking inside of a pie. Well done. But now what? Well, the filling can be covered in clingfilm and left in the fridge overnight if you want. It's one of those. It sits and matures and develops a deep, pie-like taste.

Tell the gang you're off for a swim, instead go and park the car down by the river and sit eating Snickers until you puke. Use the water you keep in the car to wet hair before going home.

(Why has pie of all things triggered a totally dark sub-story?! I love it!)

Hands up if you have a selection of little white enamel pie tins from the 1960s. No? Oh, that's a shame, I do. (I have five.) I love them though. That cool blue rim. They look great in a Sunday lunch setting, different tins full of different, tasty veg and Yorkshires. It's called Falconware. It's so nice. I love it as it ages, it chips and corrodes and seems to impart a continuity of taste. The pie you're about to cook is sat in the same dish as it's great, great, great, great, great, great, great, great, great grandpie sat in. For me, that's kind of romantic in a way, but I'm just cute like that.

When folk ask me if my pastry is homemade, my reply is always 'yes'. As a desperate people-pleaser I have a desire for people to not only like me but to be deeply impressed by me. It is pointless and spiritually exhausting. The real answer is 'FUCK. NO.' Go to the shop and buy pastry. Soz. I really can't tell a massive difference, tbh.

Can I make my own shortcrust, yes I can, and if I like my guests enough, maybe I'll go that extra mile, but usually I want them in and out so me and my lunacy can settle in for the night editing photos of dead mice I find and sit them in a selection of tiny chairs I own. (When you put a beautiful dead mouse in a tiny reproduction of the classic Karuselli chair they end up looking like 1960s Bond villains.)

Turn your oven up to 180°C. From the fridge, take the chicken mixture and set it on the side. You could do this an hour in advance, you want to bring it up to room temperature. Grab your pie tins. Grab a baking tray. Grab a little ramekin and fill it with either milk or a cracked, beaten egg. This will be used to paint the top of the pies before they cook, ensuring a lovely brown lid.

I always double-crust my pies. Always have, always will. My mum dc'd her pies, her mum dc'd her pies, her mum dc'd her pies as did her mum. Now her mum did NOT dc her pies. She was a bullish, ogre of a women who hailed from Northern Canada, and was tragically killed when a sleeping grizzly bear fell out of a tree and landed on her head. Would that awful fate still have befallen her had she only dc'd her pies? Would she still be alive today? I guess we'll never know. What a shame. I like to think yes.

It should, essentially, be a pastry sarcophagus which houses a Pharaoh of Meat. My double-crust is, usually, shortcrust at the bottom, puff pastry on top. I just like the juxtaposition of that fractured, buttery, delicate pastry on top, like a fascinator made of lace and the no-nonsense workhorse of the pastry world doing all the heavy lifting, shortcrust.

Cooking a pie from scratch is a faff. There are so many different cooking techniques we've used thus far to get to this point. We sautéed our mirepoix. We roasted chicken thighs. We deglazed a pan. We reduced a sauce. It's a real undertaking. Lots of things cooked from scratch are, that's the nature of creation. It's difficult.

A pie is like a Sunday lunch, like a decent full English breakfast, like a Moussaka, like a Tarte fucking Tatin, like a Pineapple Upside Cake, Curry, Stuffed Fried Courgette Blossoms, etc. Done correctly and with care and a passion for excellence, they take a lot of effort. It isn't easy (it's also a dying art, sadly). And, for me, it shows your friends or your family or guests that you love them. Why do all this work for people you don't love? That feels like lunacy. The way my brain is, the trauma and anxiety it not only saw but the shit I put it through, means sometimes I'm fucking cross, and moody and reactive and frightened and nervous and lonely and alone. I may not be able to necessarily say sorry straight away or tell you just how much you fucking mean to me, how I couldn't and wouldn't want to do this without you. I may not be able to tell you how good a mother you are, how I appreciate what you do, how good a friend you are and how much fucking effort you put into the children, sometimes I can't do that. What I can do, though, is spend a couple of hours carefully and thoughtfully preparing a delicious, nutritious, aesthetically pleasing meal I know you will absolutely love. I know in the moment we all dig in and talking stops, and we sit, silently, and regard the day and how fucking lucky we are, you hear my apology. You taste my apology.

That's what cooking is for me, that's how important and powerful it is, and it's not just difficult things, effort and thought can, and should, be put into beans on toast, should be put into a decent jacket spud. I get if it's not your thing. Even cheese on toast can seem hard and boring and a chore and that's fine. Fuck it, life's too short. But know if you come to my house and you eat something, I have put all my effort into that thing, and you're welcome in my home and I trust you and in some tiny way, perhaps I even love you. (Do me a favour, go back and read those last four or five paragraphs again but in the voice of Morgan Freeman.)

Before using pastry, make sure you have a lot of room in the kitchen. You need it to be clean, have some flour to hand, make sure there's space in your fridge to receive pies, have a rolling pin ready and a fork and a small, sharp knife. You need a little bowl or ramekin filled with some milk or a beaten egg, this will be painted on to the pastry before you put it in the oven. It'll make it golden and super crispy. If the kids reach up to grab at the pastry and plead with you, 'Daddy, please can I help?', tell them to fuck off. Don't pull your punches. I know it seems harsh but in the long run they'll respect the clarity of your message as a parent. Trust me.

I'm trying to make the next step of the preparation as easy as possible for you, making sure it's all clean and you've plenty of room and perhaps some light summery reggae wafting in as unless you're used to working with pastry, it can be stressful, weird and confusing. That's why I also suggest doing the filling one day and the pastry the next. A few times in the past I fucked up the pastry and panicked so badly and got so stressed and angry that I ended up fucking it off into the garden. That's one of a few explosive releases my ADHD and my fear and stress

and anger tend to take. I am so overstimulated that I just open the back door and throw the pastry as far as I can. Sometimes I'll chase it down and finish it off with a hammer. One of my other releases, which people find funny and confusing, and I guess also frightening and a bit intimidating, is I'll grasp the neck of my T-shirt and I'll rip it into two pieces. I've lost a lot of clothes this way. It's ridiculous. Writing this now, I feel ashamed and a bit embarrassed. It's like I have to do it in order to release a build-up of anger and fear, fear maybe of losing control, of letting people down.

Once many years ago me and my ex-wife Chris were at the Barbican to see a play put on by a friend. We'd driven and I was stressed and my jeans, I hate jeans, kept slipping down under the heel of my shoes. I kept pulling them up and they kept catching and I began overloading, and it evolved into an issue I have with myself and being so fucking fat that my clothes can't fit. Me and Chris are stressed out and we're sniping at one another and it builds into such a crescendo of emotion that I reach down, grasp the hem of my jeans and using all of my strength, I explode and rip the jeans completely into two pieces. I'm now stood alone in the reception area of the Barbican wearing a pair of chaps. Me and Chris walk back to the car in silence, having not seen the play.

If you end up launching a fat ball of pastry down the garden, and I'm not condoning this, worry not, for supper, instead of pie, you have buttery mash potato and stew. Delicious, nutritious stew.

This is what I do when I make a pie. It is the best way I

find. It's not messy, it's peaceful, I don't rush and at the end the place is spotless. Work clean. Love dirty. (Does seductive wink to the 12 women who've bought this book.) Let's do the base first. Get it out of the box and plastic, and if you've left it for a few minutes to come to temperature, it won't tear and rip as you unroll it. Another trigger, while I remember it ... Cold butter tearing fresh white bread. Oh my, I'm angry just writing that.

The pastry can pose a challenge: you need it cold enough to be able to handle it, but if you handle it too much it becomes so warm and fragile it can just kind of blob away and melt. So, if you feel it getting away from you, physically or emotionally, just leave it. Put it back in the fridge for five minutes. Chill out. When you're ready, remove from the fridge and continue.

The more I make pie, the better and more confident I become. Now, I hardly need to refrigerate at all. Unroll the pastry and pluff a nice handful of flour across your work surface. Take your pie dish or tin, take your pastry and lay it on the top of the dish. Does it fit? Is it too big? Is it too small?

I take the pastry and I pluff flour on to it and also some on the rolling pin. I then, gently but firmly, roll and turn and flour, and roll, and ridge maybe and roll until I can see by eye that this will not just fit but all parts of the tin are overlapped by pastry. I roll the pastry up with my rolling pin and then unroll it out on to the dish. This is great.

For me, one of the nicest things I get to do in all of cooking is what I'm going to do next. I get so much pleasure and peace and joy from it: trimming the pastry. I lift the tin with my left hand and with my right I grasp the little knife and trim all the excess pastry from around the edge of the tin. Take the freshly trimmed pie and pop it in the fridge for a few minutes.

Using a lovely big spoon, fill the pastry bottom with your tasty pie filling. Now the lid. Using the tin, work out how much pastry you'll need and roll, refrigerate, roll, then cut until it's the right size to fit on the pie. Before you position it take a little of the egg wash and brush it all over the rim of the pie. This will help glue the puff pastry lid into position.

Roll up the puff pastry using your rolling pin and then unroll on to the top of the pie. Don't ever fear this. Relax, you're doing great. Take a moment to place it perfectly. You now get a second chance for a little trim. Trim the excess lid away. Then, using a fork, press the teeth all the way around the rim. This not only looks nice and professional, but it seals the two parts of the pie together. Take a sharp knife and stab a tiny cross into the middle of the pie – this will allow steam to escape as it cooks. Use your egg wash and brush the pie all over ... We did it. We fucking did it!!! Put the pie into the oven on a baking tray at 180°C to cook for about 45 minutes, or until it's crisp and brown and just absolutely desirable.

If you're a people-pleasing show-off like me, you can use the offcuts of pastry to make little shapes that you glue to the pie using the egg wash before it cooks. I like to do little leaf designs, or initials or a heart – I've even done a dick! That's the basic way to top and bottom a pie. I enjoy the feeling of bringing a lovely crispy pie to the table and then you've still got to do the best bit: eat the fucker.

Once you've got the grasp of making a pie and using pastry, what you put into it is up to you. Instead of leek, mushroom is another winner at home. You prepare it in exactly the same way but instead of frying a load of leeks, you do it with mushrooms. Any kind you want. A nice mix of chestnut, farmhouse and a portobello works nicely, I find.

I like minced beef and onion. Delish. If I'm getting a pie in a chip shop, it'll always be a Peter's Minced Beef & Onion Pie. At home I try to recreate that taste, so I chop an onion, finely dice a carrot, fry them off, add however much decent mince, always get mince with a decent amount of fat in it – 15–20 per cent feels good. It adds so much frigging flavour. Fry the mince hard with the veg so it's nice and brown and then pour in an amount of good, low-salt beef stock and simmer. Now I add a couple of small shallots, peeled, sliced fairly thick. They cook down as the mince cooks and adds a nice – God, I hate to say it – umami. Again, if the juice level in the mince drops too low, slowly add a little stock here and there until the mince is really soft and gentle.

I've worked out a couple of different methods to move my minced beef and onion pie (Peter's rip-off, at least) forward. If the mince and onion mix is cooked and soft and tasty, I remove it all with a slotted spoon, leave in a nice bowl to one side, then provided you have a lot of nice, stocky gravy, you can turn the heat up under the stock and reduce the liquid down to amplify that flavour. Constantly taste. Salt and pepper. Pour that liquid back into the mince, mix it all together and do the pastry thang. Mince and mash was one of our family favourites as kids. Mum would do the mince very much like the above and then the mash would be blobbed out into white semi-spheres using an ice-cream scoop.

There's a little cheat I've employed here from time to time, and I'll let you in on it … I add a heaped tablespoon of Bisto Gravy Granules. Please don't tell my partner. It adds a cheapness to the taste. It also thickens it a bit. It gives me a more 'chip shop'-style pie. It's lovely.

The last kind of pie I do in the rotation is the more steak and beer/kidney/ale/Guinness kind of thing. Although not being a drinker or a great fan of organ fruit, I tend not to really bother. Technically, though, you're making a stew and then wrapping it in pastry.

Using small chunks or chuck steak, I'd fry them in butter until they were brown, remove from the pan. Slice a big white onion, add a knob of butter to the pan and then fry the onions until brown and caramelised, turn up the heat, add one tablespoon of tomato purée, stir it to cook out. Take a nice dark beer, Guinness or a bitter, and empty a whole can into the onion mixture. It will bubble and boil, use a wooden spoon to scrape all the bits off the bottom, turn the heat down and add a few big ladles of beef stock. Return your beef and any liquid to the pan. Lastly, take maybe two big, sweet carrots and cut into chunks, toss into the pan and slowly cook this pie filling/ stew until the beef is falling apart and the carrots are really soft and incredibly sweet.

I'd remove all the meat and veg with a slotted spoon and leave to one side in a bowl. Cover with foil. Turn up the heat under the pan and stir gently until the sauce the beef has cooked in is a rich and thick gravy. Tip back over the beef and carrots and taste, season and whack it in the pastry and cook. It'll be crazy tasty.

I'm thinking about that whole 'learn techniques vibe', not individual recipes kind of thing. The method for the pie filling is definitely one of those. Veg fried, meat fried, stock or wine reduced down, and then good stock slowly simmered and reduced over a number of hours. There's a shitload of food prepared this way. If you understand what's happening during this cooking method, you can use it to prepare a lot.

FISH PIE

Fish Pie is a good thing to know. It's complicated and again takes ages, and you employ many different cooking skills to make a good one, but it's absolutely worth it. Mine comes from Trudy, my ex-mother-in-law. I'd never tasted a fish pie before hers, and it was so good I taught myself her recipe. I thought I must be losing my mind when I saw her putting hard-boiled eggs in. I couldn't believe it.

I use prawns, cod, salmon and smoked mackerel. These are my fishy elements. I take sweet young leeks, halve and slice them finely. I take a carrot and plank it out, slice the planks, turn and finely slice them. Leave to one side.

Now, I take a big pan of whole milk, and put a gentle

heat through it – other people at this point would add bay leaves and peppercorns. I don't. I hate bay leaves and we can grind pepper in later. What you're going to do with this milk is use it to gently poach the fish. Not the prawns or the smoked mackerel, which is usually cooked. Once it's warm enough, add the cod and salmon and poach until cooked. Lift out on to a plate and leave to one side.

Do not throw away this milk. We're going to use it later. Bring a large pan of water to the boil and once it's rolling lower four eggs into the maelstrom. Set your phone timer to five minutes. Have a bowl of cold water ready and after five minutes lift the eggs out and drop them in the cold water bowl. I want them to stop cooking immediately. In theory, you could poach them for a little bit less as they're going to go in the fish pie and if you time it right, they come out of the fish pie still a bit runny.

I've never made a Scotch egg but I've eaten a few, I can tell you. In fact, in my whole life, at this point 50 years, I've eaten 23 Scotch eggs. Which is a pretty good total. I bet there are folk who have had hundreds of Scotch eggs. Thousands even. Why am I talking about Scotch eggs? Oh yeah, once the egg is boiled and peeled they freeze it before laying it in its cape of meat. This ensures that when it's fried it just brings the egg back to hot and runny again and it doesn't cook it any further than the original boiling point. It's the same idea with fish pie.

Don't peel the eggs yet. They're so fucking hot. Stick them in a little bowl and then stick them in the fridge. Grab a phat knob of butter and a glug of olive oil and start to heat it up. Get your leeks and your carrots and fry them off gently. They should thoroughly enjoy this. Take your fish milk and put a light on underneath it. It shouldn't boil but you want it hot. You're going to add ladlefuls of it to the leek and carrot and butter and flour mixture and you don't want the liquid to stop everything from cooking.

I jumped the gun slightly. Into the butter and the oil and the leek and the carrot, stir in and cook out thoroughly a large tablespoon of flour. This is almost exactly the method I use to make gravy but when you use milk instead of stock what you've made is a kind of béchamel.

So, this is the same deal. Remember, the more flour you put in, the more liquid it can take or the thicker you can make it. I like it thick for a fish pie. I want all that lovely leek and fish hanging, nicely suspended, in the cheesy sauce.

Using the milk you poached the fish in to make the béchamel so nice and rich kicks the flavour up a notch or two. Keep stirring and making it thicker and cook that flour out. Have a taste. Nice? Well done! How I finish this sauce off is like this ... I stir in a large glug of dry sherry. I add a fair bit of grated Parmesan, I turn in a fair bit of cracked black pepper and then I finely chop a bunch of chives and put them in.

The sauce can be turned off now. It should taste amazing, rich, a bit cheesy, a bit sherry, a bit gentle soft chives. Does it need salt? No. Good, there should also be a hint of warm cod somewhere in there too. When I say 'fishy', people hate that shit – it shouldn't taste like a kilo of prawns you hid under the floor of some horrible prick you used to live with as a farewell present smells. I just mean it should taste a bit like the delicious fresh fish you're going to eat.

I have a really nice round clay dish from Spain, it's brown and shiny and it has a lip and two clay handles. It's probably three or four inches deep and 15–18 inches across. It's perfect for this. Peel your eggs, leave them to one side. Take all the fish you're going to turn into a pie and place it in the dish. You could literally just fuck all the fish in randomly and it'd be fine but my creative brain and OCD and ADHD means it all has to look nice.

I lay pieces of cod all around and then a layer of salmon and a few plump, raw prawns pushed in-between and I flake pieces of mackerel in between everything else. It should look really tasty and ready to eat right there and then. Now ... Take your sauce and pour it all over the fish, until it's covered everything in the dish. I sometimes use a little knife to rearrange the layer of fish so the sauce easily drips down between. I'd also say this: no matter how thick this sauce is, it will definitely turn runnier as it cooks. It will defo get into all the nooks and fish crannies. (I'm sure that phrase should've been caught by my editor.)

That big delish bowl of fish and soft sweet leeks and Dutchman Ds and sherry and Parmesan and a cracking velouté can be put to one side until you've completed the next step... Mash...

Here's another chance to add more flavour into the pie. Every mouthful should be just a wonderful dance with the poached fish being held by the sauce and the whole lot of it being protected by a buttery, billion-dollar mash wearing a crusty helmet of Cheddar (another phrase that should not have slipped through the editing process).

I always use a potato ricer, it changed my mash game. Don't bother with a masher. Use a ricer, it's fun and really easy. There's another gadget I've seen people use called a mouli. It's essentially a machine you drop boiled spuds into and then you turn a handle and fine potato drops out of the bottom.

I used to boil my potatoes too, peeling them and then boiling in water. Fuck that nonsense. Never again. The only time I boil spuds is for roast potatoes. I hate peeling spuds. I'm the only one that ever does it. Everyone else pretends they can't use the peeler or their arms are tired. Hayley is so slow and my impatience means that it's a challenge for me to watch. She knows I'll eventually get triggered and have to step in to finish the job. I shouldn't though. That feels like a defect of character.

I was watching a bunch of fairly decent chefs chatting on YouTube and when they made mash none of them peeled and boiled their spuds. They put them on a baking tray and essentially made jacket potatoes first and then scooped out the flesh and stuck that through a ricer, then finished like normal, with a ton of butter and a splash of milk. It's so much easier. So, do that. Take 1.5kg of big spuds, wash them, prick them all over with a fork into a baking tray, bit of salt and I splash a bit of oil over them and then into the oven at about 180ºC for like one and a half hours. I like this kind of cooking because it enables me to bring something amazing to the table and have a very tidy kitchen at the same time. You did everything else earlier/yesterday. You're making mash, you're topping the pie with it and you're done. If we have people round, I don't even put it into the oven until they get there. It's cooked in 45 minutes. It can be sat out waiting to cook and all the prep and the washing up is done. People will think you went to COOK and bought it!

Once the potatoes are cooked, cut them in half, spoon out the white meat of the potatoes and push it all through a ricer and into a big bowl. Add huge knob of butter and, using a wooden spoon or even a hand mixer, beat the soft mash into next week, taste for more butter, add some milk, taste again, it should be amazing. If it isn't you're a fucking baboon.

'What happened to the eggs we did earlier?'

'Who said that?'

'Me.'

'Get your shit together and leave, it's for the best.'

'But I'm reading this in bed, in my house.'

'It's not your house any more, Sarah. The bank sent you all those letters that you refused to open and you just hid down the back of the cupboard in the hall.'

'I just couldn't face them.'

'I get it but you have to go.'

'Okay. Bye.'

'Leave the book. Santander own that too now.'

Take the eggs, the peeled eggs and slice them in half and push them gently into the lovely fish pie filling, they should be nestled right up to their shoulders, lucky eggiest. The egg yolks should also be very liquid and bright orange. I take my pepper stick and give each yolk their own individual grate. I love the black dots of pepper on a bright orange yolk. Maybe that would be my flag if I was ever in the position to own/become a country. People would say, 'Oh, do the black specs represent a constellation?' 'No, it's pepper. It represents pepper.'

There are three things left to do with this pie ... Using a palette knife (google it), spread the mash all over the top of the saucyfishegg. Then, using just the tip of the palette knife, I always do a pattern on top that represents the scales of the fish. Then grate strong Cheddar all over it. Done. You did it. Cook in the oven at 180°C for at least 45 minutes until the cheese has melted all over. In that time, boil water, salt and cook a load of petits pois. For me, peas is all this dish needs. Once you bring it out, serve it on a board on the table. Listen to the pie plip and sing. Don't spoon any out for at least five minutes. Let it start to settle back down. Serve and enjoy.

If I drank, and you'll see in a moment why I don't, I'd drink with this a pint of really cold white wine or a dry rosé, Whispering Angel maybe. Or a huge flagon of that nice English champagne, Nyetimber. Delicious. Why can't I drink any more? Because of all those people I hurt. Oh yeah. Maybe it'll be different this time – I don't even get to finish that sentence when my inside me walks out laughing. Prick. I fire one last shot across his judgey bow as he leaves ... 'I don't and never have identified as an alcoholic! That was Mum. Not me.' There's a pause and then the laughter doubles, no, maybe trebles, in both volume and verve. I hear the car door slam as he gets in his spirit vehicle and drives off back into hell.

My kitchen is clean and my table has some lovely people sat around it, drinking cold wine and eating expensive crisps from M&S. I've dropped a large Danish bowl that was fired sometime in 1970 full of juicy peas on to the table. I wave my head at H, she knows the head wave means 'Can you take the heatproof thing from that drawer in the table and put in on the table, ready for the pie?' I then bring the pie over, I can't tell you how proud and shy and awkward and important and smug and nervous and fatherly I feel at this moment. People like that the pie looks like fish scales, it's so easy and people love it. A fish pie that looks like a fish … That's Heston shit right there.

I never serve at the table. Let someone else be Mother. I've got some lovely bowls from a company called Finlandia, who make Scandi bowls and plates and dishes. It's amazing. (That said, this fish pie is so good you could eat it out of a hubcap and it would still taste amazing. What an awful boast. Sorry.)

Just while I remember … Hunks of thickly buttered crusty baguette are a perfect side order to ANY DISH that has either gravy/jus/juice/sauce/emulsion. Some of my greatest culinary memories have been made while 'mopping up' some rich gravy with a log of salty buttered French stick. Mmmmm … That is all.

Simple Methods To Not Only Keep You Alive, But Also Impress Lovers

There is nothing nicer for me than a quiet, clean kitchen. Maybe the radio is on. The back doors are open and the cat is being a fuckhead as usual. It's mine. It's all mine. I like to take all the veg and food that needs preparing and get them ready. I pull all the little bowls and containers I'll need for their preparation. I then get my favourite knife and I wash and sharpen it. Gently. I sharpen those knives a lot. Every time I use a knife I'll sharpen it before and after I use it. I sometimes catch my cleaner, Jeta, looking at me funny. I'll wave the knife at her and scream, 'Who wants a second anus?!!' We always lol so hard as she runs off pretending to scream!

When everything is out and ready, I begin. I LOVE to stand and chop and slice, mince, grate. I love it. Sometimes if I'm particularly anxious or depressed, I'll buy vegetables just to slice them. Just to mechanically do a movement that I know my brain likes.

Everything I'm going to cook with has its own container to live in once it's been prepped. I wipe the counter and the knife and my board between each job. Then it's done. The prep, the mise en place, is complete. We can cook. And the kitchen ... is absolutely spotless. Spotless. I guess working in commercial kitchens and a heavy dose of OCD and ADHD mean that the anal preparation of food (what?) is right up my street.

When I started working in kitchens, the bit that took the most getting used to, apart from the heat and crushing stress levels, was the clean-up. I used to hate it! It seemed so alien to break everything down and pull everything out and apart so we could clean inside and behind fridges and ovens. I guess my brain was like, fuck it, let's cut corners ... But we didn't. We put so much energy and effort into making that kitchen smile and be bright and happy that at the end you could have eaten your dinner off it. Some people even did.

What I'm trying to get across is clean as you go. It makes cooking so much easier. So much less stressful. If your environment is clean and calm and ordered in a way that you can quietly get on with something you may or may not be into, it makes life so much easier. You could come to my house on a Sunday afternoon minutes before a Sunday lunch was being served and you might not even be aware a massive lunch is moments from being served. Don't be messy. Watching Hayley prepare the simplest thing is a test. Just a simple boiled egg and some toast and you'd think by the state of the kitchen she had roasted a whole camel for 200 passing Berbers.

SCALLOPS

I friggin' love scallops. I really like them. I never really eat them though and I've no idea why. There's a really good fishmonger's in Twickenham called Sandy's. It's amazing. At Christmas the line for fish and lobsters and salmon goes out of the shop and at least 200 metres down the high street. They have people coming out with glasses of glögg and mince pies. It's so nice and Christmassy. I've never once driven past that massive queue and not laughed under my breath though ... 'You fucking idiots.' I wouldn't queue for anything. This could be a defect of character. I'm really impatient. Last week I went to get a haircut twice and ended up walking out both times. Couldn't wait.

Back to scallops ...

I like the big scallops. If you can cook them nicely, again this is something you can store in your in-brain cookbook. This is how I cook them ...

Frying pan. Hot. Butter. Little bit of oil.

Imagine we're talking about six fat scallops. Place them in the hot pan.

Don't touch them. Let them brown. Then turn them over and do exactly the same thing on the other side. Spoon over a little of the hot butter as you cook. Remove from the pan and turn off the hob!

Don't forget to turn the friggin' hob off! My brain is wired in such a way that I'll often take a pan off the hob and just wander off. Burners still burning. Or I'll turn the tap on and drift away into another room ... not cool.

So, these scallops ...

You could glug a drop of olive oil on to these babies and a tiny pinch of salt and they'd be lovely. A lovely, ice-white sea-plum just popped into my mouth. So nice. But ... these could be used with lots of things. I've done them before as a starter sat atop a blanket of cauliflower purée.

In my mind I absolutely love the idea of cauliflower. In practice I think I fucking hate it. But I do crave it. Cauli-flower cheese, fritters, soup, purée. Oh, lovely disgusting cauliflower. How I hate-fuck your dirty florets ... I used to know where I stood. Cauliflower stank, it stank the house up, stank up my clothes, my hair. Bloody cauliflower. But secretly I wanted cauliflower. I watched it. I knew it worked in my local Sainsbury's and I'd pretend we'd run out of milk so I could drive by and see it. I hid the results of my Google searches because I would've been mortified if they'd found out what I looked at when I was alone.

The affair, the physical affair, started with a crispy fritter, dipped in a sauce. The point of no return was seeing it, leaves off, pale white skin wet from her hot bath, dressed in a pale yellow quilt of vintage Cheddar, oh my God, I couldn't fucking wait to put you in my mouth. As my love for you deepened, I wanted you deeper and deeper inside me. I wanted you inside my cells.

I took three of you and I stripped you down and peeled off that bright green dress and I took you to pieces and plopped you into a bath of beefy stock. God we laughed. I was so happy. I watched you roll and giggle as the bubbles tickled under your arms. I know I shouldn't have done it but I took a thin knife and I pushed it into you and it went all the way through. Your eyes were wide with a crackly disbelief. Sorry. I'm sorry.

I quickly used a big, slotted spoon to help you out of the bath and into a big saucepan. You told me you were getting cold, so I drenched you in ladlefuls of the beef stock you'd been swimming in. I think it got in your eyes and down your throat because you weren't smiling any more. You were coughing and seemed angry. It was now that you saw what I was hiding behind my back. A hand blender. 'Sorry. I want you inside me.'

So, use the hand blender to blend all the cauliflower smooth. If it's too thick, add a little more beef stock. Season and then taste. I'd finish this with a little single cream and a dredge of white pepper. Put her inside your soul. Well? Delicious! Enjoy! That's for cauliflower soup, but here we want purée, so it's slightly different.

CAULIFLOWER PUREE

I take a big cauliflower. Cut into florets. Big pan of salted, boiling water. Drop them in and simmer gently until a knife can easily go through them. Instead of plain old water you could even poach them in beef stock. Mmmm. Yum. Do that instead.

Put all the soft florets and some of the poaching stock into a container. I guess talk of a container made me think about what a regular human would use to put cauliflower and beef stock in. Find something nice and big and roomy.

Take a hand blender and plunge it into and around the cauliflower until it's completely mushed up. Don't put loads of stock in at first, otherwise you'll have soup. (Delicious/horrible.) You need just enough to help the blender do its work.

Push the cauliflower through a fine meshed sieve, you may need the help of some kind of kitchen 'implement' for this. Like a spatula.

Obviously you've put a bowl under the sieve to capture the purée ...

At this point, taste. It will defo need salt and pepper. I've even heard of little cubes of salted butter going in to make it rich. You could even add Parmesan. Delish. This is your finished Cauliflower Purée. It should be rich and smooth (like Pierce Brosnan). It should also taste fucking amazing.

One plate. Spoonful of the cauliflower dressed on to it. Three nice, fried scallops on top, pepper. Serve. It's a very cool starter to bring to a table. And so easy and so tasty.

Apart from cauliflower you can also purée other veg: carrots, sweet potatoes, broccoli. All delish.

You could also use those little queen scallops too. They're the really small ones. The only time I really use these is to finish off a seafood risotto ... just a handful popped in at the end with the butter and Parmesan, just to heat through. Yes! Would also work great in the fish pie.

I know a lot of people say shit like 'You should never use Parmesan on risottos that contain seafood'. I say, 'Mind your own fucking beeswax!'

I've also served these scallops with thin asparagus cooked on a griddle. Also, samphire is delish. Scallops and pepper and egg yolk is good too. Crispy bacon? Scallops LOVE bacon. I remember about 15 years ago there was a movement amongst chefs to cook scallops so they're soft in the middle. It's not for me. It makes me heave a little bit. I need it cooked all the way through. There are other things that I like generally, but if prepared slightly under, my mind rejects them. One of these is scrambled eggs. For me, there is definitely a great, middle place here when it comes to prep. I don't want the eggs desiccated but I also don't want the eggs barely formed into a blanket of just held-together albumen. *heave. (*heave denotes I've heaved during writing.) *heave – there's another one. In fact, eggs, as much as I love a nice fried egg, especially with a full English, are a real trigger for my heave response. If I think about eating an unfertilised hen foetus (*heave), I generally have to stop.

GREMOLATA/CHIMICHURRI

So even though slightly different, there are lots of overlapping elements to these two sauces. I think they're good staples to have in your locker. They're really easy to make and when served with a nice salad and say, a plate of little barbecued lamb chops, or a nice crispy sea bass, or salmon fillets, or scallops, or slices of sirloin steak, they lift the whole thing. They're one of those super simple things that make normal people think you're a fucking wizard.

So ...

handful of flat-leaf parsley

garlic

lemon zest (use 1 lemon at first)

You could use a nice sharp knife to chop this all to fuck, or you could stick it all in a processor. Blend it up. Job done. That's your gremolata.

Now if you exclude the lemon zest and add olive oil, a little vinegar (red wine/balsamic – little of both maybe?) and pepper flakes, you have a very basic chimichurri.

Both of these work in the same way. Cheap, simple and super tasty.

GRAVY

I love gravy. I like jus, and sauce. I'm alright with drizzle but gravy, ooh la la.

This is the gravy I make when I do a Sunday roast. Depending on what meat you use, this will taste different and the colour will change. Beef usually is a nice, rich nut brown colour, same with lamb, and then chicken is a nice blonde colour.

The key to this is what the meat sits on when it cooks. As the meat roasts away, it releases juice and that mixes with the veg it sits on, which in turn slowly roasts and withers down and the taste and flavour and liquid intertwine and make gentle love under its sexy blanket of flesh.

I use a decent roasting tray. Thick bottom and something that can be put straight on to a flame at the end to finish and thicken the gravy.

Take two large red onions, cut into slices and toss them into the pan. Then two or three carrots, cut into thick slices, into the tray. Whole bulb of garlic. Chop in half, toss in both halves.

Leek. Usually, I make cheesy leeks to go with the roasts. Which means I top and tail the leeks before I clean them and rather than throw these scraps away, I use

them for the gravy. They're perfect. Chop them into bits. Toss into the pan.

Two tomatoes cut in half, toss them into the pan.

Celery, I hate it. So, I use very little ... one stick. Or sometimes I use the soft leaves in the middle. Looks cute. You could even put a little sprig of thyme here at this point.

The trivet of vegetables should by now look really beautiful and colourful. I make a little space in the middle of it for my beef/lamb/chicken/porkie to sit in, snuggle it down in there and stick it in the oven to sleep. No not sleep, it transforms, it morphs, it lives, it sits in its protective cocoon of leeks and flourishes into a beautiful meatmoth that flutters across the kitchen and lands on your tongue, immediately ppppppfffffuinnnng into a liquid that drips into your memory. Gravy.

If I'm cooking a piece of beef, a rib of beef, a small one, like 1kg, if only three people eat beef, then I'll put a little oil on the trivet and some salt and pepper and I'll roast it alone, without the beef, for at least 20 minutes. It gives the veg time to properly wilt and render down. After 20 minutes you stick your beef in and then cook as you would a single rib of beef.

Sometimes you're cooking something bigger than a single rib of beef that takes two to three hours to cook, so you don't need to pre-wilt the veggies.

The flip to this is sometimes you may roast something that requires you to, at some point one and a half hours in, pull the whole tray out and empty a big pint of cold water into the trivet. You don't want the veg to turn and burn. It'll taste like shit. What you want at the end of the process are roasted sweet, gently tanned, moist, juice-filled jewels of swollen pre-gravy, ready to be turned into a brown sauce your children will remember and talk about long after you're dead. It's simple and really that important. I can close my eyes and taste my dad's gravy right now, even though it's 25 years since I physically tasted it.

If we're talking about beef here, take the beef out of the tray. Wrap it up tightly with foil. Set aside. Word of warning here: as that meat rests it'll continue to gently cook and it'll give out loads of bloody juice. (Hopefully.) So, with this in mind, be careful how you store it. Make sure should your foil dam fail, the juice doesn't just leak on to the floor and then ants move in. Save that juice at all costs. For me, it's sarcophagus of foil and then in a little dish.

Now what you're left with is a tray of beautifully cooked vegetables. They're going to be sweet and brown and withered and juicy. Which is nice. Give yourself a treat and eat a piece of the carrot. Lovely.

What you're going to need next is a source of liquid. You're going to need a stock of some kind. Beef stock, veal stock, vegetable stock, chicken stock. You're also potentially going to need a drop of nice dark beer, a bottle of wine maybe, use something which is okay. Don't use shit. Have all this ready to go. For me, I use one of those nice jellified stocks I get from the good butcher and I'll probably cut it with some water. Watch for salt levels in all stocks. I've also made gravy with the vegetables in the tray and water, that works too. It tastes like shit but it's usable. If you're feeding three Alsatians, I'd use water.

Put the tray directly on your heat and bring it to a sizzle. Watch it though, don't burn it now. After a couple of minutes sizzling, add into the tray at least two phat tablespoons of flour, doesn't matter which for me. Stir it all around to cook it out a bit. This will suck up any moisture you may have had left in the pan. Don't panic. Keep stirring, it should be hot but it shouldn't be burning.

If you're using wine, now is the time to empty it into the hot pan. This is tricky as I know you'll probably only have two hands but stir throughout this move, the flour and vegetables should hiss and steam as the wine deglazes the pan and all the little burnt and delicious crispy bits come away. Turn the heat down at this point. Keep stirring.

What you want to do now is control your heat, stirring the boiling wine liquid until it gets very thick. Once it's very thick, add a ladleful of beef stock, stir until it thickens, then add more stock, stir, thicken, add stock, stir, thicken ... blah, blah, blah. At the point when you add the flour is the time you decide how much gravy you're going to make. Don't be stingy. People love gravy. The more flour you add, the more stock it'll take, and the more gravy you can make. I've been doing it for 25 years now, so I can sense exactly the amounts needed by eyeing it.

If you've reached a point where those tray-roasted vegetables have turned into a pan with lots of nice, not floury, fragrant brown, winey liquid, you may have just created a gravy. Congratulations. But we're not quite finished. Grab a little saucepan and a conical strainer/ chinois. Stick the strainer into your saucepan and pour the tray-roasted veg and browny liquid into it. We want

A SLICE OF FRIED GOLD

to separate the veg from the liquid. This step can be annoying. Make sure the saucepan is deep enough to take the strainer and that the gravy isn't going to wobble out of the top. If necessary, do it in two steps.

With a wooden spoon, push the liquid through the strainer. Having done this, now stop. Take a minute. The veg, having given every last drop of flavour, are dead. They can now be binned. Put the roasting tray to one side. Breathe. In front of you should be a saucepan, and in that saucepan should be a rich, brown, clear, tasty, tasty liquid. Taste it. Dip a spoon in. Nice? How does it taste? Does it need salt? Is it too runny? Too thick? If it's too runny, let's put the pan on a medium heat, bring it to the boil and reduce that sucker. Only once it has reduced, add salt. If you've added a shitload of salt before and you reduce it you'll make it super salty.

If you're not reducing it, put it on a gentle heat to keep warm. There's one more thing to do ... In terms of timing, it always kind of works out for me that the time it takes to make the gravy is the exact time needed to rest the meat. Unwrap the foil-covered meat and any juice you find there, pour it straight into the gravy. The taste from all this liquid is a joy to add to gravy, it should just make it better, richer, deeper.

At this point, if you need to season it, season it. I now stand at the hob dipping a spoon into this sublime meat magma, tasting it for ages (I'm actually drinking it). If it's delicious, I'm generally pretty fucking smug at this point. Good gravy is a gift and one you'll never forget how to create. There are lots of steps to getting good gravy and

sometimes things go wrong, fuck it. It's only gravy. I leave the saucepan on a very low heat so it's just bubbling away and ready to be used at a moment's notice.

I've been places for Sunday lunch where a) the gravy is a light-coloured watery piss and b) (which may be worse) there's not enough gravy. Just watching the jug going round the table and you know that's it. You'll never see it again. There's no more. Having to wolf down roast potatoes so you can get a couple more and try and get a bit of gravy from the bottom. What a shame.

Also, parents who don't control their kids at a Sunday lunch ... I don't care if they're moody and don't want to eat, fuck off into the front room and watch *Chuggington*, leave us alone to eat in peace. That's okay, what's worse are the kids who eat tons and don't give a shit about anyone else. I've watched them grabbing at all the Yorkshires and clumsily drenching them in litres of gravy. Are you fucking kidding me? Now there's none for the rest of us. Fuck me. I grab Hayley under the table and whisper in her ear, 'Come on babe, we're leaving.' She reminds me that it's our house, we can't leave. We could, but we shouldn't. It's better to have a load left over. My kids, all of them, love the gravy. I also think it's really good for them. (If you're a doctor or a dietician and you know for a fact gravy isn't good for kids, keep it to yourself please.) How can a liquid made from vegetables and meat liquor not be good for you? I love watching my eight-month-old smashing spoonfuls of gravy. Her big mouth wide open ready for another delivery. God bless her. All my kids loved that. It made me very proud to be able to do that.

Obviously, that was gravy made from a joint of beef and red wine. My old man would use the exact same method but instead of wine, he'd put a can of McEwan's beer in. It tasted amazing. I remember standing next to him while he poured a can of beer into the pan. What?! What manner of magic is this?! I felt like he was a fucking wizard. I couldn't believe it. He can control fire! The pan would spit and sizzle, he'd let me have a taste. Wow. It was magic. I ate a big mouthful of my dad's hot magic.

Re-reading that last sentence it seems weird ...

If I was doing a chicken, instead of red wine, I'd use white wine and chicken or vegetable stock – you get a lovely light, blonde gravy. Blonde Gravy could be my porn name.

This technique of frying or roasting veg and then adding flour to thicken it, or reducing it using heat, is a way to make a lot of different sauces. Going back to my dad, he also made a lovely sauce that we'd have with steak. Rump steak, it was relatively cheap and tasty as fuck. We'd only have steak on a Saturday, but he'd fry it in a saucepan, then he'd leave it to rest on a plate covered in foil. Then, in the same pan he'd add a big knob of butter, which would deglaze it a bit, before frying slices of mushroom in the foamy, steaky butter. Then, he'd add a little wine, or stock, and reduce slightly and he'd finish it by taking it off the heat and stirring double cream into the mushroom sauce. He would end with a big slug of Worcestershire sauce. Man, it was delish. Big bit of rump steak, mushroom and cream sauce, and we'd have a big hunk of baguette heavily slavered with salty butter. Oh man. I can feel this right now. Mopping up that steaky liquid with that bread watching *Metal Mickey* or good old Tom Baker's *Doctor Who*. Yes please, take me back there.

There was a lot of negative shit in my life at that time. Negative shit that, sadly, left scars all over me. I was like a man who worked with cactuses. These things though are the things that made me the man I am today. Sadly. There are also a few good memories though. Cooking with my dad is one of those things. Maybe now looking back I've always used food and eating as a way to hide. Hopefully they won't notice me. I'll just watch the hatred and drinking and violence unfold around me.

I certainly know now, being 50, not only do I use cooking as a way of showing off, I also definitely use it as a way of hiding. I get very anxious when people come over for lunch or dinner. Even friends I've known for 25 years I struggle with. It's terrible. I hate it. This is why I spend so much time on my own. I think there's a massive self-esteem issue coupled with elements of my neurodiversity where I struggle to think about what I will say to people, even friends. How do I do this? When will they leave? When will it just be us again?

That sounds awful. I love my friends and I love cooking for them but mentally it takes a toll on me. I get all ticky and fidgety and my girl has to hold my hand or come and find me in the downstairs toilet where I hide with the light off. Sometimes I breathe deeply and then inside my brain I say, 'Right, you have to get out there!' Before I head back out, I need to think of some amusing non sequitur or fact I can casually drop to my guests to hide the fact I've been gone ten minutes. I must get back to the safety of the oven.

The cooking connects me to the people I'm cooking for. I feel that maybe it's even an apology sometimes. 'Sorry I'm like this.'

When I do a Sunday lunch, I'll often do a cauliflower cheese or a broccoli cheese, but everyone's favourite is a cheesy leek. Hayley loves it. This begins by frying slices of leek in butter. I'll always take a few of the slices of buttered leek and pop them aside in a little ramekin. Then, once I've finished the cheese sauce, I'll pop a great big spoonful of cheese on top of the few slices of leek I retained. Turn of pepper. I then take the tiny version of the leek gratin into her as a gift. As a way of saying 'I like you', 'I love you', 'I'm sorry'. I couldn't do that without food.

I'm also super shit at any kind of small talk. Filler. I'll nod and say 'Yes' when human dialogue says I should say yes. All the time I'll be backing up towards the safety of the gas burners. With cooking, I know about it. I know if I do this, then this will happen. I know cooking doesn't gossip, it doesn't want my opinion, it doesn't tell me off for being weird ... you know. I hide in plain sight, and work and cook and hopefully serve up something lovely that they take home and talk about later. Even if that conversation begins with 'Nick seemed quiet', hopefully it'll end with, 'That gravy was delicious though!'

AUBERGINE PARMIGIANA

I've been making this a long while and I have both a long version and an easy one. It's delicious. And if you serve it in a lovely Greek/ Spanish earthenware dish, it makes it taste better. (What am I talking about? More cookbook bullshit here. I even used the term 'earthenware', fuck me! It does taste better though.)

This is something great to learn to do and tweak and develop over time. It's basically fried aubergines, tomato sauce and cheese. Yum. It's also a great deal more than that. It's something you'll have forever. It's something that goes with a ton of different things. Cod, BBQ, steak, hens and three other things. Vegetarians also love it because it makes them feel like you give a shit. Learn how to make this and you will get laid. Tops and fingers at the very least! Who doesn't like tops and fingers?!

To business! I've done this a couple of different ways – here are the differences: sometimes I slice the aubergines, brush them with oil and do them on a hot griddle. A few minutes on each side to get that nice colour and griddle taste. Or you can slice the aubergine and actually fry them in a couple of inches of hot oil in a frying pan. Either way, once that is done, lay all the slices out on pieces of kitchen paper and pat dry. I'd be tempted to salt gently and turn a pepper stick above them.

I don't know what the best version of this is. Frying the aubergines tastes good but it's a bit oily, the griddle is super nice. That's what I do now. So, let's assume that is what you've done, cause I'm fab and why wouldn't you just blindly do what I tell you?

I'd do the sauce before anything else. It can just sit there then. You could do it the day before. Easy. I know lots of us are Busy Mums who don't have the time to produce a world-beating Aubergine Parmigiana. (*Does that thing all Busy Mums do in adverts where they brush a strand of errant hair out of their eyes with the back of her hand. She may even blow hair upwards as well at the same time just to underline her workload and the eternal struggle to keep this FUCKING HOUSE CLEAN!!! IAN!!!)

The tomato sauce is the same one I'd do for the Tuna Pasta (see pages 13–5), but before the tuna goes in. Obvs.

So, in front of you now, you should have: lots of slices of seasoned, fried/griddled aubergines; a container with good, homemade tomato sauce; a ladle; good Parmesan and slices/pieces of mozzarella. Don't use the mozzarella that comes in a bag of liquid. It's too posh and it makes the whole thing too wet. Try and find the cheap pre-grated shit. It works great for this.

I have this weird thing I've always done where I imagine I'm the only survivor of a plane crash. We've gone down in the middle of the Sahara Desert, so I guess I'm travelling from Londres to Lagos. Flight's gone down, I emerge looking for supplies. For days, I crawl, burnt to shit by the relentless African sun until in the distance I see what looks to be a wooden packing crate. It is ... it's a packing crate, with the last of my strength I wrench the lid off ...

(Here's where you can play too ...) What would be the worst liquid you could find in there? You have to drink it or you'll die ... Mine are always: bags of mozzarella water or amaretto. Also, aftershave *heave.

I always use a nice rectangular dish to put all the ingredients in. You get a great build in a nice rectangular earthenware dish. It's easier to portion too. I buy all my earthenware cooking vessels from a Greek Monk called Papa Ricky. He has a hand-built kiln deep inside the anus of Mount Olympus. That's what it claims on his Insta page anyway. It might also explain why the bowls smell like donkey fudge.

The layering of the Parmigiana, much like a lasagne, goes like this: couple of ladles of tomato sauce, blob of mozzarella, fistful of Parmesan, turn of pepper, slices of aubergine. Repeat until all the sauce and all the aubergines are gone. The whole dish should be covered in the sauce that's left. Mozzarella and loads of Parmesan on top.

Put it on the top shelf in the oven at about 180°C. When it's done, it's going to be bubbly and the cheese will be melted and stringy and saucy. It's lovely. Don't eat it immediately, let it sit for at least five minutes, AT LEAST, to just rest a bit. It's been through a hell of a change from its earthly form into what you now see bubbling before you. So pretty. My favourite thing to serve this with is slow-cooked lamb. It's a whole Greek vibe.

SLOW-COOKED LAMB

Fuck it. Here's the lamb too. I shouldn't, but I will ...

In a roasting tray, slice loads of big white onions (I use about five or six big 'uns). Then cut a whole bulb of garlic in half and pop the two halves, cut-side up, in the pan. Add to this some fresh thyme sprigs, salt and pepper. This is the base that a leg or a shoulder of lamb will sit on upwards of at least five hours.

Heavily salt and pepper the meat. Lay it on the onions and wrap the whole thing up good and tight with thick, strong foil. Put it in an oven which has been preheated to 120°C.

After two hours, get the lamb out of the oven. Unwrap it gently and into the roasting tray pour at least 1 pint of cold water. Reseal with the foil and put the lamb back in the oven. After every hour or so, repeat. Don't let this well dry out. I'd cook it for six hours ...

Take the lamb out of the roasting tray, put it on a plate and cover with the foil you used to cook it in. Roast not, waste not. It will be fragile and so fucking wet and moist, maybe even a couple of golden beads of fat dribbling out of its main bone cavity.

The onions, if you've kept them nice and moist through-out cooking, will taste absolutely delicious. All the fat will have rendered down from the lamb into these onions. They'll have so much flavour. I imagine these onions flexing flavour all over your wife while you just stand by, helpless and weak, resigned to it happening again. You watch these onions do 30 press-ups, nae bother, to a very impressed and giggly wife. 'Your onions haven't tasted like this for years Ian, you weak bastard.' She gulps down another brothy blam of onion sauce. Ian runs into the boot room and screams into a deep Butler sink. The laughter from the sitting room doubles as Helen takes another hearty mouthful of fatty lamb squirt. C'est fini.

Either ...

1. Get a hand mixer in there and blend it all to fuck. It tastes lovely. Onions and lamb and garlic and fat and salt. The only downside I've had with this method is the liquor goes a weird grey colour. It tasted great but it looked weird. I had to eat it with a hood on. It was really messy. People got hurt. Badly.

Or ...

2. Pass the liquid through a strainer, toss the onions and then, in a small pan, reduce the liquid to intensify the flavour. Delish.

All these things, these steps, can absolutely be done at least a day before. (Wipes errant hair from brow.) Take it easy. Cooking, producing edible magic – as an aside I'd say edible magic doesn't have to be Michelin-starred food, although it definitely is – can just as easily be beans and Cheddar on toast. With a milky cup of tea to wash it down, and everything in between these two poles. Producing good, tasty food should not make you want to kill yourself. If you can't cook something simple without your kitchen looking like an category EF 4 tornado has torn through your house, honestly, don't bother. Get a Deliveroo.

But if you want to bother, be gentle, take your time, know your limitations, you're meant to enjoy it too. I'm sure friends and family would rather chat and have a laugh with a host who casually produces gleaming spaghetti hoops on toast. Lolz. You'd be a hero in my eyes.

Also, and this is something I've done a few times over the years in my drive to impress people, usually a father-in-law or a fancy lady, is that you're so ambitious you run out of dishes to use and then you eat and pretend to listen to them with one eye on all the fucking cleaning that'll need to be done. It's not fun. The Aubergine Parmigiana is sat resting on a nice little plank you found for just these occasions. The onion liquid is nice and brothy and warm and deeply onioned, all that's left is the meat ...

The lamb will be really fragile. Like my self-esteem. Treat it gently. Transfer it on to a baking sheet. Either turn the oven up really blazing and high, like 220°C or 240°C, or fire up the grill. Either way, try not to burn this shit. Not now.

Slam in the lamb and watch it. I want it hot and crisp. I know when it comes to crackling, pork is the prom queen, but I'm a big fan of crispy lamb skin. It's so underrated, as a prom date it would be the nerdy chick who plays bass guitar and collects Charizard Pokémon cards and never speaks. You arrive to pick her up, she opens the door without her glasses on ... wha wha wee Wah!!! Taste sensation!!!

Once the lamb is hot and its skin is brown and crispy, you're done. Stick it on a nice Scandinavian platter and take it to the table. Boom! Crispy, slow-cooked shoulder/ leg of lamb. Aubergine Parmigiana with a rich onion broth. Enjoy. Also, a fresh, green, crispy element is nice with this. A decent coleslaw? Fried moth carapace? Some pak choi thing with garlic and soy? Yes, please. Crispy white cabbage ... You do the math. I don't have all the answers!

I also mentioned an easy version of the parmigiana too ... Fuck slicing the aubergines and pre-frying them/ all that layering shit. Take them and just halve them, and halve again and chop into chunks. Pour oil into a frying pan and fry the aubergines until they're nice and brown. Then you'll need the tomato sauce. Pour it over the top of the aubergines, turn the gas flame down a bit and let plip away for maybe 30 minutes. Crumble/grate cheese on top, whatever cheese you want this time. Cover with foil and then cook for 15 minutes more or until the cheese has melted. Et voilà! Pour a rich, spicy bottle of St Fartington's into a pint glass and sit in a small dark toilet, door locked with the taps running at full blast so they can't hear your lonely sobs and down the lot. Bonne chance!!!

The next couple of recipes should definitely be something to have in your locker for lunches and early summer suppers.

(I'm so fucking mad at myself.) Early summer suppers, go and fuck yourself. Let me say there's something about overly earnest TV chefs telling us how picturesque their childhoods were. I hate it. It always sounds like a lie. You know? There's a thing I do, and I suspect it's because my brain is broken, where if there's something on the TV that I hate so much it triggers an 'episode', I have to rewind and watch it at least 30 times. It doesn't always have to be a TV show. Once, on a plane with Hayley, I got into a hate-loop with the word/place RUNNYMEDE!!! I must have said it 200 times.

There's something in the hatred that I love. Me and my mate Greg Fleet used to call it logginess. Logginess was something so awful and earnest and embarrassing that essentially your toenails grew out and round into a circle, growing back through your calves and then Loggi would kind of roll around saying 'Loggi' in a very high-pitched voice. What am I talking about?

Nigel Slater triggered one such terrible bout of logginess. I was watching him talking about spring rhubarb and explaining how, when he was a little boy, he'd grab stalks of young, pink rhubarb and steal father's sugar bag, greedily dipping the raw rhubarb into the sugar and eating it. Even just writing this, I'm literally on the brink of smashing an old plate on my head. If I close my eyes, I can actually imagine the resonant click of the ancient porcelain as it snaps over my skull. What the fuck

are you talking about?!! Father's sugar bag? What?
WHAT?!!! FUCKING WHAT?!!! Father's sugar bag!!!
(It's happening.) FATHER'S. SUGAR. BAG. His father
had a specific bag for sugar. For sugar. Why? It
just sounds like a lie. I mean if it isn't, then fair dos.
I guess a sachet of sugar with one end ripped off
would count, right? That's essentially a sugar bag.
Although you couldn't fit a small stalk of pink spring
rhubarb into it. I wonder if that's one of the criteria
for an official nineteenth-century 'Sugar bag? ' It's
just a lie. Surely?! Please let it be a lie. If it isn't, I
don't know what I'll do. I can't resent my parents
more. No one I know either growing up or now has
ever mentioned this being a thing. Like, 'We have a
family sugar bag. For special occasions. For the end
of Lent. Or to mark St Fuckheads Dagen.' It sounds
preposterous to me. I'm imagining his father to be
a powerful landowner and a savage drunkard and
wife beater. One day he returns from a day lurcher
hunting, hammered and feisty. After swinging his
fat leather fists around and injuring a butler, he
slumps into his chair, unconscious, guffing almost
constantly. His sturdy day coat drops to the floor
revealing a silvery glint, the key to the chest that
contains Father's sugar bag!!! Little Nigel creeps
over and gingerly steals the key from the alcoholic
behemoth, he tiptoes over and opens the chest.
Inside, Father's sugar bag ... For some reason,
Nigel's fingers have now been replaced by actual
stalks of new season Runnymede ... No matter, he

takes the long central stalk, sucks on it like an elf's dick and deeply fingers the bag of sweet white, pulling out the rhubarb, now covered in sugar he greedily crunches off his own fingers. He cums meringue all over the parlour ceiling.

He turns to see Father, covered in meringue, (cum), very much awake, Father screams,

'SEIZE HIM!!!'

Nigel jumps on to his banana bike and cycles off into the air like the end of *E.T.*

NEW POTATOES

So, like I said, this is a staple in late spring/early summer. I hate everything about that sentence. I hate myself for writing it. I didn't even for a second imagine when I signed a book deal for a food memoir I'd be writing such disgusting prose. About a fucking new potato. I've spent a long time hating potatoes in this format. I always thought 'meh', but since getting to hang out in Scandinavia a lot over the last 20 years, I've kind of grown to love them.

Place a big pan of cold water on to the flames that live on top of your cooker. If you only have an ion stove or the uncovered fuel rods of a fission reactor, that should also work but you may have to adapt your cooking time.

Once the water is rolling, throw the spuds in and cook them until they're cooked. Probably 20 minutes? Maybe less? If you can push the point of a knife through them, they're done.

Drain ... Now I put a huge fat knob of salted butter in

the hot pan and toss them in the melted butter. Pepper heavily.

In Sweden I've had these with a load of shredded dill. It's nice and I'm not really a fan of dill. You can also do this with mint. If you're using salted butter, I wouldn't salt the spuds. If not, salt. A small spoon of smoked paprika would also be delicious. (Smoked paprika and salty butter!)

In terms of being a staple, it will always be delicious and it's so easy. Again, this can be rolled out to accompany steak done on the BBQ, jerk chicken thighs, trout, salmon, skate wings. I'd absolutely introduce some kind of raw/pickled red onion into this party too or pickled cucumber, BBQ'd teriyaki chicken thighs and little buttery boiled potatoes. If you have leftovers in the fridge, smash them flat and either fry them until crispy, or roast on a baking tray, at a high temperature, until crispy. So nice. Loads of salt. My kids love them. (Maybe not so much salt with the kids eating.) (On the other hand, salt tastes nice, and their kidneys are young, so fuck 'em. Put their kidneys under a little bit of pressure, see if they leak.) Bon appétit!!!

LITTLE CRUNCHY POTATOES

Use potatoes, not sure what kind. Just potatoes. What about Maris Piper? I SAID I DON'T KNOW, PATTY! Cut them into little bits. Like the size of a small eraser. Random. Imagine someone had taken a potato and with a sharp knife had cut the potato into smaller bits. That! That's what you're looking for.

Don't bother parboiling them. Oven on at about 180°C.

Baking tray, potatoes on it. Garlic pieces, slices of lemon zest, plenty of olive oil, salt and pepper.

Roast them for about 40 minutes. You can also fry them in a big sauté pan, too. If you're roasting in the oven, turn them over every 20 minutes. They should come out crisp and soft and salty and lovely. They go really well with Chicken Paprika (see pages 39–42). They actually go well with lots and lots of things. Enjoy!!!

CRAB THING ...

I like crab and crab culture very much. I like them alive and doing their shit in rock pools. I like them dead and about to be in my tummy. Writing this I'm getting a weird sensation about being unbothered by eating other live things. You know what I mean? I really love the taste of lamb and chicken and eel and I shouldn't be ashamed of that. Should I? I'm now imagining I'm lying on a beach in Pembrokeshire and my mouth is very wide open and the entry to my mouth is covered with flags and ticker tape. A procession is going on, crabs of all shapes and sizes riding in open-top vehicles and little motorbikes are riding directly into my mouth, while locals wave Welsh flags and the mellow pang of a Caribbean steel-pan choir can be heard sounding out a soft calypso.

Have you ever seen French people eating the Ortolan? They eat it under a huge napkin, such is the deliciousness and cruelty of the delicacy. It's so horrible yet so tasty that they cover their faces so God can't see!!! It makes me want to try it if I'm honest. I may sit in my car and eat a McDonald's Double Cheeseburger with a cloth on my head.

The Ortolan, cute little thing by the way (tasty and cute, poor fucker), is apparently caught and then either kept in darkness, or blinded! This makes them react by eating, not just eating, but gorging themselves on grain and juicy figs until they've doubled in weight. This is the shit bit (you know things are going to be shit if getting blinded isn't the shit bit ...): the cute, horny, tasty, très fuckable Ortolan is then drowned in brandy. (I'm so horny right now.) They're then quickly plucked and roasted. Diners cover their heads with a napkin, pick the drunk roasted bird up and pop the whole thing in their mouths, crunching through halfway. Apparently it has no culinary equal. The burst of flesh and hot fat and fig and brandy and organs is meant to be incredible. Ooh la la!!!

I know it's cunty. I get it. But is it any more cunty than killing it in the first place? Surely basic death is the real enemy here. Once I'm dead, I don't give a fig what you do with me. Not a fuck. You could leave me on a beach and let flies and seabirds peck my dick off if you want. Tiny crabs jab and nibble at my entrances, making them wider so bigger beasts try and climb inside my tattered anus. I'm dead, I don't know any of this. I don't care. If I had my way, I'd want to be tied to the back of a powerful scrambler and have one of the older kids from the estate drag me around over a bit of waste ground while other fat, spectrum kids laugh and throw pieces of shit-stained breeze blocks at my tattered genitals. That's how Dad went. And his dad. If it was good enough for them ...

I get my crab meat from Sandy's in Twickenham. I've talked about Sandy's already, massive Christmas queue. Great produce. Nice people. My white crab meat to dark crab meat ratio for this thing is 2:1, white:dark. Also, what is this thing I'm making? I'm

suggesting this is a very tasty late spring lu
garden maybe. I'd roll this out if I was trying to impress
mother-in-law, or friends my girl went to university with.

It's very easy. It takes no time and very little skill and you get a
lot of bang for your buck. If a boy was trying to date my daughter
and he put this in front of me, along with an ice-cold Coke Zero ...
I'm in. You can take her to Feltham Megabowl. (But she needs to
be back by 9pm. Please.)

Take a nice big bowl. A shiny metal one. Into it empty the
crab, and into that add, and I'm guessing here, three large
dollops of mayonnaise. Hellman's is fine. Don't use the
low-fat one. Use regular. You could make your own mayo,
but fuck that. Just buy it. I mean by all means learn to
make mayonnaise, it's a great staple to have on the books
but just use store-bought. No one likes a show-off.

Zest half a lemon. Finely dice half a mild chilli and one
quarter of a red onion. Chop up a fist-sized bush of flat-
leaf parsley. Grate a large piece of good Parmesan cheese
until it's not as large as it was before you started grating it.

Put all these things into the bowl with the crab. Mix
it up. Squeeze half the lemon into the meat. Add salt and
pepper. Taste it. It should taste very nice. You may need
a bit more mayo if it's too dry. If you're happy and
confident this is ready, cover it with clingfilm and pop
it in the fridge. Until later.

Later ... Take the crab out of the fridge at least 30
minutes before eating it. I just don't like it super cold. Get
a bunch of spring onions, or even chives, and chop them
nice and finely. If you're using the spring onions, just use

... en off. Keep it in a dish to
... of slices of sourdough toast ...

RAB PASTA

... 's lovely. Another use for crab. Head to
San... ...ouple of containers of white and one of
brown. T... ...to a bowl and stir so it's all one meat.

Take a big, mild red chilli. Slice it and then finely dice it. Leave to one side.

Boil a big pan of salted water. Once it's rolling, toss in enough linguine for you and another human that you know. Maybe they're a friend, perhaps they're a lover you hate who's mortally allergic to crab meat. I'll fucking show you. They're my kids, too.

Once the pasta is cooked, strain but leave a little bit of water, it'll help make the sauce. Empty the crab meat into the lovely warm pasta. Stir, toss in the red chilli, squeeze half a lemon into the pasta, empty a big glug of oil, grate Parmesan heavily on top. Pepper, some salt? Maybe. Stir in and eat. It's delicious. So summery.

There's a thing that I've done before with this recipe where you take a load of breadcrumbs and you fry them until they're crispy. Into them you toss some lemon zest, garlic and the red chilli too. Then you dump it on to the crab pasta at the end. It looks great and it's a nice crunchy texture as well. It's good. Yeah, do that. It must have a name. Let's call it ... Crab Pasta with Red Chilli Crumble. (I hate me.)

TOAST FOR THE CRAB ... (FINALLY!)

You use what you want. What I use is a nice rustic sourdough, but I don't put it in the toaster, I do it on the griddle pan! What?!

I brush it with a little bit of oil and I cook it on the griddle until both sides are crisp and toasty.

For one person:

1 nice plate

2 little slices of sourdough

1 big spoonful of your delicious crab mixture on each piece of toast

a drizzle of good olive oil

a turn of pepper

Then a light snowfall of either chopped spring onions or chives. Enjoy.

AMAZING THAI-STYLE SALAD

I love this salad so much, I could probably, I should probably, eat this every day. It's crisp and sour and sweet and hot and, fuck it, I'll say it, umami. God, that felt good. It's umami, it's UMAMI!!! And it's absolutely amazing. And easy ... UMAMEASY!!! Someone stop me. Close the book and light a candle inside the geode, put it out with your fingers and then smear the ash over the cover. This should seal my spirit deep inside a plum.

I never really ate veg, apart from potatoes and maybe the odd bit of carrot and swede, so I only ever ate root veg until I was about 32. The thought of veg made me physically heave. I have no idea why, my parents never pushed me and so I never pushed myself. I liked onions, in kebabs or cheeseburgers, and sometimes I ate lettuce. A lot of lettuce was used to garnish our Mexican food at Chiquito's, so if it was drenched in melted Cheddar and green enchilada sauce, I'd eat it. Apart from that, I ate very little. I'm amazed I didn't have rickets. Or scurvy. Maybe I did. I'm a stubborn sod, so once I had that thing in my mind where I couldn't eat something, I then usually didn't eat something.

It was only after getting with my ex-wife Chris that my mind began to change about things that weren't root veg or fried or not meat. My mind slowly opened wide and suddenly I found myself desperate for things that were crisp and green or juicy and red or fruit. Lovely fruit! Radish! Cabbage! Coriander! Oh my God, I couldn't live without green herbs now. My wife now, Hayley (not wife but we have two kids and 'girlfriend' doesn't really cover it, so wife it is) is a vegetarian, so again, my mind is way open on the green front. In fact, some meals I don't have meat at all. Not at all. UMAMEASY!!! (My spirit has escaped the geode.) Trap me inside a melon. Say the spell you'll find inside the cover. At the bottom.

Ingredients (you're a grown-up now, I don't need to tell you how much of anything you will need) ...

carrots

onion

cucumber

red pepper

red chilli

white cabbage

coriander

flat-leaf parsley

limes

sesame seeds

toasted sesame oil

How to do it ... Get a lovely big bowl. As big as you can get. It may seem a bit much but I want you to use the size to toss the whole salad in later. Trust me.

Take a couple of big, peeled carrots. Then, using the peeler, do that thing where you're essentially peeling planks of carrot. You know what I mean? Does it help if I say imagine you needed to turn these carrots into a floor in the house of a local chinchilla. Does it help? Planks of carrot. After you've planked up the carrots, then stack them on top of one another and finely slice the planks into nice thin strips. (Strips is not the right word.) Squirms? Square worms, is it a better word? Yes. Slice across the planks into squirms. Toss them into the huge bowl.

Halve an onion, slice it finely. Toss it in. (In terms of onion, or any of these ingredients, if you want more of one, or less of something, go for it. My amounts are just guidelines.)

Take a nice girthy cucumber. Using your peeler, peel some of the skin off. We don't need too much skin. Then, use the peeler to again plank the cucumber. Throw the planks in as they are. Don't squirm them up. They should be long and wet like a Saint Bernard's tongue.

Red pepper – cut two faces off the pepper and slice them into fine batons. Julienne if you will.

Red chilli, cut the lid off and get rid of all the seeds and pith. Cut it into slices, throw them in. These look nice sliced and round.

White cabbage – a small one of these goes a long way. Quarter it and using either a cheap Japanese mandolin, or a very big sharp knife, turn it into very thin slices. The cabbage should be the main event in the bowl. It should be the most of all our veg. The body if you will ... Watch your fingers when you chop or slice using that mandolin. I get bored of listening to chefs bang on about how sharp mandolins are, but they're really sharp as fuck. Hayley bought me one years ago but it was a really beautiful one made out of stainless steel, too good for me. What I wanted was a £12 plastic one. I got one this year for Christmas and I love it. It's super sharp though. If you're using one, please be careful. Or not. Whatever.

Coriander – a whole bunch – chop, medium, not too fine, toss into the bowl.

Parsley – flat-leaf, not the pubey type. Again, chop like the coriander. Toss into the bowl.

Squeeze the juice of one lime into the bowl. Salt. Big slug of sesame oil. (I absolutely LOVE sesame oil.) Super urmermoo. Now, using your arms, toss all the ingredients over and over until they're all super mixed together. Take a bit and cram it into your beautiful soft mouth. Well? More oil? More lime? Salt? Tinker until thrilled. Pour from huge bowl into a cute serving plate/bowl. Then sprinkle sesame seeds over the top. I tend to use the last lime and cut it into chunks and serve a piece with each portion.

This is like the Thai salad that's got papaya in it, which I adore but can be fucking hot. You can even whizz up some peanuts in the food processor and sprinkle them on top too.

Learn this so you don't need a recipe book when you prep it and people think you're a genius. It goes with everything. If you serve this in a big bowl with fresh oily hummus, warm pitta and BBQ'd chicken thighs or pan-fried salmon with crispy skin, or a big juicy sirloin steak, it's a winner. It's so nice and so easy and people will go away saying nice things about you.

FRENCH ONION SOUP

I always use French Onion Soup as a great example of food chemistry. Just onion soup generally, but I could have chosen hundreds of dishes. Thousands of dishes. Every culture that cooks must have hundreds of examples, and that's the simplest recipes they have. I like to think that if you asked cuisine where it lived it would tell you 'On the corner of art and chemistry.' But that wouldn't be true, it lives in Leytonstone near the big cemetery.

If you slice onions it releases a protective juice that makes you cry. Fuck you onions. Slice up loads of them, put loads of butter into a big pan and then fry them until they're all soft and brown. Add some water and a large amount of good, rich, beef stock. Turn the heat down and just let all those amazing, soft, caramelised, fried onions simmer for a bit. Then, taste that liquid. That's frigging amazing. That's onion soup. Delicious. What magic.

CHILLI CON CARNE

Who else needs a little Flavor Flav right about now up in their shit? You do, well nosh on this sweet Chilli con Carne. YEAH ROY!!! From Flavor Flav to Chuck D or chuck steak I should say (I may take the rest of the day off after that segue. See you all Monday).

Get a kilo of steak and chop it into cubes, little cubes. Like a ragù/Bolognese, you can do this with mince or actual meat which melts down over a long cooking time. Use beef which is a bit fatty, don't fear fat in meat. Long, slow cooking renders it out and adds a terrific flavour to finished dishes.

Butter and oil in the bottom of a big pan, this is a one-pot deal, we're cooking everything in this pot. Fry the beef hard, I want to see brown bits all over the meat and bits sticking to the pan. Fry in batches, please.

If you put too much meat in a pot it brings the temperature down and things tend to boil more than fry. Once cooked, lift out with a spoon and leave to one side.

For the next bit, two sliced onions. Four big nuggets of garlic. One red pepper, chopped, one green pepper, chopped, one large mild red chilli, chopped, one small and fiery pepper, something from Thailand perhaps or Trinidad, toss it in whole. Then, when the chilli is finished you can lift the hot chilli out and that way you get the flavour and not all the nutty heat.

When it comes to spices, I tend to look through the cupboard like a coked-up scaffolder scanning xHamster. Generally, the spices I'd put in my chilli are: cumin, loads, it's a real Mexican flavour. Smoked paprika. Cayenne pepper, then find a nice mild chilli powder or mild chilli flakes, like Aleppo. So nice. Warm and complicated, rich. I'm trying to layer different flavours. You could definitely open up a tin of those green chopped chillies I got on Amazon. I buy a lot of my tinned chillies on Amazon. This Chilli con Carne would absolutely love them.

A word about Amazon, you can get loads of stuff for good Mexican food on Amazon. They do these things like sweet, dried chillies, vacuum packed. All you do is rehydrate them in water and chop them up and stick them into a chilli. You can buy traditional spices too, if you want to cook something a little more authentic. You could buy everything needed to make a lovely red or green enchilada sauce. Delicious. Not just Mexican food either, curries, Thai food, Chinese, etc. I know lots of people who are also a bit like, 'I shan't be giving Monsieur Bezos any more of my hard-earned cash ...' Let me tell you two things: 1) Eat shit chilli. 2) Jeff doesn't give a fuck about your £2.60.

Back to our chilli, sponsored by Amazon Food and ChemMunitions Inc! With the brown steak cubes resting, toss into the pan the veg and use the liquid and steam it produces as it cooks to deglaze the pan of beef bits. Lid on for a couple of minutes, then lid off and use your spoon to get all the burnt bits off the bottom. Cook it out until the onions are soft and sweet and translucent. Now pump in two gwelps of tomato purée. Turn up the heat and stir while the tomato purée cooks out.

Once all the onions and chillies and peppers are coated red, tip in 1 litre of water. I always boil a kettle and use that. Turn up the heat. Stir. Put the meat and any delicious juice back in. Slowly bring it up to a nice confident puttpit. Take your big bunch of coriander you have in the fridge, top and tail it. Put the leaves back in the fridge and, as finely as you can, take the stalks and chop. Throw them in the pan and stir. If it's now boiling, turn it right down. Reduce that sauce, slowly, slowly. If it catches, stir it and add more water. It's ready when the meat literally just falls to pieces when you squash it under a spoon. This should also coincide with the sauce that should now be super thick and glossy and taste rich and spicy and cheeky. If you wanted to stick a tin of black beans in, now's the time to do it but I wouldn't. What I would do now though is season it. Stand over it like an old clockwork flamingo and dip your beak in and whistle and squawk until you get it right. Lovely.

A lovely Chilli con Carne is a very beautiful thing. Historically, British people tended to serve dry mince, which was either bland or hot as fuck, and it would nestle atop an atoll of badly cooked rice. But no more, no ma'am. Not on my watch. We've spent upwards of three hours slowly making something that's really lovely to eat, let's not spoil it now. I have a little tip here for how we're going to serve it ...

Firstly, chop that coriander up. Toss it in. Keep a few bits back to use as a garnish. Stir. Take a lime and squeeze the juice in. Now into some lovely little side bowls add the following items:

soured cream

mature Cheddar

lime chunks

slices of bright red radish

slices of pickled jalapeño

slices of spring onion

slices of red onion

Grab a pack of flour tortillas and slice every tortilla into six, put on a baking sheet and toast in a hot oven until crisp. You'll have to turn them all over a few times. Don't let them burn. My brain tells me that I have to constantly set timers and alarms on my phone. There'll be one set for eight minutes and when it beeps it'll remind me to turn the tortillas over. I like to take a really nice clean simple white tea towel and wrap them in that and serve them in this simple shroud. Then put on the table all the little bowls of sides, or 'fixings' as they call them in the south of the States. And, finally, a lovely pan of incredible Chilli con Carne. As you can see, not a grain of rice in sight. It doesn't need it. Dig in. If anyone mentions rice, indignantly get them to leave. I don't care if it's your girlfriend's father, get his coat and lead him out. Tell him you'll talk about this on Sunday.

PICKLES

In Mexico and Mexican-themed restaurants, they sometimes offer a drink in a nice, long, thin glass bottle called Jarritos. They do a green grapefruit one. It's so cold and fresh and sweet. I love citrus a lot. I'd love to wash down a crispy tortilla which now finds itself home to a cube of delicately spiced unctuous, juicy chilli and mature Cheddar and a dollop of soured cream with a circle of jalapeño on top, with an ice-cold Jarrito. Let's eat and then get in the sea and have a nice swim. Then let's go back to the room and put NHK World-Japan on in the background and we can make love and then snooze until 5pm. Then let's get up and shower and go out for a cocktail before dinner ... I'm liking this flight of fancy a lot ...

Now, I hadn't pickled anything before 2020. It was just not a thing in my life. Then Covid happened and I, like millions of others, decided to use the time given to them to learn new things. I wanted to fill gaps in my repertoire (and there are many). I could live for 200 years and I'd still not even bruise the surface. Is that the saying? Dent the lid? I'd still not even bend the film atop a Greek-style set yoghurt. That's it. What I'm trying to say is I could live for 200 years and I'd still not even bend the film atop a Greek-style set yoghurt when it comes to knowing all there is to know about food. I mean there's a LOT to learn about food. It's amazing.

With pickles and pickling, I knew nothing except it was used as a way to increase the longevity of some ingredients. Usually, fruit and vegetables. Also, an egg. I used to drink in an old boozer that had a jar of pickled eggs sat on the bar. I never got it. I never once, in all the thousands of pints I sat there and inhaled, thought 'I want more than anything the pickled foetus of a dead chicken.'

I follow a lot of Michelin-starred chefs and I could see many years ago a tide turned and pickling began to be a new thing again, and fermentation, even though it was actually a really old thing.

Food went from the 1980s and the difficulty of trying to tear itself away from Mama France's loving bosom, to the 1990s which was all cash and coke and flash fuckers eating Lamborghinis made from caviar. Then further on a bit from about 2005 onwards, there was a nice break from tradition and a fresh breeze pushing us towards sustainability and seasonality. Then Copenhagen got involved somewhere there and the El Bulli geezer and the nice Italian one from Modena (Parmesan and Ferraris) and the whole culinary world started to change. For the better.

Food bought this big old Victorian doer-upper in Deal, really amazing six-bed, it has so much potential but the house is kind of fucked. Only one hour and five minutes from London. Anyway, Food's wife, Patty Drink, was away with work at this fancy wine event in the Alsace tasting biodiverse Rieslings.

Food is very stubborn and when she gets a bee in her bonnet about something she must scratch that itch. Today's itch though is a huge, old cupboard they found left in the loft. Behind the cupboard is this biggish hole, from out of it a white chocolate mouse comes flying. Food yelps and drops the cupboard. Dust flies everywhere. Food, annoyed but uninjured, shakes her head. She gets down on all fours and peers into the hole to see if she can see any other mice, and just inside the hole she sees a small fruit-leatherbound book. She reaches in and pulls it out.

On the front of the book, embossed in wafer-thin carrot, is the title. The book is called *How We Used To Eat – A Memoir of Techniques Discovered (Often Quite By Chance) by Humans Both Old and New*. Food pulls the book out and unravels the liquorice cord that binds it shut. She begins to read and immediately falls headlong into the story. Into her story.

After 26 minutes, Food spies the little white chocolate mouse sneaking back into its hole, mouse isn't going to make it. Food slashes a claw out and grabs poor mouse. It squeals and fights to get away, but alas Food is merciless and hungry. (As she always is.) She swings it like an old watch on a chain before letting it drop into her mouth. She crunches down again and again until it is silent and motionless and gone. Warm salted caramel pours down Food's throat.

I should explain that when I said 'claw', it is because Food's right hand is that of a hen, her left is a lamb's hoof. One eye is a coconut, the other a pomelo, her heart a large tomato, one leg is a broad, green, vibrant leek, the other a huge garlic bread with cheese from Aldi. Her fingers are sweet potato fries and her toes are vegetarian chicken nuggets on the left foot and Young's frozen scampi on the right. I may seek the help of a neurologist ... Weren't we just talking about pickles? Yes.

Like most things in life, things always seem hard and pointless and tough until we take the time to slowly read and understand the recipe and then give it a go. I also feel this vibe when I think about bricklaying, using a defibrillator and flying a chopper. So, I tried to pickle red onions slices as I like them a lot and I wanted something crisp and vinegarish to cut through all that phat Chilli con Carne flavour.

It was easy. It tasted like shit but it was easy and an incredible starting point. I'll often ask myself, what went wrong? What was good? Could we still eat it? Would a hyena eat it? Also, I've only lost an onion if it's uneatable FFS. Take one red onion, slice in half and then slice the halves. I put it into a new fancy jar I bought from Amazon and used six times for pickling. Then get on the internet and google 'pickling liquor'. Read the thousands of responses, pick one you like, get the ingredients it tells you to. Follow the method. Faye Presto. Pickled onions to go as one of the fixings with your incredible slow-cooked Chilli con Carne. Let me ask you a question ... When you get invited to a friend's house for a meal, how many of them serve homemade pickles? None. None.

It's around about this time when the husband of one of your wife's friends who you've never really had time for, says something that you overhear in the car park of a fucking picnic you don't want to be at because you're 17 years older than them and it hurts when you have to sit on the floor, and you're so overweight you kind of crash down then roll on to first your front and then your side and

you casually pop an arm under your chin. I felt that looked not just athletic but cute. You roll on to your front and then push yourself upland, swing a knee under until you're kind of kneeling down. You take a deep breath as you attempt to ignore the message from your right knee telling you the awful news that left knee has sadly passed. Three young men have sensed your pain, both physical and other, and act as anchor points so you can haul yourself up and off the earth. You hum and whistle loudly because this is how you cope with the huge amount of pain you suffer from, daily.

I end up doing some weird charade, character shit, so I can leave them with a laugh, maybe they'll forget everything else, the walrus shit. Make it good ... What shall I choose ... ? What comedy genius dwells inside of me ... ? Yes! Got it! Here we go gang ... I do a kind of classic 'ta-da' jazz-hands thing and then, a bit overly loud I'll agree, I hit them with a very strong impression of Porky Pig 'Well That's All, Folks!!!' My mouth is open and my eyebrows are up. It's like my face is a fly trap for mirth. It's awful. The young people are just frightened and confused. Hayley leaves. Is she cross? People laugh but from other groups and at me. I can tell. 'See you.' I turn to catch her up.

As I stretch my leg and begin to hobble off, one of the group says, 'Hey dude, you forgot your bumbag.' Now they laugh. I don't get it, I thought B-bags were hot?

We walk to the car in silence. I don't want to look at her because I already know what look she has loaded. It says, 'I'm disappointed by your weakness and secretly I'd want the kids sired by a man not so fat he'd soon need a kind of wheeled trolley to live.' I have to agree with her. I notice she's stopped walking. 'What are you doing?' She's fumbling in her Balenciaga microsack for her phone. 'You go to the car darling, I'm just going hang back and take some photos of these young Brazilian men doing capoeira.' I stop limping a moment and think, smelling a rat ... 'Oh. Okay. It's just that you said we could leave so I could catch the start of the Hungarian Grand Prix ...'

'Go to the car!'

I sit in the car for two hours. At times I completely lose sight of her. Weird. Eventually her friends file back to their cars and I slump down so they can't see me, and here's the good bit: I overhear Alistair, Mandy's fella, talking about making his own pickling liquor. Cool. That's my in.

As well as pickles, which tasted delicious eventually, it took a while to get my brine just right, which is part of the fun and the joy. When at first you don't succeed, do it again until it doesn't taste like shit. Is that it? Once you get that right and tasty and you're off and running. This is info you can't unlearn. If, God willing, most of humanity suddenly ceases to exist and we're just left here (you and me), then we would have an advantage over the other dicks because we have the ability to survive through the winter when the snow is too deep for us to hunt native furred mammals or wild hens. In the eyes of these cavechick kweens, I'd be sexy as fuck. I can protect us with my brawny arms and fascination with huge razor-sharp knives. Check. Has ability to feed us throughout the winter. Check. Sexual tyrannosaur. Check. I have to believe that when society collapses, this is when I will really hit the big time. Fingers crossed.

Having a jar or jars of multiple and various different pickled veg is sexy and cool. Very often I'll finish a dish with a little pickle here or there. There's something about that crisp, fresh, vinegary, sweet feeling that sits nicely with a rich gravy or chilli. Pickles offer seaman hope. (I am willing to bet my children's eyes that that last sentence has never been written before in the history of cookbooks. Pickles offer seaman hope.)

What I've found over the last 30 years of my life is showing up is a big deal. That's 75 per cent of your final grade. Just pitch up. Push those doors open and take a seat. We saved you one. Then try, have a go, or not, you turned up. Fuck it if you fail, I fail CONSTANTLY. It keeps me humble. I'm talking about pickling a fucking red onion here. But I could easily be talking about kids. School plays. Sports days. Family meals, Ramadan, Christmas Eve drinks, a marriage. Or I might be talking about mental health. Walk through the door. Have a go. If you fuck it up, ask for help, someone will help you. Cooking will help you. Cooking helps me and art and crying. 'I always sleep best after a good cry,' said Master Frodo?

A complete aside here ... It's just come flooding back to me. It's an idea I had a long while ago when I lived in Dublin while shooting *Into the Badlands*. It's also food-based, so this book seems just the place to introduce this mind-fucking concept. When we filmed *ITB,* we had two complete units shooting independently of one another. One unit shot all the drama. One unit shot all the action and the amazing fight scenes. (How we never got any awards for the fight scenes is actually awful! I've been a fan of Hong Kong, Jackie Chan-style martial arts for 40 years and felt the work we did was outstanding.)

There was always so much dialogue for me to learn as Bajie. Daniel's character was all handsome and brooding which meant Bajie got to do all the wise talking. It was sometimes really nice not to worry about dialogue for a few days and just spend good, quality time fucking stuntmen up. I say that now. It was often the case that we'd shoot a few takes of a fight and I'd be fucking knackered! I'd look at the clock and it would be 8:36am. Only another ten hours of this!

We had our own Hong Kong stunt team; they had all come through JC's fight school in China. They were incredible fighters. We'd start the day by sitting on the set and watching Master Deedee and the other guys and girls noisily working out in Cantonese what the next fight would look like. It was very rare one had to pre-learn anything. Eventually they had the first ten moves of a very long fight that would often take a week to shoot, and the crew would cram on to the set and they'd show everyone what we were going to film.

While the first ten moves of the fight scene were being lit by the sparks, the actors and stunts would be off-set learning the hits and kicks of the sequence. If need be, we'd alter it slightly to fit in better with our characters' fighting style. Then we'd shoot it. After that we'd start the process all over again and gradually you'd build up a big, long fight. I loved it. I liked the fighting and I was not only good at it and committed, I was super careful and respectful of the stunt team.

Master Deedee didn't talk much. Not in English anyway. He was our sensei and our guru and all the actors worked their asses off trying to impress him. He only ever wore a Gucci tracksuit. Sometimes after a take Master Deedee would walk on to the set and just gently pat me on the shoulder, nodding his head in a 'Yes' motion. Man, that felt fucking good. I worked my hole off on that show to get the fighting right. (And the drama.)

On Sundays, the whole of the Hong Kong stunt team and Daniel Wu, and Mikey, the amazing first assistant director, and a bunch of other people would spend the afternoon drinking and eating amazing Chinese food. I like to think that when the stunt team arrived from HK, a young stuntman was given the job of finding the best Chinese food in Dublin. If you'd had a good week on fights you'd be invited for lunch on Sunday. (This makes it sound elitist and exclusive. It wasn't, anyone could come, but it suits my story better like this.)

I clutched a tattered business card in my hand. I'd been told to arrive at 1pm sharp. Apparently Madame Wong's was the most authentic Chinese food in all of Temple Bar. Although the business card said otherwise to me ...

For the next part of the story, let's let the beginning of *Gremlins*, and the flying noodle bar bit in *Blade Runner*, and *Big Trouble in Little China*, and the big gong in *Indiana Jones and the Temple of Doom* and the bullet noises pinging off of it, do a lot of the heavy lifting when it comes to setting the scene of just what Madame Wong's was like.

I pushed through the front door to be met by a huge fish tank with a lot of fat, tired-looking carp floating upside down. I was shown up into a secret room at the back of the restaurant and there all the team were sat.

I got a nice little cheer and some cuddles and felt a million dollars getting to hang out with these amazing, committed men and women who'd taken essentially ten months out of their lives to get the shit beaten out of themselves 14 hours a day, five days a week. I felt really spoilt getting the chance to just sit back and let them order things I would never know to order. It was an amazing experience.

I know it was just eating good Chinese food with good Chinese people but it felt special, I felt like I belonged. I was also on my own in Ireland without my family, and to feel like, only for a few hours, that I was part of theirs made me want to hit them a bit softer on Monday. I didn't, of course. You can't really. The camera sees. I also loved the fact all the Hong Kong guys every Sunday would always have brand-new trainers and tracksuits on. They were proud as punch. It was their little treat. Sometimes even Master Deedee would bowl in wearing an ice-white pair of box-fresh Air Max.

Here's the whole reason for my overly dramatised story. Let me cut to the chase. It was while I was tackling a rather delicious and particularly *noodle-heavy* broth that I had this idea. (Which I own by the way, so fuck off.) I enjoyed the noodle aspect and the veg and little pieces of rich roast pork, my issue was this ... I have to put my chopsticks down and pick up this huge mandolin of a spoon and use it to drink my broth with, or God forbid, we drink straight from the bowl! No bloody chance, where do you think I hail from ... Gansu province? (If this was stand-up, the audience in Shanghai now would be creasing up!!!) Finally, the point of this charming tale ... Here's the thought that struck me. I turned to the stunt team ...

'Guys ... Hey, everyone, sorry to interrupt but I'm one of the main cast, Nick Frost. I should be regarded.' They stop and listen ...

'Thanks, guys, I just had this amazing idea ... What if the chopsticks were hollow? So, you could eat the noodles, and then just suck any gravy up after?' I'm smug as fuck right now.

Let that sink in for a bit if you want. My other ADHD brain lodger, Dennis, quick as a fox says, 'Surely all the little delicious bits would clog up the straw and you'd not be able to suck the soup through it?' It's a good point.

Answer ... The hollow chopstick has a tiny grate over the bottom that stops rice and other matter from clogging it up. That's fucking brilliant. A chopstick which is also a straw that enables the user to simply suck up the tasty broth after you've demolished the noodles. Wow. The table sit stunned and silent for an age. Then, one by one, in silence, the chaps get up and leave.

I feel that everyone present is so frightened by this concept and its power, so frightened by what it means for China, not just as a superpower going forward but what this means culturally. How come a Western Idiot had this idea? China invented explosives and writing and maths and the restaurant. They're amazing. How could they have missed this?

The lights go out. I'm alone and it's dark. I panic. I need to get a message to my family as quickly as possible. I need to let them know that Operation Wounded Dragon is real now. It's happening. I hope Hayley remembers the checklist I tried to teach her. I know she won't. She hates that kind of shit, always accusing me of overreacting. Now who's overreacting?! Why won't she pick up? I could tell she wasn't listening. Fuck! I can tell when she's flitting around on the line looking at sites that offer pre-loved baby cardigans and reading about brawny, easygoing men from Fife who dig their own natural swimming holes and breed their OWN FUCKING SOURDOUGH STARTER!!! PICK UP!!! The plan is so easy. I've made it foolproof. I even developed it into a very simple melody and taught it to the kids.

Take out as much dosh as you can // Make crusty rolls with ham. My little baby, she likes jam. Drop 'em in a bag quick, quick. Add a little six-pack of ready salted crisps. You need a bit of water cause crisp make yoot mouth dry. Grab them sovs in my pant drawer and torch that house sky-high. Fuck that place, let's hope the cat dies. Toss the kids in the car, one, two, and race to Evesham, grab a pretty eight-berth narrowboat waiting for you. // Now live off-grid and thrive. Live off-grid. Survive. Remember, never order Chinese off Deliveroo, even if you're super hungry for that salt and pepper tofu. //

Don't re-marry during long romantic slump. If you touch another dickie, I'll have the proper ump. In a year or two when the future is clear, I'll summon ya'll by firing a flare. Pretty like you in the night sky it floats, just follow the smoke and get into the boats. A teddy bear for him, some roses for you, change that baby's shitty nappy, I'll meet you in Peru.

God, my little daughter loved that song. She'd lay in my arms gurgling the tune. Why could Hayley not learn that? It's easy. It literally might save her life.

I tailored it specifically for her. I used a lite dancehall tempo and then borrowed soft melodies and hooks from not just Styles but also Jonas. (Joe not Nick.) It's honestly like giving a donkey a fucking strawberry.

Sorry, but if I took a straw poll and asked every one of her friends' boyfriends the following question: 'How many of you have ever written a secret escape message and hidden it in a charming, catchy "calypso-style" melody, which should, in theory, make it easier to learn? Anyone?'

Out of 11 men only one other had done it! Just one.

Before the inevitable happens and China silence me forever, I begin to formulate a plan. Hang on, this is a bloody cookbook. Okay, um, one egg. There. If this plan works, like I think it might, I could buy my family and I some time.

The Chinese Secret Service intervene and I have to disappear. Honestly, I can't even really use chopsticks. I end up stabbing shit and just cramming it into my mouth and even then I sometimes miss and it wobbles out. No sir, this whole business is sure to daub the regime with a bent brush. I was never meant to accidentally discover the chopdick. I must be silenced.

I went ahead and bought a lathe and some tools and a few bits and pieces and I crafted two prototype chopdicks ... because you suck them. You suck them. Chopdicks. This shit writes itself.

I'm going to smuggle out the only two prototype chopdicks I crafted by actually sliding them first into a rubber sheath and then down, deep down inside my own urethra. It's an amazing coincidence but my 'urine duct' is perfectly built to house two pairs of chopsticks end to end. Lady Luck is smiling on me!!!

I'm going to hide a bunch of pillows under the quilt so the MSS operatives watching think I'm asleep. I even managed to barter an old dictaphone off a half-blind Tibetan monk, Rudy loudmouth. I'm like, 'Yeah, we get it, you like Buddha!' Anyway, I found a rock-hard fossilised rat shit and told him it was a piece of amber. Idiot.

I used the dictaphone to record a bed of night sounds to aid my escape attempt. It went great, the only hiccup, I thought I'd turned it off. I hadn't. Whatever. There's now a bit of bonus 'Hand Relief' content in there. I was cross at first but it actually sounds pretty good. Listening to it a lot, as I have, there's actually a wonderful realism to my error you couldn't capture if you were actually trying to. It's quite brilliant and combined with the sleep apnoea, snoring, night terrors and the actual final release-erotique itself, you've got a very convincing soundscape for me to work behind.

Once I'm through the mines and avoid the barbed wire. (It's not what you think, it's actually a section of the fence which Barbara tried to escape through last year. Snipers shot her and she landed, hung up into the wire. The camp commandant decided to leave her there as a chilling message to others. Barbara was 99 years old.) Rudy also has a battered old

Segue I've got my eye on. I don't know why or how he's amassed this mountain of electronic contraband tech. How is he allowed all this shit? It's not fucking fair. My legal team had months of back and forth just so they could send a small jar of plum jam for my 50th. It's barbaric. Once Rudy is soundly sleeping I'll beat him to death with a concrete-filled jam jar in a sock and steal the Segue. I'll drive it using my shattered, arthritis-filled knees down to the docks and from there board a container vessel bound for Tenerife via Guam.

I'll start swimming when I'm close enough to dry land and, for my above-average swimming capabilities, that ideally has to be somewhere between 1 and 1.1 nautical miles from shore. Any more than that and they'll find me washed up on Mr Han's island, bloated with crabs inside of my anus. (Insert delicious recipe for Chinese anus crab here ...)

'Any questions?'

Ten or so hands thrust upwards towards heaven. Nice engagement. I scan the room before picking someone.

'Uhhh, yes, Helen, Reuters.'

'How does one judge such a critical distance when you're hiding deep inside a ship's chimney?'

'Oh, what a great question, Helen, thanks. Um, for me I usually let myself be guided by the screech and chatter of Japanese seabirds. Once I can hear the cheeky chuckle of the wedge-tailed shearwater, I know it's time for me to abandon ship as it were.

I'll leap overboard and swim to land. Japan hopefully. Although one of the Koreas would also be fine.Taipei?'

The plan was perfect. I surfaced about 1,100 metres from the beach. The swim was easy and warm, to be honest I laughed most of the way. I fucking laughed.

I make landfall and head up the beach, which is packed full of young families. They wave and scream. Some of the younger kids misunderstand and try to lay wet towels on me thinking I am a young minke whale. I can't believe I did it! With my freedom comes a wave of unbridled emotion. I fall to my knees and sob uncontrollably. The parents try to comfort the children who have begun to turn slightly from the waving and laughing of earlier. I dry my eyes and try and make them all understand.

Pulling off my Durex allows me to easily remove the chopdick prototypes from inside my battered and flooded urethra. I don't know if they've caught sight of the sticks or it's now trademarked Brothgrate™ but everyone has gone nuts. It's amazing. I feel like one of The Beatles.

I thrust the chopdicks into the eager hands of one of the excited children. In my very broken Japanese, I officially hand over the chopdicks and remind them to let their friends use them and their friends and their children's friends. Fuck the money. Like Tim Berners-Lee and the interweb, I'm going to just let the idea loose. It's for everyone. Pick up peas or inhale broth. You decide. Bonne chance.

MEATBALLS

Badabing! Sorry. I love meatballs. It's a really good thing to have in your repertoire. You can tweak it and add finely diced chilli if you want a little kick or, like mine, I add some pine nuts that I've toasted slightly. Let me drop some science ...

400g fatty beef mince

250g veal mince

250g pork mince

½ white onion

stale breadcrumbs, soaked in milk

1 bird's egg

Parmesan cheese, grated

red chilli flakes

lemon zest

pine nuts, toasted

salt and pepper

Get a nice, big, shiny stainless-steel bowl (drool emoji). All great recipes should start like this. Stick all three meats into it and then wash your hands thoroughly. Then, make a spear shape with your fist. Imagine the meat is the face of an enemy and then repeatedly strike the meat over and over again using spearfist technique until your enemy no longer lives ... That's also the kind of time it takes for us to turn three separate meats into one well-worked 'supermeat'. Don't look for that name anywhere, you won't find it. It's patented. My three-breed supermeat is now ready to become meatballs.

Chop and fry the onion in butter, then let it cool and then add it into the supermeat. If, when doing this, you hear the meat laugh, consider it a good omen. Take a pregnancy test, you may be with child. Even the men.

Also add the milk-soaked breadcrumbs, this will help it bind. Crack the egg in too. In fact, just tip everything into the bowl and use your lovely hands to mash it all up together. Add salt and pepper. Now, I like this bit. Take a frying pan, add a little oil and pull off a little of the supermeat and fry it like a tiny burger. Once it's cool enough, eat it. Is it nice? Does it need to be seasoned? Yes? Go for it. No. Well done. You win.

I'd take a big, clean baking sheet and take your time forming your balls of supermeat. I guess there's a question about size here. The Swedish always have fairly little balls, which I kind of like. It also means less cooking time. Sometimes, in the States, I've seen very big meatballs, like the size of grapefruit, which is totally too big for me. If I'm making these for a traditional meatball and tomato sauce 'Italian'-style meal, then for me the sweet spot in size is 1½ inches across. Imagine something 12 per cent larger than a standard golf ball. If you can.

Once you've formed all the meat into balls, fry them gently in a nice, big non-stick frying pan. It's the same pan you're also going to use to make your sauce. Once they're nice and brown on the outside, remove them to a dish and cover with foil. Feel free to freeze any you think you won't use. These can last ages in the freezer. Remember when you fry the meatballs that you only need the outside to be nice and brown. These are going to sit in a bath of rich bubbly sauce for the end stage of their existence.

The pan you fried the balls in will now be crusty and a bit burnt and full of nice flavour. Add oil and butter and then we're going to make a basic tomato sauce ... Fry half a large white onion and two large nuggets of garlic – the sizzle and the moisture from the veg will deglaze the crusty meat flavour off the bottom of the pan. Now add, I dunno, 1kg ripe, red, chopped tomatoes. Cook for a while until it begins to reduce and simmer and melt down into a very easy, very delicious tomato sauce, which I've pointed out before can be used in loads of things.

At some point, add some water, which will help turn all those tomatoes into an actual live, living sauce. When you hear the high-pitched squeals of the dying toms turn into a single, deep, chesty cough of an old man, you know the transformation is complete. Now is the time to add your meatballs. I find three or four is usually enough for any guests. It's a lot with pasta and focaccia too.

I usually get 12 or 16 balls in the tomato sauce. The balls should, hopefully, have enough sauce that they are shoulder deep in the pan. Turn the heat right down, cover the frying pan with lashings of thick foil. Every now and again, remove the lid and turn the balls over. If you need to add a little water to the sauce, go for it. When you're 20 minutes out, bring a big pan of salted water to the boil and for four people, cook a whole packet of spaghetti. Once it's ready, we're ready. Let's eat.

Turn the heat off under the meatball saucepan. Leave to sit for five minutes.

How would I serve this dish? Who asked that? Abby from *Flava* magazine.

'Abby, thanks for this. I often serve this family style!'

What does that mean? It means you serve it in one huge bowl you bring to the table and then everyone helps themselves. Sweet. I have a lovely big serving platter which is ideal for this. Have you ever seen the trophy the women win at Wimbledon singles? It's that but it isn't silver, it's pottery. (In fact, I've just had to leave the laptop a moment and go and look for that plate and I can't find it. I feel it's a piece of ceramic I may have lost in my divorce. It can be hell when a marriage ends. Still, who cares about a plate, at least I got to keep my lovely big ... house ... Oh, balls.)

Drain the spaghetti, retain a little of the cooking liquid to loosen the sauce a bit. Coat the spaghetti heavily and turn it all on to the big plate. Then plop all the balls into the nest of spaghetti and finish with a load of chopped parsley and a load of finely grated Parmesan. It's so nice. People love seeing a big platter like that turn up. Open a nice rich, dark, complicated red and pour as much as you can into a pint glass. Once the nervous laughter stops, smile, down your drink and buon appetito!

SPATCHCOCKED CHICKEN

Who's ever spatchcocked a chicken. Anyone? Abby from *Flava*. Anyone else? No. Okay, I get that. I had watched a TV show and the technique of spatchcocking had come into my mind, so I went to a local butcher and he actually got proper moody that I'd want a whole chicken prepared in such a way. Guess what? ADHD bought some poultry shears online and they arrived and I fucking taught myself.

I think true spatchcocking is to take all the bones out, legs too, so you're left with a whole boneless chicken. I don't tend to remove the leg bones because I'm a lazy twat, I just take the scissors and cut the spine out. It's two cuts. Then I turn the bird over and squash it flat. Take a sharp knife and make deep cuts in the legs. Two slashes per leg, this enables lots of marinade to get in and also ensures the legs will cook evenly. I also slash the breasts too, same reason.

With a traditional roast, you'd never want to slash the bird, the point is to keep it intact and roasting to keep all that moisture inside the bird. This is not the case with spatchcocking. For me, I'm going to cook this on a hot BBQ, on a hot-as-fuck griddle pan on the hob, or at 220°C+ in the oven. Hot and quick. It should be scorched and there should be flame and juice dancing together until the dawn.

I like to marinade a spatchcocked bird too, there are a million different choices. Olive oil, lemon juice, salt/pepper, thyme. This would work. A Mexican vibe, very nice. I do a nice Japanese-style one with crispy chilli sauce, soy sauce, teriyaki sauce, red onions finely sliced, one squeeze of lime, water. I tend to stick all the marinade ingredients into a big Ziplock bag and then put Boneless Bertie into the bag as well, and that can sit in the fridge overnight if you want.

The next day can be spent preparing everything else and then, when people arrive, you have one thing to cook. It's easy. Heat up a BBQ, but be ready, the fat and sauce that comes out of the chicken will cause the flames to rise. Be ready to move and dance across the grill to ensure you don't burn it to fuck.

I catered Hayley's birthday one year and I'd done all the leg-work the day before, prepping three salads, sauces, guacamole, I even made a cake in the shape of a big H ... (how desperate am I to be loved FFS). Anyway, I'd been in contact with a great butcher from the East End and he'd sent me three amazing big côte du boeuf from a 12-year-old dairy cow who lived (and died) in Galicia. My plan was to just unveil all the sides/fixings and then cook the steaks and, when they were ready, slice them up and that was that. Easy. I could chat and enjoy basic human interaction, the kind my mother-programme used to run aboard the Evolution, long before we actually dropped.

I marinated the steaks and got them ready, hot grill, stuck them on, went back into the kitchen and plated up salads and bread and grains, and roasted beetroot with cheese, and a salad that is grated carrot and parsley and grated Cheddar! It was amazing. I was warming tortillas and I heard people calling my name so I headed out and people pointed to the BBQ which was now fully alight. I had the tongs and I waved them above my head and said something like 'Perfectomundo.' Or 'Well done for me, please!' A couple of the girls laughed. Good. Is it good? Fuck, be quick but casual. I opened up the lid and a fireball leapt on to my face. No one saw though. It says something about your place in society where you can be in your own house which has 22 strangers in it and at one point a huge fireball erupts into your face and no one sees. I actually remember flicking my burnt eyes around and realising no one had seen.

I grab my tongs and use them to move the meat to the furthest reaches of the coals. What had happened? As the fat had rendered down it caught alight. I wave one of the meat bits at the girls ... 'It's perfectly pink on the inside ladies!' I waggle my charred and charcoal-heavy eyebrow. A couple of them nod. I think one of them actually leaves. One of the girls later comes up after I've done the cake and asks for my manager's number. I'm really confused and then I realise she thinks I've been hired for the event. I try and explain but she's pissed and pretty insistent, so in the end I have to give her my manager's number.

People don't respond to that kind of comedy any more. I think it's a generational thing. I'd watched Dad do the old 'pink on the inside' burnt meat schtick very successfully in the late 1970s to Judy Bennet and old Jackie Jinx. They got it. They got comedy. The beef was fucked. I had to perform surgery on it by slicing it in a way that all the burnt bits were gone. There wasn't much left. What can we learn from this story? Be ready? Don't try and do too many things at once? Stay calm? Don't waggle burnt beef at young women? I think all of these things.

I shouldn't necessarily feel this way, but standing alone, next to a hot grill, holding the marinated body of a chicken whose spine I removed using big scissors, feels a bit like home. There's comfort here. There's a chance to relax and to impress. I drain the marinade from the bag and place the chicken, skin-side down, on to the magma-hot grill. Be prepared to move the chicken. Or, if you're clever, you create a zone within the BBQ itself which is a bit cooler than the rest. If it flares up, just move it into the chicken chillout zone for a bit. Take your time.

You have a real chance here to make something so fucking tasty and memorable people will not only remember it, but they will ask to come over to eat it! I like the fact that when I'm gone there'll be people who will remember fondly something I cooked them and smile. What a legacy! You can also combine this with a lot of different combinations – couscous and some roasted vegetables; lentils and fat red chillies sliced thin; pak choi and lime juice and feta cheese; coleslaw; curried lentils and chickpeas; noodles; rice and sauce.

When it's done it'll be soft and saucy, juicy, the meat will be white and the skin will be crispy and crunchy. How do I serve this? Well, put it in a dish to rest. It'll release loads of nice juice. Now I take a huge chopper and I wield it mercilessly until the chicken is in roughly eight bits. But wait ... there's more ... More? More chance to add some flavour. That's the game.

I slice up a big red mild chilli, I chop a big bunch of coriander, I take a lime and chop it into chunks and to this I add the amazing juice that's come out of the chicken. I shake it all together in the bag and then I tip it all over the pieces of BBQ'd chicken. It's really nice. Once again, this is a way that you can turn a theory into a lot of actual dishes out in the field.

A 'grillmaster' would know what to do. They always know what to do. They're so masculine aren't they? The grillmasters. There's nothing they don't know about the preparing and cookery of dead animals and/or sweetcorn cobs.

Grillmasters' wives leave them too. Grillmasters aren't perfect. Their wives cheat with non-grillmasters. There's more to life than low and slow.

'What about high and quick? Jude? I'm talking to you. What about high and quick, just once? Answer me, Jude. You can't do it, can you? I'm leaving. I'm sorry. I met a guy, he's not a grillmaster. Jude, he's

just a regular guy who keeps his charcoal in the
bag he bought it in, and it's a bit wet as he keeps it
outside under a chair. I like it. He did Hot Dogs and it
took eight minutes. It was amazing. Bye, Jude.'

Jude listens and the door closes softly. Jenny has
gone. Good. As much as this hurts, the thought of
another man's weak, hairless non-grillmaster hands
all over his wife is too much. He could never love
that again. Jude signs some documents and leaves
them on the thin table in the hall. He goes upstairs
and dresses in his finest grillmaster attire, the stuff
he and Jenny bought in Austin that time after the
finals of International Rib. He pulls on his Stetson and
looks in the mirror. He's ready.

Jude leaves the house and walks across the
yard and past his wonderful open kitchen, it cost a
fortune but it was worth every penny. All the times
the other grillmasters came round. Jude pushes
into the shed and there is a very big, very hot grill.
The grillmaster no.1. Jude made this with his own
hands. Designed by Him and Dad. It could essentially
slow-cook six camels at once. He tests the heat,
it's perfect. Jude takes off his boots. He stands on a
grate set in the floor and with a tremendous amount
of effort hauls a 50-gallon drum above his head.
He pulls a rope and Jude is drenched in a tsunami
of homemade BBQ sauce. Something he and Dad
designed and perfected over the years. There on
the side of the drum is the golden stamp of honour,
Winner Best Grillmaster Sauce, 2015. Dad never

got to see the award, never got to come to the ceremony. What a day. Him and Jenny had stayed in a fancy hotel down in Baton Rouge.

Jude opens one of the empty drums in the cooking silo. He takes his hat off and shuffles down inside. From out of his pocket, he takes 300 strong sleeping tablets, he shoves them into his mouth and washes them down with a glug of apple cider vinegar. Jude presses buttons on the timer and the door closes shut and the BBQ begins to slowly rotate. Inside, Jude falls asleep. He smiles. The true death of a grillmaster. Slow-cooked in their own BBQ. It was how Dad went, and his dad, and his dad before him.

A week later, 11 men and a truck full of fixings and salads arrive. Four of the men break off and silently enter the grilling chamber. It is still and warm. One of the grillmasters presses a button and the cooking silo hisses open ... Inside is a perfectly cooked, crisp and succulent man. Jude. The smile on his face not only looks amazing, but it also tastes great too. The men stand around tasting his features, snapping an ear off, checking the depth of the smoke rings. He's done to perfection. The doors are kicked open and Jude is wheeled out to be enjoyed with salad, and beans and tortillas and guacamole and some Cheddar. This is our way. The way of the South.

PORK BELLY

If you wanted to do this on the BBQ with racks of ribs ... lovely.
If you wanted to do this with a slow-cooked pork belly, totally
do-able and amazing. I'd do this one of two ways, this is just
me. Two perhaps shows the limit of my knowledge. A real chef
could probably offer eight ways. Still, I'm not a real chef, I'm
a human who likes cooking and I'm happy to learn. Progress,
not perfection ...

**I'd sit a piece of pork belly on a trivet of veg. How many
people do you have coming over? I had my sister and her
husband over yesterday, my ex-wife and our son, and
Hayley and our kids. The kids ate fuck all really, except
gravy and Yorkshire puddings. My baby daughter loves
meat. She sits at the head of the table with a big bone in her
mouth, sucking soft pork belly in. She laughs and gurgles
and eats and eats and eats ... she's amazing. She waves the
clean bone in the air, proud like a flag.**

**Four people and three kids, and I had a piece of pork
belly about 1.75kg. It'll shrink a lot when you cook it and
I had a bit left over, so judge it from that. I sit the pork
on a trivet (google it) of sliced white onion, carrot, celery,
apple and leek. As per the slow-roast method from
before (see pages 63–8), I'd cook for one hour, then fill
the roasting tin halfway up with water and wrap hard
with foil. It'll create a real sauna for that pork to cook
in. I'd take it out after four to five hours. Gingerly, and
with a sharp, long knife, slice the sheet of pork belly
(pork fat) from off the top of the roast and leave aside. If**

you've cooked it wrapped in foil, it will not have crackled. No way. The water and steam will keep it wobbly and jelly-like. Later, before you serve, have a grill ready at a super-hot temperature. Lay your psychopath's face out (the pig skin), and watch it like a hawk, grill it until the skin begins to bubble up and crisp and harden. Do not let it burn. Pull it out and chop it up and serve it with the meat. This is proper crackling.

Now the meat ... It's been skinned, it's cool. Put it into one of the big Ziplock bags and drown it in a Japanese marinade. Soy sauce, teriyaki sauce, sweet chilli, a little sesame oil, limes, coriander stalks, red chillies, a little brown sugar and a finely sliced red onion. (Maybe a bit of water too to dilute.) How long should you marinate this? Overnight? Four hours? Yeah, one of those.

Then have a BBQ ready, either gas or coal, remembering to include a built-in chillout zone, and then cook on the griddle. You want nice, hot burn marks all over it. Keep a little brush to hand and paint on more of the marinade as and when the meat needs it. It's cooked, so this process is just about getting more flavour and colour into the thing. Once you feel you've got to this place, slice and serve with the salads and remember the crackling.

Now, the other way is essentially the opposite. If that makes sense? Marinate however you see fit. Set up the BBQ for indirect grilling. Direct is straight on top of the coals/gas grill. Indirect isn't. If you had a nice round Weber grill, you'd set the coals up on only half your BBQ and stick the meat, pork belly in this case, on the other. Gas BBQs are good for this kind of cooking I've found as they're really controllable. Coal is nice, but you need to be on it in terms of checking if it's too hot, has it gone out?, taking the meat off and putting more coal on, waiting for it to heat up ...

Once the grill is ready, remove from the marinade bag and lay it on the cooler half of the BBQ. Shut the lid and cook gently for a long time. Every now and then, use a brush to paint the pork with the marinade. Once it's ready – I can't tell you when, three hours, maybe more, maybe less – take it off the BBQ and put it into the oven at a VERY HIGH TEMP, 220–250°C, until the crackling begins to puff up and pop and sizzle. Man, it'll taste so nice. Like Jude.

CHICKEN THIGHS À LA NHK

Chicken thighs are one of the greatest gifts a hen ever gave a human being. The other great gift a hen gave a human was a large green emerald. We ate it anyway. Fucking humans. There's loads of ways to use them, I think they work great in Indian recipes and if I ever do little teriyaki-glazed Japanese BBQ, it's thighs I use. If I ever use thighs in a recipe, generally I'll use the thighs that used to be on a chicken.

Here's a marinade I thought up after watching 10,000 hours of NHK World Japan. I found out the reason I watch the same things again and again, Rick Stein, *Close Encounters of the Third Kind*, NHK World Japan, etc., is that my ADHD demands to be soothed and, of course, to have little dopamine hits. Watching the same films and TV, and listening to the same music time and time again, helps me feel better. It also helped me formulate this marinade for chicken thighs. I never thought there was anything weird in the fact that as a child I had the same lunch every day, and it followed me into adulthood. I probably had the same lunch every day for 30 years. It made me feel comfortable. Happy. I called it a museum lunch because it was a lunch I'd take to a museum during a school trip.

Two crusty rolls (I call them hospital rolls because they're the kind of rolls I'd get in the canteen of a hospital, usually Withybush down in Haverfordwest). Crusty, hospital rolls, heavily buttered, ham and a lick of Dairylea cheese. As I got older, I added a huge smudge of English mustard. Bag of Wotsits and a cube of Ribena. Boom. And relax.

So ... Chicken Thighs à la NHK.

8 chicken thighs

1 jar of chilli crisp (if you know, you know. If you don't, get up on this shit. Google, Amazon, Post Office, front door, chicken thighs, BBQ, mouth, stomach, enlightenment)

teriyaki sauce

dark soy sauce

dwabs of honey

coriander

sliced medium red onion

couple of limes

Toss it all together apart from the limes in a bowl. Chop the limes and squeeze them into the marinade, drop the squeezed bits in too. Cover with clingfilm and leave in the fridge for one or two days.

When it comes to cooking these on the BBQ ... Cook them in the oven first: 180°C for 30 minutes. Many is the time someone BBQs up some chicken and then, when people are eating, you can see the meat round the bone is pink and translucent. Being hypervigilant, I notice a couple nudge each other and nod towards the uncooked chicken thigh. Balls. They'll be dead by evening. What a shame. So young.

Cooking in the oven first neutralises this threat. The chickens are already cooked when they go on the grill. All you need is 25–30 minutes to get a nice crisp skin on the thighs, a nice BBQ'd colour all over and you're done. A couple of these thighs with a Greek Salad or that Thai-style Salad (see pages 169–73), that's a gift that keeps on giving. Like Premium Bonds.

SUPER-QUICK VEGGIE SHEPHERD'S PIE

I did this yesterday so I'm writing it down before I forget it. Send the children to the shops on their bikes to buy the following items (I'd suggest following them at a discrete distance in the car):

½ leek

1 medium carrot

½ onion (white or red)

1 garlic clove

1 nice tomato

½ bag of Quorn® mince

1 tablespoon Bisto Gravy Granules

vintage Cheddar

For the mash

1 big potato

salt and pepper

milk

salted butter

You'll notice that the amounts of ingredients I've estimated to cook this are a lot smaller than our usual gluttonous feasts. We were all super busy yesterday and we didn't have a ton of time to eat so this was just a small, quick, nutritious, delicious pie.

While the kids play and watch TV and drink milk and scream and zoom their toys noisily across the table (try, not, to beat, children) ... Often you'll find me with noise-cancelling headphones on during these trying times. Yes, it looks a little weird and it's even a bit antisocial but it's better than me screaming at them for simply being kids.

Tea towel under chopping board, gentle sharpening of knife, then finely dice the leek, carrot, onion and garlic. Knob of butter in pan. Listen for frantic sizzle. Turn down gas and then begin. Place into the hot foamy pan, glug of oil and gently sauté.

Take your lovely big, ripe tomato and chop roughly. You could also just use a tin. Add to the pan. Stir, shake, whatever, then add your Quorn® mince. Turn up the heat and fry it a bit. I always cook it like I would a ragù and add some water and turn the heat down at this point. Let it gently plip for a while. This is more for the veg than for the Quorn®, which I think is kind of cooked and ready to rock straight from the bag. It's a bit like tofu I think – you feed it with tasty flavours from the shit you cook it with. Make sense? You don't have to cook it for three or four hours to make it nice and soft.

Because of the relatively short amount of cooking time, you need to find a way to add flavour. I add a tablespoon of Gravy Granules at this point. It adds flavour and it also thickens the gravy. Turn of pepper, no salt, set aside and wash up everything you've used to this point.

Peel the fucking potato (kills self). Cut it into small-ish pieces. How small? How can I help you visualise my wishes?... Okay. Imagine someone had peeled and cut a potato into small bits. Like that. That big, do that.

Bring a pan of salted water to the boil and cook the spud. The good thing about cutting potatoes small is they cook in no time. Watch the potato. It's easy to sit in the toilet crying for half an hour and then you come out to a pan of watery potarti soup.

I check by lifting a piece out on a spoon and pushing a knife through it. You'll know if it's cooked. Turn the spuds out into a sieve. Then process using a ricer back into the warm pan you've just cooked the spuds in. Add salted butter, lots if you're feeling saucy, and milk. Use a wooden spoon and stir and beat until you have a really nice mash. It's delicious.

Use your metal pie dish, then add the Quorn® mince ragù. Add the mash on top and then grate loads of vintage Cheddar on top of it. This can be wrapped in foil and kept in stasis until needed later. Cook later for 30 minutes at 180°C to warm through and to melt the cheese. It's a really nice easy meal and my kids love it. It beats a sandwich and crisps where you all sit in different rooms doing different things. We sit and have a big spoonful each and then there's ketchup and bread and butter and cold milk to drink. It feels so nice to me as a dad that we all sit and eat, and we chat and laugh and bullshit and eat. It's simple.

Although, actually, it's not that simple. This last bit feels like a horrible cooking show dream where everyone is wearing thick Christmas jumpers but it's August and they're all holding a glass of Egg Nog and Kristabelle is holding a chubby toddler, telling an amusing story about cooking a Yule Loaf for Boris Johnson. Everyone laughs. 'And we're cut.' Kristabelle hands over the fake baby and storms outside to smoke a luxury cigarelle. You know? I hate the lies and the fake pictures TV cooking shows paint.

The truth is that dinner time can actually be really stressful. Just threatening to turn the TV off can elicit screams and falling down, and the kids ... (LOLZ).

The Baby is a dream, she'll eat anything, everything, we've known her to sit for one and a half hours and just slowly, methodically, browse. It's amazing. As long as the meal ends with her triumphantly raising an empty can of Coke Zero above her head! That's her thing. She lifts it into the sky like she's won a race. Then she'll pretend to do a cheers and then she pretends it's a phone. She's amazing.

The others can often be tricky at their ages. The middle one often does a thing where he walks up to the table and looks and, on the way back to the TV, says, 'Nope.' (Soul crushing if you've been cooking for three hours.) Tough shit. We all sit together at dinner time; you don't have to eat anything but we sit together. Sometimes that means tears, or sad cuddles, or a bit of screaming, and the kids ... (Lolz. I did it again.)

Son Number 1 can be tricky too, but I can feel him emerging from that phase of only wanting meek foods you know and trust. I heard a theory that toddlers often refuse foods they don't know as a way of avoiding being poisoned. I mean not now, but thousands of years ago, I guess that was super useful. The more I learn about the body, it's amazing. Don't be confused about this, we are animals.

My ADHD can be totally triggered at mealtimes. One of the nuances of my brand of ADHD is often an inability to regulate mood and this flares up a bit when you've spent three hours preparing four or five different dishes for us all, plus little plates of berries and bread and melon, and it's essentially fucked off by a child who barely looked at it. I hate to admit it but it presses my buttons. Hayley is like a patient angel, I've learned so much from her.

My stupid, male, ADHD default position is a need to make the dog come to HEEL! You know? It's old-fashioned fathering and I was wrong and it did not work. It doesn't work. We just became enemies at dinner time. Who wants to eat dinner in that atmosphere? There's a story in this book about me not eating Jam Roly-Poly because someone shouted at me.

Why should I expect my kids to be any different? Did I learn nothing?

Hayley is so gentle with them. I'm learning though, I'm getting better. We turned a corner a few months ago when instead of butting heads, I said to Son Number 1, 'Do you want to come and have a cuddle?' Hayley raised her brows and the whole table seemed surprised, tbh ... He nodded and pitter-patted round and I lifted him up on to the table and we had a nice cuddle. It changed from then. It's a complete fallacy that because you have a child you're a father. You have to earn that shit. And it takes years and years.

I think that's why cooking something after a good day out, when the kids are knackered but happy, we're all enjoying each other, me and Hayley are being cute together and I've got an hour to whip something up feels so much like a win. If we've done the day right and they're tired and hungry and we all sit together and eat, it's loud and fun and the kids are grabbing for more cheese or ketchup or tortillas. Because often it isn't. If all three kids can eat versions of the same thing and then, for afters, we sit outside and have the fruit lollies I make – win.

I always make enough for my first wife, Christina, too. She loves her food as well, so I always make a bit more. When she comes to pick up big boy, she'll often sit and eat as well. Or she asks to take the sauce home in a container. I was alright with that at first but it's started to bug me. I'm not a restaurant. Sometimes I think this is her real regret about our divorce. No legal access to my gravy any more. Imagine if she got custody of the gravy. Every other week I had to drop a huge vat of gravy round her house. I imagine seeing Gravy run into her house with its hat on and a dragging a little case. 'I'll pick you up

Sunday evening,' I shout. It doesn't hear, it runs straight in. I notice Chris has a spoon in her hand and she dips it into Gravy's head as she runs through the door. When I pick it up on Sunday, it's not my gravy any more. It's not joy and fun and laughter. It's a clean empty pan Chris tosses into the footwell of the passenger seat.

CHICKEN BURGERS

I love a chicken burger. I love KFC, I love a chicken Zinger® Tower, I love the gravy they serve. That gravy is a great memory from my childhood. On Saturdays, in the morning, a group of us would go to the pool in Barkingside, Fulwell Leisure Centre. It was a massive pool and the water was cold and it had diving boards, big ones. These were the first high boards I ever got the courage up to jump off. I remember standing up there shaking like a shitting dog before finally flopping off the top. I remember feeling so good after I did it. I went up time and time again after that. I felt a real sense of achievement jumping off that board.

When we came out of there me and the fellas always had chips and a pot of chicken gravy from KFC. It was delicious. I just looked on Google Maps, it's still a KFC. It must have been there for 40 years! That's amazing! The gravy still tastes exactly as I remember. So rich and chickeny. That could be my desert island food. What a delicious continuity. I always use chicken thighs for chicken burgers. Boneless, please. If it comes with bones, you'll have to bone it out. YouTube it or go to a proper butcher and ask nicely. It's an easy thing to do and very rewarding once you know how to do it. (Like jumping from top board.) Learn it as part of your knife skills.

Let me do the 'You will need' thing ...

For one burger ...

2 skin-on, bone out, chicken thighs

2 slices of American cheese

good, fresh, unfussy burger bun

ketchup/mayo/mustard

1 lettuce leaf, trimmed to fit

2 slices of tomato

slices of onion

For a side

1 large sweet potato, chopped into French fry shapes

1 plate

1 knife

1 cloth for wiping face

salt and pepper

In a medium/hot oven (180°C) roast the chicken thighs for 30 minutes. Remove.

Then in a skillet or a good, thick-bottomed frying pan, fry the chicken thighs, skin-side down, until crisp. Turn over and place the slices of cheese on top of the chicken. Turn the heat off. Leave while you prepare the bun ...

Toast the bun so it's warm. Then, on the bottom half of your bun, squirt ketchup/mayo/mustard. Add the lettuce leaf, it should be like a salad boat, really. You know? Into it add tomato slices and the onion. Now lift the crispy chicken with all that delicious melting cheese on to the bottom bun and top it off with top bun. Et voilà! Salt and pepper and eat. This will be lovely.

Serve it with homemade sweet potato fries. Here's how: get your oven nice and hot (180°C). In a roasting tray, add your sweet potato fries and a drizzle of oil and salt and pepper, cook the fries and turn them every 20 minutes until you have sweet potato fries. Serve with the chicken burger, add a nice cold Coke Zero and dig in! You deserve this! You're beautiful.

CHEESEBURGERS

I LOVE cheeseburgers. I love them. A lot. They're so lovely. I know this will get a lot of hate and I don't care. My favourite cheeseburgers are either Five Guys or McDonald's. Oh my, I love McDonald's. I think a part of that is a connection to the past and the need for the dopamine a trip to McDonald's always brings.

Here are some things a cheeseburger needs to be/have to float my boat. Thin, almost crispy beef. Raw onions. Cheap as fuck American cheese. Bun without sesame seeds.

I also like the fact that cheeseburgers, good cheeseburgers, can be made at home and they taste as good as anything you get in a restaurant. There aren't many foods you can say that about. Here's my effort ...

Buy decent burgers from a good butcher. If not, take minced beef and mash it up with the spear fist you used

for meatballs. Salt and pepper. Form into patties. Chill. Them, not you. I always cook on a griddle but the other side. The flat side. Take a patty and squash it flat. Fry it so it's crispy and brown both sides. Add a slice of American cheese on top to melt a bit.

Bun ... soft, white, smooth on top ... bottom half. Tiny pump of mayo. Tiny pump of red. A slice of cheap US cheese, lay on top of that cheese the hot, thin, crispy burger, then on top of that American cheap cheese, add some finely diced, raw, white onion, then top bun. Squash a tiny bit and then sit and eat four. For me this is the perfect burger. For many years in Britain, I feel thanks to Jamie Oliver's fame and his famous Beefy-Botham-Burger, British people thought this was the paradigm of a perfect burger ... A patty as thick as a Chinese phone book. Or a massive cricket ball of meat. Burnt to fuck, then covered in lettuce and loads of other shit, pubs I'm looking at you.

I love the new American-driven push to take the burgers back to basics. Simple, beefy, crisp, cheesy, simple. Show me a better burger. I'll wait ...

I'd love to see a homemade forge/BBQ where you can buy either/both steel blades and also thin, cheap burgers, but you can also get a tattoo there or a traditional barbershop fade. You can also buy BMXs and cryptocurrency. Cold cola, home-brew beer and fleshlights. Wow. What a powerful shop. I want it. I want it now. I want it NOW. God, men are weak and obvious. Still ... I'm having my hair faded and some tats and I'm eating a cheap thin cheeseburger and I might buy an old PK Ripper BMX too in a bit. (A PK Ripper was a very cool BMX everyone wanted in 1987. Its frame was rectangular instead of round. WOW. It was so cool and a beautiful shade of powder blue.) Fuck, this is a good idea. Let's do it. Perhaps it isn't a shop. Perhaps it's a community, a town, a movement, a planet.

A whole planet of knives and meat and BBQ, and BMXs and crypto and guitars and chances to get your Pump On and trainers and beard oil and moisturiser. Can we have moisturiser? Fuck, yeah we can. All that hot steam and knives will leave our skin so dry. I guess the rule of thumb is moisturiser is fine as long as it smells like bacon or engines or other meat or weed. God, men are fucking boring and obvious. Give us meat and a fleshlight and we'll put up with anything. It's quite something really. I mean it's sad. If there was any justice, we'd die after mating. Like ants.

A SALAD BY NICK FROST

This is a winner at our house. We have it a lot and it goes with everything. Hayley loves it. I love it.

Grab a ... big bowl! (Did you guess?)

I have never really made or boiled grains. I tried couscous once and it turned out like a white cake, so I didn't want to do it again. It's like me and golf or stand-up comedy: if I can't be immediately good at it, I don't want to do it.

There are so many great, tasty grain options in the super-marché at the moment, little packets for two where you tear a corner and cook for two minutes in the microwave and then you squeeze the pouch and voilà! Grains, lovely, healthy grains, of all kinds. Grains.

For this recipe I usually use Puy lentils but feel free to mix and match all the grains you want, it's your toilet.

Let's assume we've got people coming over so this is for four.

2 packets of Puy lentils

4 pak choi

1 red onion

2 jalapeños

*radishes, traditional red or pink or gold
or a melange of all colours*

olive oil

2 lemons

pack of coriander

pack of flat-leaf parsley

1 brick of feta

Separate your grains into a bowl. Get your lovely crispy, fresh, green pak choi and chop it down into nice crispy chunks. Get it in the bowl. (Any crispy white/green salad works instead of pak choi by the way. Crispy white cabbage is nice.)

Take your onion. Peel it. Halve it. Finely slice it. Bowl it.

Take a lovely, large, deep green jalapeño chilli or two and, using your sharpest knife, slice real fine. Instead of cutting them into circles, I like to defy expectation and turn the chilli slightly, which gives me long bent hoops and if anyone out there really knows me, you'll know I love a long bent hoop. Bowl.

Chilli warning – wash your hands with warm water and washing up liquid. Enjoy the sensation of the water and the soap lathering up, and then freshen with some nice cold water. Dry in a soft, sweet-smelling towel, treat yourself, you've got time, it's cool, they're not here until 4pm. Don't skip this. From my own experience I've suffered chilli burns in not only both eyes but my penis and the balls that dwell beneath. That was all within 25 minutes of each other. It was not the best date I had ever been on let me tell you. (It also wasn't the worst.)

Take the radishes and either use a mandolin, carefully, or a very sharp knife to cut into fine discs or just cut into quarters. I only slice finely because, to me, the little white suns staring out of the salad look good. Bowl these idiots.

Go to the drawer where you keep the big spoons and take one out. Using it gently, turn all the ingredients over and over until it looks like a freshly dug field with jewels of earth poking out here and there.

Just before you serve ... Olive oil, lots of good oil is essential. Squeeze the juice of the lemons into the salad. Finely chop a handful of each herb and toss it in. Crumble your brick of feta into the bowl. Taste it now before you season, the feta could take away your need for salt. Turn over gently one last time.

Have ready a big platter directly from a mid-century table somewhere just south of Stockholm. They won't miss it. Trust me. Decant the salad on to the dish and amble over to the table. Sign autographs for 30 minutes.

'Could you put pomegranate gems into this?'

'Great question, thanks Alice. Yes, yes you could. Anyone else? Oh, Alice. Okay, sure you can have follow-up question ...?'

'What would you serve this with?'

'Alice ... you! Um, okay, anything. Seriously, like lots in this book, loads goes with loads. Slow-cooked meats, steak, chicken, lamb, any kind of chop, salmon or trout is amazing. Bowl of the salad with a little fried salmon fillet on top! Fuck, yeah! Serve that with a splash of soy sauce and a squeeze of lime before it heads to the table. That's a nice little meal. Well done! Look what you did!'

PAK CHOI ALT...

I buy a couple of packs of the little baby pak choi ... they're small and the green is super green and the white crispy bit is super white and crispy, they're lovely. Cut them in half with one firm stroke. Turn them over and brush the cut sides with some oil. Now place gently on to a hot griddle pan. Avoid turning. I want one side to be crisp and green and the front to be softened and charred by the griddle bars.

Once the nice burnt bits have happened, turn them over and place on to a nice little serving dish. I serve this on the table as a little side. Now take a fat, mild red chilli and slice and dice it until it's very finely processed. Sprinkle a little of the chilli on to each piece of pak choi. Then drop a couple of little beads of sesame oil on to each piece of pak choi too. Boom. Done. It's easy.

FRIED HALLOUMI

Another little side that everyone in the house loves is Fried Halloumi. It's easy. Grab some halloumi. Cut into slices. Get a frying pan, heat while empty. Once hot, put the cheese slices into the hot pan, leave it alone. Only turn once the first side is lovely and brown. When it is, turn over. Leave. Once both sides look the same, stick them on a plate and bring to the table. I've also served this with blobs of oil and tiny pieces of diced red chilli too. It's really good. Note to reader ... this is the only thing Hayley can cook better than me. I'll let her have this one. For now ...

LITTLE WEIRD CHEESE SALAD

I have no idea who gave me this recipe but when I close my eyes I can weirdly remember so much about the conversation which gave me it, I just can never make out where I am or who I'm with. Never mind. I remembered the salad which is the main thing.

I remember doing that thing where I was pretending to nod and be totally into the idea of a salad which is only grated Cheddar and grated carrot. I was very sceptical but at some point I took a gamble (not really a gamble, it's Cheddar and a carrot, you know?) and it was bloody lovely.

Grate some Cheddar.

Grate a carrot.

See you at the Salad BAFTAs.

CHILLI CON POLLO

What? Chilli with chicken. No ... No ... NO!!!!! (Helmet-wearing chimp is sucked out of airlock.) Don't be afraid. It's great. With Chilli con Pollo, rather than beef, I roast a whole chicken. You know what to do. I've sometimes used this step to add more flavour. This isn't a chicken that's being used for a Sunday roast, so feel free to cover with oil and rub in cumin and smoked paprika and chilli powder etc. Sit it on a bed of sliced red onions. Sprinkle the onions with chilli powder and cumin. Surround the bird with bunches of spring onions and tomatoes and garlic cloves. Slowly roast for about an hour or so at 180°C.

While the chicken cooks, let's get on with the other bits. Find these items in a local shop:

2 large white onions

2 carrots

3 celery stalks

1 red pepper

8 garlic nuggets

Handful of coriander stalks (leave the leafy bits for later)

4–5 tomatoes, roughly chopped

tin of chopped tomatoes

1 dried ancho chilli

smoked paprika

ground cumin

chilli powder (mild)

tin of kidney beans

Time this right by cooking the chicken first and wrapping it in foil and leaving it to cool on a big plate on top of the oven. You're going to be left with a great basis for a chilli here. It's absolutely delicious. In a large saucepan, add a glug of oil and a spoonful of butter and get it nice and hot.

While the pan is heating, roughly chop the white onions, carrots, celery stalks, red pepper, garlic pieces and the coriander stalks. Once the pan is hot, dump all the veg from the chicken in, turn down the heat and fry/cook/ stir until it's all soft and lovely.

Have a little nose around at all the nice rich, roasted veg the chicken sat on to roast and pick out all the onion, garlic and spring onions, which will be nice and oily, buttery and red from the spices, and add these to the veg pan. Turn up the heat for a bit. Cook and stir again.

Now add the roughly chopped tomatoes and a tin of tomatoes too. Cook and stir for a few minutes and then I add a whole kettle full of hot water into the lovely rich stew you're beginning to craft. Toss in the dried chilli and spices. This will add depth to the flavour. Ancho chillies are a spicy and complicated flavour but not that hot. After the chilli has cooked and you're ready to serve, I always remove this plump chilli-bollock.

Turn the heat down now and let all these flavours mix and meld, watch them kiss. Smell. Taste. This will definitely need seasoning but not quite yet. I guess I'm saying, taste by all means early on, but don't be surprised if there's a moment when you're like 'Oh my God, it tastes like shit.'

While the blips are blipping, turn your attention to the chicken. Have ready a bowl or a dish or some vessel capable of holding all this lovely roasted chicken. Starting at the two breasts work your way around the bird, picking the bones clean of meat. With the breasts and the leg meat, flake it and shred it down. Keep it all under cover until needed. Remember the chicken is cooked, so once you incorporate this into the tomato, chilli, cumin, paprika stew, you'll only need to cook it to heat it through. You don't have to cook the chicken more. I've found a couple of times if you overcook the chicken it becomes brittle and powdery. Do you know what I mean? Treat it gently like an addict's sense of self-esteem.

Slowly cook the tomato and chilli base until it's now thick and saucy and its flavour has condensed and has really become robust and delicious. Take your plate/ dish of roasted, saucy bird and empty it into the space. Mix thoroughly and add the kidney beans too. If it needs more water, add more water, it will reduce again as we heat it through.

After 30 minutes more, taste and season. This should be ready. I serve this in a small bowl with soured cream and lots of coriander.

This is fun, take your tortillas and cut them into corners, spread across a baking tray and cook hot until the torts are crispy and tanned. These are so nice to eat chilli with. Trust me!

I think, once again, if your eyes and ears are tuning into the theory/technique side of this book, then we're not doing anything new. It's a mirepoix, it's liquid, it's braising and reduction, it's seasoning, it's smiling and then eating. It's romancing, it's kissing, it's making love, it's marriage, it's children, it's a life well lived, it's bad news, it's inoperable, it's death, it's a funeral, it's the children, now grown up, finding this book and recreating something they all enjoyed when they were young. It's a sad silence and then it's a smile and it's Dad back at the table, loud, quaffing Coke Zero, feeding us, struggling, moody but trying to make us laugh, being silly, nourishing us, not just physically. It's memory, it's taste and smell and sound, it's a time machine, it's a gift. Don't fuck it up.

CHICKEN ESCALOPE

There's nothing nicer on a warm spring afternoon than lunch with a couple of good friends. I hate this sentence. Classic bullshit sentence you'll find in a cooking show or cookbook. Lolz. It is kind of true though. It also depends how many. Up until the age of 46, I'd never held a party in a house that I owned. Sure, I'd been to parties in the house I shared with Simon and Smiley and the South African shitheads. They were bonkers. It's only now looking back I realise how fucking cool we all were, we knew some amazingly talented, cool fucking people.

I think in hindsight I can see how much I was suffering with ADHD. I loved the idea of a party but I also remember going into my room and hiding under a quilt. I was so/I am so bad at small talk and humans generally that I would just walk around pretending to be human and malfunctioning inside gently. This was why I'd drink and get high I guess. I didn't have to talk to do drink and drugs. We just got on.

Fast forward 20 years and we have 75 people in our house, in my home. Why are they in my home? Oh God. I was sat in a dark toilet and I heard a very gentle knocking on the door. I had come in and turned the lights off so I could have some nice quiet time to eat a cheeseburger. It was Hayley knocking. She turned on the lights and shook her head. A kind of 'What are we going to do with you?' head shake (I like it when she looks at me like that. She's not disappointed, she's trying to find a solution which tells my Esteem she's here to stay).

The 'event' was over pretty quickly really if you measure it against the geological age of our planet, or the time it would take a spaceship to cross our own Milky Way (roughly 1,000,000,000 years), but it didn't feel like that at the time. Even though I totally love 97 per cent of the people who were there. I came out of the toilet and then silently DJ'd for three hours. It was a way I could hide in the light and be a good host and love you but not necessarily have to talk to you. Maybe there's nothing nicer than lunch with a couple of good friends. But just a couple mind.

I really like meat when it's been escalloped. It's easy but because you need to coat meat in breadcrumbs I think it puts people off. Don't let it put you off. Please. Yes, it's fiddly, but you also get to legitimately use the phrase 'beat your meat'. Is it juvenile? Yes, yes it is, but it's also funny.

In lunches gone by, I have escalloped chicken breast, veal chop/fillet and pork fillet/chop. For this recipe, let's stick to chicken.

Take one large, lovely chicken breast. Butterfly it out. Check online how to do it, it's fun. I had to do it thousands

of times at the restaurant every week. It's essentially taking a fat plump fillet and slicing it in half (not all the way through, though), opening it up like a butterfly, placing it between two layers of clingfilm and then beating your meat flat. It should look like a big, wide, lumpy plate made of flattened chicken or a hub cap for a butcher's car.

I like the next bit. Three large plates, one with beaten egg, one with flour and one with panko breadcrumbs. Take your flat chicken. Dip in the flour. Wash with the egg, dip in the panko. Repeat. In a frying pan, heat up an amount of oil, maybe a tablespoon. Fry the escalope. Watch the temperature of the oil here, too hot and the breadcrumbs burn and the meat within stays pink and deadly. As I've said, don't be afraid to turn the heat up and down or take it off the heat. It should just gently pop and crackle and fry on the outside while the inside cooks too.

I can't tell you how long this will take. It depends on how thick your meat is. (Don't.) A butterflied chicken breast banged flat and fried, I reckon the chicken inside will be ready after four minutes each side. (If it isn't ready and you just blindly eat it and it's uncooked and you die, it's NOT MY FAULT. I cannot/will not go to prison again, even a nice category D open prison.) This should come out of the pan and on to a plate covered in kitchen paper. Dab it all over and remove the excess oil, if there is any. From here it goes on to a plate and it should be seasoned and served hot.

What would I serve this with? A big fat wedge of lemon and a salad. There are two in my mind.

TOMATO SALAD FOR CHICKEN/ VEAL/PORK ESCALOPE

Find three or four different types and colours and shapes of tomato. Chop them all in different ways and arrange them carefully in a bowl. Olive oil the fuckers. Salt and pepper, squeeze of lemon. Chives sliced uber fine and sprinkled over the top. Et voilà!

or

Cucumber, peeled, cut in half and deseeded. In a bowl. Watercress, torn slightly, in the same bowl. Half a red onion, peeled and sliced, bowl and then make this dressing. Small glass bowl, sesame oil, light summery splash of pale Spanish sherry, few drops of bright yellow lemon juice. Season and whisk and into the bowl. Dress and serve with sizzling hot schnitzel.

À des amis!

POMMES DAUPHINOISE

In a traditional cookbook, and when I say traditional what I mean is not this one, they'd usually write things about Dauphinoise like, 'Not for the faint-hearted' or 'If you've fallen off the diet wagon' or 'I wouldn't suggest eating every day ...' What I'd say is this: 'Shut the fuck up. We're having Pommes Dauphinoise.' I feel personally, if you have not just the time, but also the inclination to peel and finely slice 1.5kg of potatoes, then you have earned the right to eat whatever the fuck you want. (Apart from an Ortolan.)

Whenever people who know a lot more about food than me

tell me what kind of potato does what, I kind of switch off. It's too much info. For this recipe, I find using potatoes works great.

300ml double cream

Pint whole milk

Block of Cheddar

Small block of Gruyère

1.5kg white spuds

1 whole garlic bulb, skinned and chopped fine as teddy bear pubes

large amounts of unsalted butter, softened

salt and pepper

Oven on to preheat to 180°C, please.

Decant the cream and the milk into a jug. Stir it. Also, if you want it creamier, add more cream and vice versa, less cream more full-fat milk.

Grate the cheese, and mix it up all together. Here, I think the vibe is more Gruyère than Cheddar. But, do whatever, put whatever cheese you want.

Peel all the spuds (even writing this line makes me tired and moody).

I've always sliced the potatoes by hand with a big sharp knife. Use the sharpest knife that you feel comfortable with. Put a cloth beneath the chopping board and let's begin.

After watching endless Keith Floyd as a child, I was always trying to cut my pots very thin and very big, like the slices were cross-sections of the whole spud, yeah? We don't have to do that though. If you can, cool; if you can't, also cool. What would work for wobbly swordsmen is if you cut all the round bits off the potato and then just cut thin little squares of spud, little rectangles. It might fit your cooking dish better anyway! Whichever way you do it, you should now have all the ingredients laid out before you. I love this stage, often the prep means the hard work is done. Now it's just assembly and cooking and then the best bit ... Eating!

Use the foil paper the butter came in and rub the dish all over, hopefully this should help it to not stick. Take a little of the garlic and sprinkle across the now-buttered dish's silky bumbum. Now, carefully, line the whole bottom of the dish with the thinly sliced spuds, sprinkle with a little garlic, sprinkle a little cheese all over too and a few tiny blobs of butter. I'd also like you to season every layer too. Little salt. Little pepper. Do this again and again until the spud layers finish an inch from the top.

Well done! You should now have a big, ovenproof dish full of thinly sliced potatoes and butter and garlic and cheese and S and P (sorry). Take your cream/milk jug and pour it into one little corner of the dish, it'll rise up through the potato layers, flooding them like decks on the *Titanic*. The cream should cover the whole dish eventually, although when it cooks the cream and milk evaporate and reduce and get sucked up by the potato, essentially leaving nothing by the end. If you've done it right, the potato will be so soft because of the cooking and the liquid you flooded its decks with.

On the top of the dish add your final layer of cheese and place it in the hot oven for at least an hour. At least!

Hints and tips ... Have some foil at the ready. If the cheese browns and the potatoes are still hard, cover the top with foil to stop it burning any further. If you're unsure if it's ready, take a thin blade or a skewer and pass it through the dish. If there's tension, it's not done. If it slides through easily, it's done. The flip of the foil trick is if the spuds feel ready but the cheese hasn't melted, turn the heat up to brown the cheese.

Your phone alarm goes off and the Pommes Dauphinoise is complete. The cooking stage is anyway. Don't touch it for ten minutes. Leave it. Let it settle and cool a bit and relax. Its metamorphosis has been a long and difficult one. A long time ago we'd braised some lamb shanks, remember? They're on that plate still under the foil. See? Good! Let's go.

A few tender green beans, some amazing lamb with the sauce generously lapped on top, accompanied by a beautiful soft, buttery, cheesy, saucy square of rich Pommes Dauphinoise. Yes, please! Don't scrimp on that gravy neither. You would have to be either already deceased or a plankton not to enjoy this meal. Also, a vegan or someone who didn't like lamb. Fuck! Yes, okay, I get it ... Let me whittle it down ...

If you like beans and potatoes and slow-cooked meats and unctuous, complex sauces served in three styles, you'll love this. And, also, I know I mentioned a mouse in the sauce earlier but I defo didn't leave it in, no way, not my thing. Good luck and enjoy!

As soon as people know you like cooking or you can cook, a lot of the time their first question is: 'What's your signature dish?' It's such a stupid fucking question. I hate it. Signature dish? I'm not a restaurant in Florida specialising in Shrimp and Grits. Or a small NYC hole in the wall that only sells amazing, thin, crunchy, soft bun cheeseburgers. I'm a home cook. Your question is like going on a date and with nothing else to say you awkwardly ask, 'So, do you have any hobbies?' (Do you? I collect Pokémon cards.)

A while ago I figured out that learning to cook individual dishes and recipes was kind of like trying to sleep with every human woman on earth. Delicious? Yes. Pointless. Also, yes. No, what keeps me coming back is learning the science and the techniques behind the recipes, wherever they are from.

RAGÙ

Let's look at ragù. It's gently frying a selection of vegetables and then adding a meat, covering it in a liquid and then slowly reducing the whole thing for an amount of time until you're left with an incredible end result.

Be it Chilli con Carne, or ragù, or even a curry, I guess, it's kind of the same technique, only the ingredients change. This way of teaching myself how to cook, I found opened up SO MANY different dishes to me. I found that if I could make a decent ragù, then I could serve it with pasta, I could use it in a lasagne, then the same technique meant I could make moussaka, cannelloni, shepherd's pie, cottage pie, curries, chilli con carne, slow-cooked pork for tacos, etc. You feel me? Learn the techniques. It opens so many doors.

Anyway ... for my ragù I use (and this probably makes enough for a massive lasagne or six bowls of penne and ragù):

4 beef short ribs

2 pig cheeks

6 meaty pieces of oxtail

Add butter and oil to a big stockpot or big Le Creuset. Remember, there's a lot to go in the pan so use a big 'un. Get it hot but don't burn the butter, please. In batches, fry all the meat so it's lovely and brown, crusty, caramelised. Again, all the little burnt bits that caught on the pan will be released when you fry off the veg. Put the meat to one side. It will release magic liquid. Save it.

Now, in the same pan/pot/casserole ... Hang on, could you do this in a slow cooker/pressure cooker? Sure. Do I know how to do that? No. Sorry. Someone asked me the other day if I had a slow cooker. I don't. My issue is I've no idea where I'd put it. I'd hate to think of me hating it because it clutters up the kitchen. It doesn't deserve that. I'd end up fucking it off down the garden by its cord.

My in-laws bought me a spice grinder for Christmas. No idea where to put it. I won't use it. Twenty years ago, I'd have put it to work breaking down a pound of skunk but not today. Those days are LONG GONE. (Thank fuck.)

The veg you'll need is this:

2 Dutchman's dicks (carrots)

2 onions

3 celery stalks (I also like using the inside ones with the pretty, soft, light green leaves – I've always thought it would make a nice paint colour for a child's nursery)

3 nuggets of garlic (I use garlic – I like it but I'm sure some Italian chefs would spit in my face or do an Italian swear thing like, oh I don't know, biting the end of their thumb or crushing an apricot with a flip-flop)

*1 massive squirty worm of tomato purée
(maybe 3 or 4 tablespoons)*

about 1 litre water or nice beef stock (I couldn't tell you how much, maybe 1 litre to start with but you'll be cooking this for ages and later on may need a little top-up)

Now, I LOVE to prepare the veg. Mise en place it's called (I think) and specifically what we're going to make here is what Bianca's Dad would call a soffritto. The French version is called a mirepoix. What a lovely word. The English call it veg chopped up really small.

I have been chopping, dicing, slicing vegetables of all shapes and sizes for nearly 30 years. I love it. I love doing it. Maybe this would be my YouTube channel, although, let's be honest, it probably exists already. Companies who make knives could pay me just to chop vegetables in slow motion either with or without my shirt on. Maybe on my OnlyFans I could chop soft fruit and mushrooms with a blade pushed into my banana?

I can chop veg really quick. My kids whoop with delight when I chop things fast as fuck. It's impressive. I think. So, getting the chance to spend 30 minutes finely dicing down the veg into a beautiful soffritto is an absolute joy for me. Slice down all the veg into a beautiful soffritto. Take your time. Use a very sharp knife. Use a steady, wooden board. Plant your feet shoulder-width apart but remember to get up on the balls of your feet, you should be mobile, fluid, it should be rhythmic and fun. It should feel nice. Like hitting an ace in tennis, or an effortless boundary in cricket.

Add a glug of oil to the pan and dump in all the veg and the garlic. Stir it round and then put the lid on. It needs to steam and braise a bit. Turn the heat down, don't let it burn. Every five to ten minutes or so, check the heat and stir the veg. Turn the heat up and add in the tomato purée. Keep stirring and cook out the purée. When all the soft veg are coated in the purée, pour all the water or beef stock into the pan. Bring to the boil. Take the lovely meat and the magic juice and carefully tip it all into the stock and tomato and soffritto. The liquid should cover the meat. You need to turn the heat down at this point so it just blips away, nicely bubbling – it should sound relaxing and tickly.

Cover the liquid and young ragù with a circle of foil or greaseproof paper – this is called a cartouche. Now this can be cooked for hours. The last one I did was for six hours. What I need is the meat to be so cooked it's barely hanging together. I then transfer it to a big bowl, cover with foil or clingfilm and I leave it. What I need to do then is assess the sauce. Do I need to reduce it slightly? Do I need to add water? Once I put the meat back in it wants to be saucy and gravy-coated but not overly wet. The sauce needs to be thick enough so it could cling on to a piece of hot pasta.

Once the meat is cool enough to be handled, either use your hands or forks to separate it into tiny meaty flakes. Add it back to the sauce. Stir so it's all incorporated. Taste. Season with salt (if needed) and black pepper.

This is my ragù. There are so many different versions of this and ways it could now be used. But knowing this recipe or a version you can make with mince for a simpler 'Spag Bol' type thing is lovely. You'll tweak it and adapt it and perfect it in a way that suits you and yours, and you'll use it forever.

I use mine in a couple of different ways. It goes into a lasagne ... I know it's long process for a lasagne but it's

TOTALLY WORTH IT. Do it on a Saturday morning before the idiots are up. Cook it all day. This can be prepared and sit in the fridge for a couple of days. Its taste develops and deepens.

Or I serve it with penne or pappardelle and loads of good Parmigiana. Again, I understand the cheese choice may be an issue too in terms of Parmesan v Grand Padano v Pecorino but I live in Teddington, so fuck it. I've watched the kids grate Cheddar on top! This could also be served with a nice buttery mash and if I was doing that, I wouldn't break the meat up quite so completely. Enjoy the process of cooking. Get to know why you're doing what you're doing. What does each bit add? What does it all do? And then you get the joy of sitting down and eating something that tastes like magic. This is what fascinates me about the process: you cut these things like this and put these bits in with this, you add that, cook for how long and boom ... Slow-cooked, delicious, incredible Ragù. Buon appetito!

Whenever I post a picture of the ragù on Instagram, I get a bunch of people leaving comments like 'It isn't traditional ragù', or 'I wouldn't use such and such an ingredient', blah, blah, blah ... Whatever.

No, I'm not Italian. Would a 77-year-old nonna from Emilia-Romagna do it differently? Yeah, maybe. But would that same old lady taste my version of ragù and gently close her eyes, while its rich taste took her back to a remembrance of her first clandestine

kiss that night after Cousin Silvio's wedding? The
time all the children ran wild through the dark fields
of wheat. The sound of the brass band and laughter
filling the warm night.

She chased the giddy children through the barn.
He was there waiting for her. She turned to leave
and he reached out and grabbed her hand, stopping
her. She turned back, trying to seem put out,
cross, but that exterior belied the butterflies she
felt inside.

'*Che cosa*?' She acted dumb. She knew. They both
knew. It had been building for so long. He smiled.

'*Sai.*' He pulled her into him. He didn't have to pull
hard. The magnets between their hearts activated
and suddenly they were kissing. They were kissing.

'Bianca!!!' It was the booming voice of her papa.
He'd left the party to search for her when she didn't
return with the others. She knew this would mean
trouble for Marco if they were discovered. She pulled
away and ducked under the arch into the courtyard,
rushing to placate her drunken father.

Hey ...,' Marco whispered.

She stopped and turned back.

'*Posso chiamarti*?' She flashed an incredible smile;
it fizzed out of her like fireworks. She couldn't help
herself.

'*No!*'

She grinned. Her answer surprised both of them.
He smiled and burst out laughing. She rushed back
and kissed him once again, sloppily, passionately,

before fixing her dress, winking and running out to find her beloved father. Once again a child. Marco knew then that one day he would marry her.

You'll be pleased to hear that Bianca and Marco married and had six bright and healthy, cheeky, chubby daughters and lived happily ever after. Unlike her father who died at 61 of alcohol-induced liver failure. Swings and roundabouts, innit?

GNOCCHI

Here's another way and a great reason to make a lovely tomato sauce. I also LOVE the fact you can make it with leftovers ... Gnocchi. It means 'knuckles', which is pretty cool. I lost a few gnocchi over the years being rowdy and drunk and angry, another trait I never knew was part of living inside my head with Anne, David, Helen and Dean. Not being able to self-regulate my emotions ... Check. Angry as fuck and just somehow not being able to stop myself exploding with rage. Check. Poor people around me. Poor me. Now I can, most of the time, control it. I know what it is, I feel it coming, I sit, I breathe, I put my headphones on and may listen to the soothing noise of heavy rain for a while. It'll pass.

Before I knew I had ADHD and all the other shit, sometimes it didn't pass. It exploded in bouts of broken hands and toes. I suffer now, and will suffer badly I imagine, with arthritis. I've only got a few knuckles left. My hands are bent and broken and scarred from when I hit walls or took nails or knives and scratched my hands so badly it left deep, lifelong scars. I look at them a lot. It makes me feel ashamed, sad. I was so frightened when I was in that state but fortunately for other people and myself I was never a violent person when it came to other people. My violence was always directed at me.

I never ever wanted to hurt anyone. Yes I've had a handful of 'fights', but I was always so afraid of killing someone. Being heavy and powerful and quick and agile and flexible always made me feel a great responsibility to not unleash it on another human. So, I unleashed it on myself. Where was I? Ah, yes ... cookbook.

Take two knuckles of garlic. Smash them flat and remove the paper, write the word 'help' on one of them and 'love' on the other, burn these in a small stone bowl in the garden. Ring a gong, once finished, go back into the kitchen and slice and finely chop a small onion, I don't care what colour. Heat some oil in a frying pan and drop in the onion and garlic, brown a bit, not too hot, don't burn the garlic.

Grab your lovely tomatoes, sniff them deeply. If ever you're caught deeply sniffing tomatoes, always offer the person who caught you a sniff too. It's polite and basic. No one has ever accepted my offer. Chop your tomatoes into nice big chunks. Half and then at least half again. Once the garlic and onions are ready to receive the tomatoes, drive them over and make the introduction.

Let them all swim together, turn down the heat now. Stir or shake the pan and after a further five to ten minutes, add an amount of water as yet to be announced. What I can say is it'll be between 200 and 350ml water. The last couple of goes making this sauce for gnocchi,

I've done it slightly differently from my proper tomato sauce in as much as I cook it to a certain point, 25– 30 minutes after the water goes in, and then I turn it off and let it sit and mature and steep.

The next sauce stage comes a bit later once you're cooking the gnocchi. Stay tuned. Please. For all of our sakes. Stay tuned.

I had a load of white potatoes that were sitting in the bowl and they'd started to sprout a bit. I never want to throw spuds away, or any food actually – I do, but it's a shame. My mum, whenever she used to throw bread away, would kiss it before tossing it in the bin. I asked why she did it once. She said, 'I'm kissing the bread of life.' I liked that. She offered me the bag and I kissed it too. This is probably one of the nicest childhood memories I have. Kissing a mouldy bag of bread. (Not quite true, but you feel me.)

Grab a metal dish, fill it with the potatoes and put it in a hot oven (180°C) for perhaps an hour. If they're big, a bit longer. If they're small, you can fish them out and leave them to cool while they're waiting for the bigger ones. When making these gnocchi, I find you need space and time. Get to a point where all the spuds are done, turn your oven off and fish them out. Leave them to cool for a while. Cut the potatoes in half and, using a little paring knife and with a spoon, remove as much white spud meat as you can into a bowl. Throw the skins away. You should now have a lovely big bowl of cool potato. Push this through a ricer, or if you don't have one, push it through a sieve. You'll be left with very fine worms of mash, essentially. With your fingers or the fingers of a good friend, form the worms into a circle. Like the caldera of a dormant stratovolcano. (Google it.)

This next bit is a hit-and-miss operation for me as I didn't follow a recipe, I just read the method of gnocchi enough to know what to do. I take some flour, a handful at first, my hand or the hand of a friend, and dust it around the circle of potato. I then crack a big egg in the middle. Use your hands to bring it all in together. Knead the dough, because now that it feels wet it's dough, add flour, a little flour, little by little.

Knead this as little as possible. Bring it together, add flour, knead it, little flour, knead ... etc. You know it's ready when the ball of mash and egg and flour has turned into a very beautiful, tactile, lovely ball of, essentially, pasta. Press your finger into it. Watch the pasta ball push the finger print back out. It's done.

Pop into a clean, lightly floured bowl, cover with clingfilm, set it somewhere cool. Put the kettle on and while it is boiling, clean up. They'll be spuds and egg and flour everywhere. Clean up. Drink tea, dunk into the tea the first of six sneaky Hobnobs. Sorry if six biccies seems excessive. I sadly don't make the rules. ADHD. I need a dopamine hit. (Sad face.)

Once you've finished your tea, clean the mug and put it away. Let's hustle. It's 4:15pm, we have 45 minutes before the animals need feeding. Take your lovely big ball of pasta/dough, have flour to hand to dust the work surface, also have a big, flour-dusted, baking sheet on which to hold and rest the gnocchi once made. I didn't salt and pepper these. Do that or do it when you serve. It's all good.

Chop the ball of pasta into four pieces. Dust your piece with flour and using your hands, in a roly-roly motion turn the dough into a long sausage, the thickness should be about a cigar. Or a Richmond banger. For cigars, I'd say imagine the ones Churchill smoked, not a slim Panetella, not the kind Clint Eastwood used to suck on. Think Cuban, not Café Crème.

Then chop the long sausages into chunks, maybe 1 by ½ inch. Work fast too, if you can. Gnocchi is known for having little fork marks on top of it. These, unsurprisingly, are made by squashing it with a fork. It's nice and fun to do. I don't quite have the knack yet. When I push the fork in it kind of flattens out. Writing this now I have a flash come across my mind ... Rest them in the fridge before marking them. Of course ... Of course... (That may not be right. Let's ask YouTube. Let me know. It'll also be amazing watching old Italian ladies making pasta. What skill! It takes a lifetime of doing something to make it look so easy. It's fun to watch.)

A huge ball of gnocchi dough is a lot of gnocchi. I usually chop it in half and freeze half the dough and make gnocchi from the other half. That gives my five probably a decent portion of six bits of gnocchi each. They all want more after, so maybe I don't do enough. Rest your dough on the baking sheet, sprinkle with flour and prepare to cook.

Take a massive pot, fill with water and bring to the boil, salt and olive oil in the water. Now, head back to the tomato thing … Take your stick blender and blend the onions and garlic and tomato together. Pour it into a frying pan and slowly heat the sauce.

Once the water is boiling, take the gnocchi and drop them into the boiling water. After four minutes or so the gnocchi begin to rise and swirl in the briney maelstrom. Pull them out with a slotted spoon and place them straight into the sauce to stay warm. Once they're all in, shake the sauce all over the gnocchi and then serve. A little oil on top for the adults, salt, pepper, a ton of Parmesan. Enjoy. Well done. It should taste wonderful. Again, if it doesn't, bin and enjoy a mug full of Rice Krispies. You obviously didn't do it right. You obviously couldn't follow my incoherent ramblings.

If you got it right. Hey! Well done. I love you. Nicky wuv woo. Gnocchi should be learned and remembered and stored. It's a lifetime of pleasure.

Sauces I've been thinking about when I think about gnocchi … These are just from my brain. I could just look in a book I guess, but this feels more fun.

Ragù & Parmesan. Obvious.

Mushroom Sauce. Kind of like a Heinz-ish mushroom soup sauce but homemade. Yummo.

Butter & Sage. Yes, please! (Not my idea, I think I heard it before or have eaten it before.)

Butter, Sage & Sausage. Not those fennel-based, fancy, home-made, hand-reared sausages I hate so much. Gimme a fucking Richmond banger any day. Hunks of sausage fried and served with the Butter & Sage sauce.

Why don't you have a go... Okay? Good, right here we go ... What's that you're saying? A rich, cheesy béchamel with cubes of smoked ham? (Sounds of a fork falling to the floor of a fancy hotel kitchen.)

'Who the fuck said cheesy béchamel with cubes of smoked ham?'

No one brave enough to step forward.

'WHO THE FUCK SAID IT?!!!'

'I did you cock, it's Nick. I'm writing the book you live in.'

And, just like that, the sketch was over!

I suppose what I'm getting at is there must be literally HUNDREDS of toppings for gnocchi, just like pasta. Clever Italians. What food geniuses they are. Actually, you could probably say the same of the French and Chinese, Spanish, Indians, Mexicans, Koreans, Turkish, Japanese, Greeks. In fact, all that food out there, every single country having thousands of individual ways to prepare the ingredients that grew or they could get hold of in that country. Food and cooking is amazing.

RISOTTO

I never understood what risotto was. I never got it. And then when I tried and saw how easy it was, I was hooked. If you're serious about cooking, learn the technique behind this and learn how to make a nice risotto. I know it feels a bit 1970s but it's delicious and I think there's a timeless quality to something being totally delicious. Before the rest of the dish, let's start with the mushrooms. (Because we're making a Mushroom Risotto. I should've said.) We can prepare before time, cover with clingfilm and set aside. Once you get into the cycle of stirring the risotto and adding liquid, you won't have the time to fry mushrooms and your life will be shitty for three years.

I need bespoke mushrooms for three different stages of this risotto. Firstly, something big and flavoursome to chop finely and fry with the other veg. It makes a nice mushroom base for what is, after all, a mushroom risotto. Secondly, I need lots of lovely mushrooms that I'll fry in butter and fold into the risotto towards the end – this will make up the bulk of the mushroom taste. I use chestnut and bog standard mushrooms and thick slices of fried portobello.

Slice them and fry them in butter. Splash a couple of drops of Worcestershire sauce into this and add to this a couple of sprigs of thyme. Toss and fry at a high heat until the mushrooms are cooked and brown and amazing. Taste a few. Nice? Put into a bowl and set aside. Not in the fridge, please.

My third element du champignon is the mushrooms I'm going to use as a garnish. When I make this dish, I try and find a big juicy cep. They're so pretty and woody and beautiful. If you ever get a chance to stick your head in a basket of these, you should. It's quite something. They're so umami. It transports me into the wilds of the forests that surround Frensham Ponds, one of my favourite places in the world. I spent a long time walking those pine-laden hills, digging around, looking for mushrooms.

At the end of cooking a risotto, I always leave it to sit for a few minutes. I let it relax. It's been stirred constantly for 40 minutes, it deserves a break, but while it rests, I don't. This is when I prepare the garnish. Using your lovely phat cep or porcini as it's also known, slice it quite thick. Choose the middle of the shroom to get yourself a nice fat steak bit. In a little frying pan, bring some butter up to temperature and fry the mushroom slices so they're brown and gorgeous. Please bear in mind this mushroom will be the one that makes people go 'Ohhhhhhh, a mushroom.'

You need to either make a great fresh stock or buy one, low salt please, and add a bit of water to it. I have a very large pot of stock on the stove, sitting, warm, waiting to be used. 'Soon my liquidy darling, soon.'

I'm going to make a Mushroom Risotto. I love it. Hayley loves it. These are the ingredients I would use:

For the stock

good stock (I'd probably use beef stock for Mushroom Risotto but I'd want it a bit beefy. You choose whatever you want. I've done a spring onion and Parmesan risotto a few times too and that's nice with a clear, golden veggie stock. You do you, doll.

For the mirepoix

1 onion, finely chopped

1 celery stalk, finely chopped

1 fat carrot, peeled and finely chopped

1 nugget of garlic, smashed flat and finely diced

Here I introduce my first shroomy element. It is a mushroom risotto after all. My intention is to take two or three different kinds of mushroom and fry them up and stir them into the risotto later but here is a chance to add some mushrooms now. I use a big portobello at this point. Chop it really finely, like the same size of the rest of the mirepoix. Once you've chopped all this veg you will not only be chilled and Zen, but you'll also be ready to do this.

Frying pan, big one, skillet, high-sided, or a big deep saucepan, remember a lot of liquid is going to be put in this pan. Big knob of butter, glug of oil. Turn the heat up beneath your stock, you'll need it soon. It shouldn't boil. It should just be hot and steamy. I have my risotto pan in front of me and the burner behind the frying pan has the hot stock on it. Complete with ladle.

Gently fry your mirepoix. I don't want it browned. Stir and then lid to keep the steam in. After a few minutes, it's done. It'll look nice, white onions and little green and orange nibs and the mushrooms. Nice.

Into the pan add a small knob of beurre and turn the temperature up. It's time to add the rice, obviously use risotto rice, I usually use arborio but you may use whatever you wish. Once the pan is hot, add the rice and stir around in the fat and the veg until you can hear the rice pods snap, crackle and pop, then lash in your first ladleful of stock. It will hiss and bubble and steam, the liquid will pretty much evaporate away pretty quickly. Add another ladleful, the same thing will happen but less violently and the liquid will again evaporate. Turn the heat down now slightly and add another ladle of stock and begin the stir. It begins ...

So, what's happening here is this ... The rice will drink up all the stock and all the flavour from the mushrooms and by stirring constantly the rice releases its starch, which makes the risotto thick and creamy eventually. You will do this next section a lot ...

Rice and mushrooms bubble and plip, we stir until all the liquid has either evaporated away or has been sucked up by the rice, add a ladleful of stock.

Rice and mushrooms bubble and plip, we stir until all the liquid has either evaporated away or has been sucked up by the rice, add a ladleful of stock.

Rice and mushrooms bubble and plip, we stir until all the liquid has either evaporated away or has been sucked up by the rice, add a ladleful of stock.

Do this gently and respectfully and use all/most of that stock. The dish will look and feel really different from when you began. It'll be lovely and unctuous and creamy and saucy. There's a lot of chat about how wet you should make a risotto. I feel it's all about personal preference and what you have going into it. Taste it and season, please.

At this point, I empty my beautiful bowl of fried mushrooms into the rice, stir them in, gently, there we go. Wow. It looks great. There's one last, very important stage here. Before I leave it to sit for a couple of minutes, I finish by adding a few cubes of cold butter and a LOT of freshly grated Parmigiana! Stir them in and leave it. Get your bowls ready. Ladle of risotto into the bowl. Now add your cep slice on top. I usually take a little bunch of chives at this point and very finely slice them, then sprinkle on top of the dish and the shroom and then a light grating on top with more Parmesan. Get it on the table and eat. It's amazing.

There's also a way here to add a little extra flavour and that is this: use dry ceps and rehydrate them in a jug of warm water. Once they are again full of health-liquid, pull them out and squeeze the liquid into the jug you used to hydrate the shrooms. These mushrooms can be chopped and fried with the other shrooms for the body of the risotto.

More tastily the dark brown crystal liquid that has come out of the ceps can be added to the stock to add a real depth of flavour.

Other risottos I've made:

Spring Onion & Parmesan

Crab & Scallop – this is nice because you fry scallops and serve them on top as a garnish.

Chorizo & Smoked Paprika

Turkey & Bacon (Boxing Day Risotto)

There must be literally hundreds of different risottos. The technique is generally the same. Learn the technique and you will unlock hundreds of potential dishes. Hundreds.

Sometimes I've made a little risotto and put something on top of it. If you make a basic fish-style risotto using fish stock and saffron, then adding a chubby, well-cooked salmon fillet is a lovely, tasty addition. This also works for trout and plump white cod or even a piece of fried monkfish tail.

Find what you like and make it. You could learn a risotto a week.

You could leaf through a risotto manual and make whatever one takes your fancy. Google it. They're amazing and cheap to make, if you don't add a kilo of Parmesan, and friggin' tasty.

GREEK SALAD

When we shot *Paul* in Santa Fe, New Mexico, I hosted the whole crew one afternoon on a Sunday. On the Saturday, I went out with a bunch of cast and crew and got so hammered after watching children ride big sheep at a local rodeo that I ended up insulting, completely accidentally, a local MDMA dealer. He was angry that I had come into his club and not paid tribute to him by joining him for a drink. He was weird and aggressive and at one point the safety pod in my brain told me to get in so we could jettison to safety. What this actually meant was me running out of a back door and into a waiting rickshaw. A rickshaw piloted by a tiny blonde girl. Poor woman. It took about five minutes to actually move but once we got going we hit a terrific top speed. 2mph. It took us one and a half hours to get home, 800 metres away.

I woke up late on Sunday and then had a weird headachey something-to-do vibe and then I remembered I had offered to cater for 75 people in three hours' time. FUCKBALLS!!! With a hangover banging deep inside my spine flaps and horrible memories of screaming children, their weak, tiny hands clinging on to dusty, lanolin-rich wool inked into the rodeo cortex of my middle lobe, I precooked 20lb of BBQ chicken wings and 20 racks of pork ribs. I stank. I heaved and sweated all over that food. Then I stood and made a huge Greek salad that no one would touch and a bunch of other things they would. A few times

over the past five years I made a really big Greek Salad, amongst
other things, to fill out a BBQ or a something I had catered. No
one touched it. I mean they pecked at it a bit but I had so much
left over. It was actually a lovely afternoon. Getting to hang with
the crew and eat together and laugh and share stories and gossip
about horrible actors we'd worked with ... Man it was fun. I loved
living in Santa Fe. The food was great. The film was fun to make
too. It was a bit like *Hot Fuzz* too in as much as we took over a
whole town. I love making films. What a lucky man I am. Find
something you love and let it kill you. I think the author of that
meant drink or drugs. I used to think work. Maybe now I think
the answer is life. Let life kill you.

NB: If you served me up cucumber with its thick, verdant skin
on, I'd honk. The only way I can eat raw cucumber is if I take a
peeler and take 91 per cent of the skin off. I then take a little spoon
and pull out the seeds. Only then will the cucumber pass my
mouth's 'Puke Test'.

**Grab a lovely big cucumber, the kind that makes lesser
men nervous ... Peel it so 91 per cent of the skin has been
removed, pull out the seeds and chop it into pieces the
size of an eight-notch Lego brick. Slide into a big bowl.
Take a large red onion the size of a cricket ball, undress
it, cut in half and then slice thinly. Bowl. Core out a red
pepper, slice and chop, add to bowl. Now, I feel the heart of
a Greek Salad is the tomatoes, the ones you get in Greece
and the Med in general are big and red and sweet. We
can get them here like that but it takes a real hunt. I also
leave big, tom-smelling toms out in the open for a while,
hopefully in the sun. It gets domestic toms very close to**

their Mediterranean cousins. Chop them however you like. I slice in half and then half again. Add to the bowl. Now toss in the black olives, no stone. Kalamata. Delish. Gently, have a nice toss. Mix it all up. Be gentle.

I'd suggest taking some really nice olive oil and dressing the salad now. Also, some good flakes of sea salt over the top. The salt brings out liquid from the tomatoes and it adds to this lovely amalgam of juice at the bottom of the bowl. Mopping this up with nice bread is a little gem that humans can enjoy for free. It will make you live longer.

I add the feta cheese at the very end. In some parts of Greece they stick it whole on top. I usually break it up and stick it in when I'm tossing. That's basically it. The only thing you could add at this point is a dusting of dried oregano. A Greek salad. Add this gem to your inventory. It goes well with everything. Meat, veggie burgers, monkfish, salmon, BBQ. Everything. What a dream. *YAMAS*!!

I love Greece. I also love *Grease*. The country and the musical with John Travolta. *Grease* was the first film I ever went to see with my parents. I've always owned the soundtrack too. I actually remember my dad carrying a very sleepy me out of the cinema. I tend to watch the same films and TV shows over and over again. It's a way to self-soothe my ever clucking brain.

Hayley often asks, 'How many times have you seen this?' She's always surprised when I say something

like, 'Two hundred.' She can't understand how a
person could watch anything more than once. For
me and my brain it's about watching something I not
only love, but more importantly, I know. I know it. No
surprises. I know the dialogue, I know how it ends.
I know all the music. I know and love little sounds
(machine-gun bullets on massive gong in *Indiana
Jones and the Temple of Doom*).

I often rewind something many times to watch a
particular section. I'm the same with music. (On the
drive to work yesterday, I listened to the Frank Ocean
song 'Chanel' 16 times.) I'm the same with food ...

Here is a brief list of TV and films I watch all
the time:

Close Encounters of the Third Kind, I've probably
watched this 250 times. My beautiful Auntie Melanie
used to date an American serviceman many years
ago. I think I was 10 or 11 at the time. He came over
to her small council house in Haverfordwest and he
brought with him two things. A VHS copy of *Close
Encounters of the Third Kind*. And the other thing he
brought was from the restaurant on the naval base. It
was in a kind of box I'd never seen before, a big flat
square box and inside they told me was something
called a PIZZA. That was the first time I ever tried
pizza. And *Close Encounters*. What a day!

The first three *Star Wars* films.

A New Hope – hundreds.

The Empire Strikes Back – hundreds.

Return of the Jedi – hundreds.

Raiders of the Lost Ark – hundreds.

E.T. – hundreds.

Poltergeist – hundreds.

Every TV show Rick Stein has ever made. (Recorded so I can watch, sometimes every day. Rick Stein can work as an aid to sleep, or if I'm anxious or if I'm writing. Just to have him in the background while I'm working feels so nice.) Same goes for Michael Palin and Michael Portillo and Fred Dibnah.

Northern Exposure.

The X-Files.

Snakes in the City.

Aussie Gold Hunters.

Outback Opal Hunters.

Outback Truckers.

Below Deck.

Endless Pokémon booster box openings.

Culvert drain unblockings.

Hours of tsunami footage.

NHK World Japan – A Japanese language TV station from Tokyo. In my day-to-day life this is what I watch the most. It's gentle, informative TV with the best kind of programming. Imagine a Western man who speaks fluent Japanese cycles around Kochi province taking in the scenery when he happens across a 95-year-old lady harvesting radishes. They talk briefly and then he helps her for three hours. She thanks him by making him a green tea and her friends come round and they all bill and coo over how good his Japanese is and then he gets back on his bike and they wave him off as he continues his journey south. So nice! Also, a thing called Bento Express – a camera travels around an office and people show it their lunch. Fun. And Sumo! We've come a long way from Greece the country! It's funny how the brain does that. My mind is like a girl chasing a bright butterfly across a warm summer meadow.

When me and Hayley go to Greece, the food, day in day out, is generally the same, which is great for Alan, Debbie, Helen and David. It suits me fine. It also means that when I prepare it here, the old brain thinks I'm in Greece. (What an idiot!) If you put me out in a garden, stood next to a hot BBQ, in any format, gently grilling some meat cubes to accompany a delicious salad I've made, I'm happy. There's also a certain, same old, same old, my brain desires. The prep is the same wherever you go. I'm so proud of my brain sometimes. I don't say that much but the ability to plan and make big meals for lots of people and take into consideration all of their food likes and dislikes, then to shop, then to have bags of produce and to silently work through it all in a tidy, ordered manner to prep everything without looking at a book and then to cook it all, so everything is ready and hot at the same time! Wow! Well done brain ... Where's that butterfly? There!

A MARINADE FOR MEAT

Take a big bowl. Take a chopping board and on to it smash and then finely dice 2 nuggets of garlic, grate a piece of ginger the size of a thumb, add both of these to a bowl. Finely dice a very mild red chilli. Bowl. Peel and finely slice half a red onion. Bowl. Take a bouquet of coriander and chop it in half. Some of you may be thinking 'What the fuck does that mean?' And you'd be right to think that ... What I mean is: cut the woody stalky bits off and keep the nice leafy bits, put them back in the fridge. Chop the stalks up and stick them in the bowl. Now, two phat tablespoons of chilli crisp sauce. (If you know, you know.) Then at least half a bottle of soy sauce (light), same of teriyaki sauce. Halve and squeeze two limes and then either some light brown sugar (two tablespoons) or a healthy squeeze of honey into the marinade bowl. Flurry of mild chilli flakes and also a few whole spice bombs, like Sichuan peppers. Even a few black peppercorns is nice. Now add a little olive oil here to loosen the whole mixture up.

Stir it up. Have a taste, No? TASTE THE FUCKER! Set aside.

Take chicken or pork and cut it into really small bits. Add these to the marinade and mix in well. Leave all day. Or overnight.

Thread the meat on to skewers. You want loads of meat on each skewer, pack it on. Because they're nice small bits, they cook really nicely. Better than big cubes of meat cook. The Japanese are so clever with their lovely yakitori.

(Which is what we just made!) Let's all close our eyes and imagine for a minute this ...

You've spent a great day on the beach. You come back around 2pm-ish and lay on the bed in the air con. You're both kind of sun-horny, so you fuck, it's amazing, like old times. You nod off and when you wake up, they're in the shower. You make a list on your phone of stuff you need for dinner. Then you both head out in the little car you hired to the cute little village to pick up food. 'Shall we have little sundowner?' FUCK, YEAH!!! You sit in a nice silence and drink ice-cold Mythos. A waitress brings over some weird nut things that your partner loves, you hate them but it's cool. There's a huge fish that lives in the harbour and she LOVES THEM. You toss the nuts in and watch the seamonster extend its mouth tube and take the spicy wasabi-covered nut out of the water. 'Thank you,' it says in Greek. A cat called Peter comes over and watches.

Back at the house, the BBQ is hot and ready. One of you preps the salad while the other places the amazing skewers you just made on to the grill. Freeze. Remember this moment right now forever. Look at what you have. Wow. Even if you've been arguing all week, let that go. Forget home, forget work or lack of, forget everything except right now ...

Look at the deep golden orange colour the sky has turned as the sun sets.

Look at the beautiful little cat, not Peter, a different cat you guys have befriended. He's so cheeky and funny and cute. You called him Lipstick!

Close your eyes and listen to the sea gently lapping on to the soft golden beach beyond. Look at the swallows swooping down and drinking the water from the swimming pool. (Poor them, you had a bunk-up in that earlier, it was like omelettes floating around by the time you climbed out.)

Look at each other. You're both beautiful, all tanned brown and red and cute and tired and hungry. Now close your eyes and inhale slowly and deeply. Smell the wild herbs in the hedgerow, smell the sea, smell the moisturiser on your skin. Smell the chicken skewers you've spent the day marinating. They're almost ready. On the table outside the farmhouse near the beach are some salads and some warm pitta and a hummus you bought and a tzatziki you made. Your partner brushes past you and smells amazing and looks so beautiful and we smile and all there is, is now. Look how lucky we are. That was the point to this rambling. Just feel. Breathe. Fuck! You're so lucky.

It's easy to forget that week or two we get every year, it's not just here on the sun-soaked shores of the Aegean that we get a chance to breathe and to feel genuine gratitude to be alive. You know? We may not have the swallows and swifts diving down and getting their beaks gummed up with our congealed pool fuck, but what we do have are these skewers. Open your eyes. I'm in my garden, the kids are screaming, the cat has my youngest by the face and it's biting her nose. I look at the grill and there is the holiday. Let's eat! *YAMAS*!!!

TZATZIKI

milk

Greek yoghurt

cucumber

garlic

dill

mint

salt

pepper

I use a little milk and add it to the yoghurt just to make it less thick, how thick is up to you. To the yoghurt, add: cucumber. I peel it. I chop it in half. I use a spoon to scrape out the seeds and then I slice/chop, whatever you fancy. Add to yog. Smash up a couple of big garlic nuggets and chop finely, add to yog. Get a bunch of dill and a bunch of mint, not loads, and chop it finely, add to the yoghurt and stir. Season and bring to the table.

I'm having a moment now but I sit and I have a warm pitta in front of me. I pull off some amazing, well-cooked souvlaki and wrap them up inside the bread. I reach past my wonderful, loud, triggering kids and splurge a spoonful of fresh tzatziki on to the chicken ... God, I'm lucky.

Mexico

I make a lot of Mexican food at home. Everyone loves it. Here comes a huge claim: I feel at one point I was making the best Mexican food in Twickenham. I've banged on about Chiquito's a lot, so I won't keep banging on, but I was there when our store, in fact all Chiquitos, were taken over by a mega-conglomerate called City Centre Restaurants. Their corporate aim was to install a paradigm they called 'Brand Standard'. This meant the food you ate in Dorset tasted the same as the food you ate in Manchester, which tasted the same as the food you ate in Watford.

What it meant to me though was instead of our prep kitchen making fresh sauces every day, everything was shipped in frozen and defrosted. It was awful. I came into the kitchen at the end of the old-style prep, the proper way. I asked to not be a waiter any more because people were rude and fucking stupid. I moved into the kitchen, when three prep chefs would come in each morning and check in a huge pallet full of fruit and veg and then we'd work through the day's 'prep list', checking out what we'd need to make. Every recipe would start with a kind of 'you will need' list and then you gathered what the recipe wanted and then you made the sauces.

They tasted amazing. Fresh, traditional, spicy, clean. Every one tasted a tiny bit different depending on who made it. Which is what City Centre didn't want. But it's what made Chiquito's great back then. That was a long time ago, sadly ,but having been one of those prep chefs, I managed to remember a few little tips and tricks. Sadly, I didn't steal a prep recipe book when I left. I'd love to get all those recipes. Some of those sauces were incredible. I still think about them today. The only place that's come close are proper Tex-Mex places I've eaten at in New Mexico or Austin. What a shame when a corporate dick decides to get involved and, overnight, fucks everything up. But it's all about the dollar baby. Am I right? Don't leave me hanging, baby?! It's all about the Benjamins ... Guys ...?

It's not all about the Benjamins. It's about relationships and experience and joy and pleasure. Some of it is about the Benjamins. But not all.

GUACAMOLE

I love guacamole. Hayley loves it too. This is exactly the original guacamole recipe as I remember it from that prep kitchen and it's delicious. You will need ...

2 large ripe avocados

½ juicy tomato

½ red onion

1 nugget of garlic

½ mild red chilli

Whizz all these things down into a lovely bright green 'guac'-style paste. Taste it at this point. You'll be surprised how boring and tasteless it is. Hold yourself, I've got some flavour for you. Now add in:

some salt

some white pepper

a splash of Tabasco sauce

a splash of Worcestershire sauce

Finely chop a bunch of coriander (I fucking love it!) and stick it in. Then, take a fine juicy green lime, and squeeze that in too.

Have you ever peeled and eaten a lime the way one would an orange? It takes ages. I became obsessed with peeling other citrus fruits for a while, four years ago. I began peeling and eating lemons really casually during meetings. People are like, 'Did he just peel and eat a lemon?' Yes, yes I did. It breaks people's minds. I remember being sat on a packed tube carriage 28 years ago and watching a guy peel and casually eat a huge orange. My overarching memory was thinking he must be hugely endowed. Only a Phat D can be that confident, so casual. 'What am I doing? Why, I'm peeling and eating a huge orange. Oh, and by the way, here's a mammoth dong.'

Now, eat your baby hard till her legs are trembling. (What I mean by that is, taste the guacamole.) It's completely different. It's now a proper guacamole. Obviously you can tinker with these flavours, add little by little. I'd stick this in the fridge for a bit. To serve it, take it out of the fridge, unless you have a big fridge, then you can all get inside to eat. Slice a red chilli into thin rings and place three on top of the guac and serve with a big bowl of salty corn chips. Get up into my insides. So nice. Coronas and Cadillacs go great with this.

This is a recipe you can fiddle with and keep forever. You can use it in a lot of different ways. I've served it with pieces of fried salmon and fajitas and big sirloin steaks too. It's lovely and takes no time.

FAJITAS

Fajitas are nice. They always feel a bit special and people enjoy the ceremony. At Chiquito's we served them sizzling at the table! It always amazed me how many times you'd say to customers, 'Hey guys, this skillet is white hot, please don't touch it.' And then people would just reach over and immediately touch it. They'd really squeal and leap. When you worked in the kitchen, as I did, after my waitering career came to an end, the busiest section and by far the hottest was the broiler.

You stood at a huge BBQ-style broiler and just cooked endless banks of different meats. I liked it very much. Anyway, one of the first things I'd do is turn on a huge double gas burner that sat next to the griddle and I'd put on about 30 thick, iron skillets. They'd sit there all day until they were needed for fajitas.

When a waiter called for the fajitas to be 'fired', the broiler-man would prepare the dish for the table. If it was chicken, it would be chopped into slices and then the waiter shouted, 'FIRE ME SINGLE CHICKEN!' Single chicken was one breast of chicken, double was a pair of breasts, you could also have prawns or steak and veg. You could even have a combo of any pair of the two. I'd then grab a handful of onions and pepper slices, dip them in a bucket of melted butter and stick them straight on to the iron skillet, it would spit and scream and burst into flames. I'd lay it on a disc of burnt wood and out it would go to the guest. People loved it. It also tasted really good.

At this point I was 23, give or take. I worked there from 21/22 until I was 27 or 28. I had no money at all. I had no notion of saving or the future or a career, a family, a house ... I earned money from tips and I spent them the night I earned them, generally. It was absolutely hand to mouth.

On my days off, I'd head into the restaurant to eat. If my mate Flea was working in the kitchen, I'd head into the restaurant at around 3pm-ish so as to miss the lunch rush and I'd sit quietly and invisibly in one of the corner booths and I'd let the waiter know he should tell Flea that I was in. Wink, wink. Flea would always sort me out. Sometimes it was laughable the amount of food that would come out. You'd have to let the manager know you were coming in but they'd hardly ever come over or they didn't give a shit at the amount of free/stolen food/margaritas that was disappearing.

I'd get the waiter to ring through a Single Chicken Fajita £7.95 (special order ...) and Flea would take care of the rest. It would be a huge pile of juicy prawns at its heart with a blanket of chicken covering one side and a blanket of steak blanketing the other. That's like £35 worth of meat. He'd send out endless Guacamole and a ton of Chilli con Queso (a rich, chilli, unctuous cheese sauce that's just an amazing thing a human can put in its mouth). It was quite a lunch. I'd have to pay for my first margarita too but after that the bartenders would send endless jugs over. What a lunch. I'd leave a couple of hours later, arseholed! Or Flea would finish and we'd hit a local pub in Kilburn. I would've spent next to nothing. We looked after each other back then.

Shall we have fajitas? Let's have steak and chicken. The fajitas we used to do at Chiquito's were butterflied out and left to marinate in a lovely secret blend of Mexican spices. Back then you couldn't get hardly any Mexican ingredients in shops. Maybe flour tortillas or refried beans at a push. Over the years, in my search to recreate fajitas, I stumbled upon a company called Discovery, who make a packet of dust called Fajita Mix. It's pretty good. It tastes a bit old school.

Turn a packet of dust into a bowl and glug olive oil on top, mix with a spoon and then prepare the meat. I take a lovely chicken breast and butterfly it open. YouTube it. It takes a while to get comfortable doing it but when you can it feels great.

Don't butterfly the steak. Use it as is. I'd suggest using a nice bit of rump steak. Cheap, tasty, good on the griddle. You could also use flank. Stick them in the bowl with the dust and the oil. Use your hands to work the marinade into the meat. Refrigerate this for at least a couple of hours.

Wash your filthy, oily, weak hands. Fajitas always come with a dish full of nice things to stuff a soft flour tortilla with. Guacamole. (This you know.) Soured cream, shredded iceberg lettuce, Cheddar cheese and a little tomato salsa called Pico de Gallo, which is finely diced tomato, white onion and jalapeños. Make it in a big bowl,

add lime juice and a little salt. Lovely. It's crisp and clean, slightly spicy. Have lots of each of these little additions ready. Part of a busy Saturday shift in the restaurant involved putting together loads of these side dishes ready to be sent out with the sizzling meats.

For the meat, I'd suggest either doing this on a very hot griddle pan in the kitchen or on a white-hot BBQ. My extractor fan is FUCKED ... I cannot griddle anything without the kitchen filling with the intense blue smoke uniquely given off by once-living flesh basted in flavoured oils. (What a creepy sentence.) I've had three sets of different 'men' come round and all have said different things about why it doesn't work. One even thought there wasn't an exterior vent. Sad.

In the house I used to live in, before the house I live in now, I was in the fortunate position of not having to live in it while I had a big extension put on to the kitchen to turn it into a big kitchen living room/dining room. It was beautiful. I'd just done a big job and had the budget for a bespoke kitchen. A chef I knew who has stars linked me with a company that makes bespoke kitchens for restaurants, so that's what I had. It was amazing. I had my own Athanor cook suite. It had a huge slab of iron in the middle of the stove and either side of that induction hobs. It did everything. I had ovens and warming plates and fucking salamanders ... The cream of the crop for me was an industrial cooker hood. It was super sucky; you could've set fire to a gallon of crude oil in the kitchen and a person in the front room would be none the wiser.

I always miss that hood. Here's the kicker ... Soon after the kitchen was finished my divorce kind of forced me to sell the house. Man, that kitchen was amazing. It's odd to think the people who own that house inherited that incredible kitchen. I miss her. The kitchen, not my ex-wife.

So, I'd use the BBQ. I've got a gas-fired one but it's away from the house and I get lonely/Hayley thinks I'm avoiding the children. I bought a little Japanese tabletop grill, which is amazing but it takes ages to get ready to use, but it's all I've got, so I'll use that. Whatever you choose, get it super-hot and then cook the chicken and steak super-quick and super-hot. I want char marks all over the steak and chicken. Once they're cooked, pull them off the griddle and rest them for a few minutes. This gives you time to take a huge stack of flour tortillas and heat them in the oven. Once warm, stick them on a plate, and with the side bowls, put them on the table. Now, if you want to recreate restaurant-style fajitas, you can quickly fry slices of pepper and onion and put them on a plate and then put the steak and chicken on top of this. Serve and enjoy. Fajitas are fucking lush.

I got an idea for a prawn dish after watching an episode of *Man v. Food*. I say idea, I mean that I essentially just ripped it the fuck off. If I make Prawn Fajitas, this is how I do it ... We've got the Guac and the bowls of Pico de Gallo and Cheddar, etc. We've got an oven full of warm flour tortillas. Check.

1 red onion, chopped coarsely

1 bunch of spring onions. Finely chop the whites and then turn and chop the greens too

2 nuggets of garlic

1 sweet red pepper, chopped

ground cumin

cayenne pepper

chilli powder (a bit hot)

smoked paprika

4 ripe, sun-smelling, sweet tomatoes

1kg good fresh prawns (What weird, beautiful, odd, tasty things prawns are? That line was written by Keats when he lived in Corsica and spent his time sniffing glue and eating prawns.)

½ green pepper, chopped

1 bunch of coriander

2 limes

This is a lot like the stew you made for Big Vern and put the spicy sausages in (see pages 35–9). I had a very similar plate of prawns in this kind of sauce when I went to Key West once. Fry your onion, white spring onions and your garlic kind of hard, it's cool if they catch and go brown. Toss in your red pepper, cook it until soft. Then toss in a glug more oil and into it stir in a heaped teaspoon of cumin, cayenne, chilli powder and then maybe 1 spoon plus a bit of smoked paprika, stir and cook it all out. Then, chop your tomatoes into little chunks and toss them in the hot oil with the onion and pepper, this'll sizzle and you can turn it down at this point. Now I want it to slowly cook down and simmer until it reduces into a nice tomato-rich, paprika tang'd, fajita stew. If you need to add a little splash of water here and there, absolutely go for it. The end product can be a little fluid.

Now toss in the prawns. A word about prawns' anuses and the shit duct ... Growing up, I was always under the impression that the black line that ran down the back of prawns was a bag of sea plops that should be avoided at all cost. Is that still the case? It's been a long time since I teased a packed shitbox out of a prawn.

Just toss them in. They will turn from grey and see-through to pink when they're cooked. Stir them all in. Toss in the green pepper; this will soften but not cook entirely. I like the taste of green pepper like this. A bit fresh, while everything else is saucy. Chop and toss in loads of coriander, squeeze the lime juice into the sauce and, as soon as the prawns are cooked and pink, I finish by whacking a big knob of butter in and stirring it all together. It tastes so nice with the guac and the lettuce and the soured cream and mature Cheddar in a warm tortilla. Lovely.

BURRITOS

If you were to take the griddled chicken or the steak or the prawns and not send them to the table as fajitas, you could use them for the filling of a lovely burrito instead. You could use all the trimmings as well. Instead of using a small tortilla, this time you want to use the big guns. There's even a way to use two large tortillas to make a super-uberritto. It's huge. In Cally and all over the West Coast, you usually get the choice of filling your burrito with red rice, a Mexican rice you can make with onion and carrot and a stock with tomato purée instead of water (there's a bit more to it than that but that's it essentially) or refried beans. Delish. I prefer not to pack my burritos out with either of those things as I tend to use them as little accompaniments on the plate when I serve. This is good news for my guests as it means they get a good solid, meat-filled burrito. I'm going to focus on steak for this recipe.

A decent bit of rump, 350g or more, flattened and marinated in that Discovery powder. Griddle hot and quick. I like mine medium rare, so once it's done, I rest it under foil.

Take your flour tortilla and fill it with lovely food. What an annoying recipe style of writing. Imagine if all recipes were so vague and obtuse. Take some nice food and add these other foods in a specific order and it'll become another different third kind of food and then eat it with some cutlery and it'll nourish you. Goodnight.

I'm not going to waste pages of me trying to tell you how to fold tortillas to make it a burrito, or how then to turn that into a Chimichanga ... YouTube it. If you're anything like me, you'll have to see it and be able to pause and rewind. Do that. Maybe I'll do a YouTube channel that's in conjunction with the book so you can actually see me turning perfectly good ingredients into inedible plates of hatred.

I use a big spoonful of refried beans to kind of anchor the rest of the ingredients together and add a bit of moisture

to the whole thing, no one wants a dry burrito. No one. Maybe Nazis. Typical dry-burrito Nazis. Fuck them.

On top of the beans, add some strands of shredded iceberg lettuce, then a little Pico de Gallo that you prepared earlier. Take your steak and chop it into slices, then turn them and chop into chunks. Stick the beef inside. Grate over a shitload of Cheddar and spread a big dollop of guac on top. Little turn of black pepper and then fold that tortilla up. Roll it up until it looks like two cans of Coke end to end, but instead of flimsy aluminum it's made from Mexican bread. Weird description.

Stick it in a really hot oven. I like mine to go brown and crispy and I like it when the Cheddar starts to bubble out and melt all over the interior of your burrito. While that bakes, get ready to plate up ... Get a plate. In one quadrant, place a big hot dollop of refried beans. Add grated Cheddar on top. In another platter-quadrant, place a big spoonful of red rice. I'm finding it very jarring that I'm describing the plating up process using the word 'quadrant'. I bet Mary Berry never described a plate of food using the word quadrant. I'd use some finely chopped spring onion tops to dress the rice.

Then you use the other half of the plate, quadrant A1 through A2 (inclusive), to house the burrito itself. I then take a bit more shredded lettuce and top it with Pico de Gallo. Finally, top your burrito with a big spoon of soured cream and another big spoon of guacamole! Get it on the table. Boom! That's how we do it at the restaurant. That way to dress a plate was what we'd do most plates like in the restaurant. Lettuce, pico, beans and melted cheese and rice. It goes with everything. It's clean and delicious. I love the juxtaposition (sorry) of melting cheese and steak and crisp lettuce and Pico de Gallo.

If you wanted to do a chimichanga instead of a burrito, everything is the same except the cooking method. I'd secure the edges of the burritos with a toothpick and then instead of baking them, you deep-fry them in oil. Please secure the burrito with toothpicks! I've seen them puff up and unroll and dump all their filling out into the hot oil. Dirty.

I must say, I have a soft spot for the chimichanga. It used to be one of the items on the staff menu we could have, free, before our shift. But it was good. Of course, the kitchen boys would always make special hybrid foods for fellow staff members. It wasn't uncommon to see a chimichanga filled with another chimichanga on top of a cheeseburger, hidden under a kilogramme of prawns, secreted 'neath six sizzling steak fajitas. As I said before, we took care of each other.

The nicest thing we served was, and I've drooled over this memory for 20 years, a cheesy sauce called Chilli con Queso. When we made it from scratch, we'd get a huge block of solid yellow cheese from an American company called Kraft. It was like a giant's eraser. Having lived in the States, I realised the whole queso thing was kind of everywhere – not in London though, apart from Chiquito's.

Very often as a waiter, I'd nip into the kitchen and casually lean through the line, steal a few tortilla chips and then saunter up to the sauce section, leaning through, trying to get as much cheesy queso sauce into me as I could.

There was a dish on the menu which was a burrito smothered in that sauce but the sauce was expensive to make, so it wasn't on the staff menu. All the staff were constantly on the hunt for little offcuts and bits of this and that. We were all paid so little that any food you didn't have to buy outside of work meant you could spend more on drink and other saucy items. All I remember eating at that point was food from the restaurant or curry from the Pink Rupee.

Pink Rupee was an amazing Indian/Nepalese place that would stay open late and usually we'd head there Friday and Saturday after our shift to eat and drink and drink and flirt and drink. We kind of bossed the place a bit, we really loved the owners and always tipped huge and they would look after us in return. Everything happened there – kissing, drinks, love affairs, rumours, gossip, fights with other guests and, apart from the excellent and memorable Butter Chicken, the other very important thing to happen there was my confirmation that I had fallen in love with Simon Pegg.

Simon didn't work at Chiquito's, his GF did, and so he'd often join us at the Pink Rupee. We'd been spending a lot of time together and I knew we were falling for each other. One night after a shift, we were sat, heads together, having a laugh and a beer and chatting about *Star Wars*, as we often did, when he grabbed a salt shaker and whizzed it around the table, making the noise of a robot. I knew EXACTLY what he was on about. No one had ever got that before. That was it. I felt the world slow and it was just me and him and that salt shaker and a Butter Chicken. That's all we needed back then. It was 1995.

I wished I had kept the secret for the Queso sauce. Back then, though, there was no general access to that kind of cheese.

I remember at times during the prep of the sauce, me and the prep team, usually Flea and a lovely Ugandan fella called Chris, would be stood around with a 10kg block of orange 'cheese', just passing it around so everyone could see it. It was confusing to all of us, especially our Ugandan kitchen team. They'd talk in hushed whispers about the cheese. They had never seen anything like it. Every now and then someone would have a sniff or even have a nibble, leaving a huge bite mark in it. It honestly tasted like nothing-shit. How on earth it could become yellow heaven was completely beyond me at the time. I miss lovely Chris; he had such a sunny outlook on life. We'd all listen to the radio and laugh and chop veg and stir huge vats of gently frying veggies. It was a really easy, nice, fun, simple time. I miss that. My life is so fucking complicated and frightening and stressful now.

That's a bit sad. I know there'll be a number of people who read this book actually thinking about people who'll bother to read a book versus people who say this thing to me, there's not many people in the centre of this Venn diagram. What I'm not describing very well is that the few humans who might see some of the films I've done or the TV shows or online magazines, may just assume I'm a billionaire with no problems in my life and that all this shit came easy to me. All I'd say to those people is: don't assume you know anything about my life until you've walked a mile in my shoe. I'm only letting you have one of them. Just one shoe. Unless they chose to take me up on my offer one of the days I'm so anxious and tired and mentally completely fucking broken that I can't leave my front room. If you come then, you can actually have both shoes. I don't want to appear churlish.

I remember several different types of tinned chopped chilli peppers. Onion in some form, it may have been onion powder actually ... and then that big yellow, bite-marked, super rubber. It would melt down and mix with all that chilli to form something amazing. Maybe that Chilli con Queso isn't the best example of culinary magic. (Maybe it is?) Reading this book you'll realise, hopefully, that I love my family and although being around humans can be really fucking difficult for me, I love my friends so much too. I don't have many but the ones I have are my fucking heroes. Apart from this, I also love food. I know there'll be people who can barely read saying now, 'Yeah, we can see that fatty...' But I love not just eating it but every aspect of it. What's the famous saying 'Blah blah blah, Death and taxes ...'? I always feel it should include food in some way. Food is so important to every human being. Not always in a good way either, I get that. People struggle with food. Struggle to actually find food, to have enough food for themselves and their families, struggle to eat food, struggle to barely look at food, struggle to walk through a supermarket without having a fucking panic attack, struggle to not stick their fingers down their throats in order for them to feel good about the way they look.

Food is also something you can get addicted to. I've struggled to not hide food and not lie about my food intake, to not hide Snickers bars, to not hide cakes, to not make some excuse to drive the car out and park down by the river and, in a darkened vehicle, eat seven fucking Wispas. You can get addicted to food. It's easy to just shrug that off because it's just food, it's not like it's cocaine, right? Wrong. It's exactly the same. I feel it could even be worse in a way as you can hide all that tasty sugary shit in plain sight. 'Oh, bless him, he's always had a sweet tooth, hasn't he?' 'Yeah, life with Mum and Dad was so awful I used biscuits to make myself feel better.' And that's cool except he now has a heart the size of a bison's. You see how that happens? It's easy. Any addiction that drives a person to lie and hide shit ... Can kill you.

Food and the history of food is also as old as human beings. What an obvious thing to say. What was the first prepared meal? A soup? Or cooking meat? A soufflé? I heard a rumour that the Pyramids were actually giant factories originally used to produce thousands of gallons of hummus every day but I think that's a load of horse shit.

What I also love about the food we eat now is its evolution. It's thousands, no tens of thousands of years old, in some cases. Humans all over the world have become so fucking good at preparing food, so many amazing accidents along the way have happened to make the thing they were preparing ten times better.

There's also that wilder element found in South America, sub-Saharan Africa and Australia where you hear people talking about how to prepare food that, if done wrong, will absolutely kill you. I'm always astonished when you hear old Aboriginal chefs saying things like, 'This must now be pounded nine times so the juice runs clear or you die.' WHAT!!! How many people died finding that out? Why wouldn't you prepare that once and then your mum's eyes bulge and she starts to seize and she drops the baby and all the kids are thoroughly broken watching her shake and foamy-mouth herself to death, and the community gather round and eventually one of them says ... 'Let's not prepare that again. This woman died and now her children will have to be eaten too.' The kids' ears prick up. 'What was that last bit?' 'Nothing, kids,' says Rick.

They didn't say that. They were like 'How many times did Gwen pound those Death Beans?' (Jesus Christ, they're even called Death Beans for fuck's sake. What was Gwen doing?)

One of the older, uneaten kids hollers out, 'Once, Mum pounded them once.'

The locals all chatter and whisper like Ugandans chatting about a magic cube of bright yellow cheese in a hot, noisy market in the North of Kampala, and then they say to everyone ... 'Okay gang, we've had a conflab and it's been decided that whoever cooks Death Beans next should pound them not once, but twice. That should do it. That should make them tasty and edible ...' But it didn't ... it made them worse, the Death Beans pounded twice made people spontaneously combust, just burst into flames right there. Terrible. This is the kind of thing children never get over. It didn't stop there though. That happened another seven times. SEVEN FUCKING TIMES before the mother didn't seize to death or burst into flames or drown, or have a huge aneurism or shit themselves to death, or just wander off into the bush and have a crocodile eat them, or was struck blind and walked in front of an ox cart, or wobbled around seemingly drunk and wandered on to a resting spear.

Why did they keep going? There are so many kinds of this example in cooking. Who ate the first mushroom and didn't die? The whole world of fungi seems like a game of roulette to me. Hundreds of thousands of people must have died trying mushrooms. Maybe old-time humans used prisoners to test the mushrooms. If you died, you were set free, but if you lived and the mushroom was edible, you were put to death for stealing an edible mushroom. That doesn't seem fair really.

I like to imagine what the first human being who ate a lobster looked like ... Someone found this 'thing' trapped by the receding tide in a rock pool and pulled it out while it flapped and snapped its claws to defend itself, even at times releasing a terrifying scream, and thought, 'I'm going to eat this little fucker.'

Here's how it happened ... It was very dark on the island; the beach was littered with broken leaves and smashed coral after the mighty storm that tore up the place. Andy and Lulu were sat huddled by the fire trying to get warm after losing everything in the tsunami, when out of the night crawled a dazed and massive lobster from the darkness. The lobster, dazzled by the flame but also sadly compelled by it too, just kind of wandered into the fire.

Andy screams and Lulu reaches for her stick and smashes the long crab with a log and a bit of its sizzling claw juice flies out and straight into Andy's mouth. 'Mmmm, that tastes nice,' says Andy. Lulu makes to hit it again and Andy stops her and explains that the liquid tastes nice, they're interested now. The lobster is clearly dead and it's turned an orangey red in the fire, and the two humans poke and jab at it and the air is filled with a delicious flavour. As Lulu reaches in and begins pulling it out, the front bit gets caught in a log and the tail snaps off in her hands and it's fucking hot, so she drops it into the sea with a scream.

What Lulu has just done is she's seasoned food for the first time. Andy grabs it and they both sniff and poke at the ice-white lobster tail, curious as to what the fuck is happening right now.

'Go on ...,' says Andy.

'Fuck off, you do it.'

Lulu has such a way with words. Andy shoves a sharp stick into the tail and pulls out a piece of the sea meat and pops it in his mouth ... Horny, but slightly less hungry, he turns to Lulu.

'It's fucking lush, babe. It's not only tasty, but I also weirdly want to try and have children.'

They begin to furiously fuck and eat a lobster at the same time ... I don't know if this is exactly how it happened, but I think it was. How could it have happened any other way? It's impossible. There must be endless stories which are a bit like this.

Do you get what I'm saying about food, though? Everything humans eat has a history ... I'm just about to google a question and I'll give you the answer. The question is this: How many dishes can eggs be turned into? Oh, apparently it's four. Hang on, that can't be right. Okay, there's like over 100 ways to use an egg. That still seems low to me. I'm not sure that takes into account 'foreign' egg users ... I'm looking at you, Mexico. Whatever, I'm right about the death and taxes thing. Can you all make sure people know that it was me that said it. Fried gold was mine too.

Chilli con Queso was Kraft cheese, garlic and chillies, splash of milk. That's easy. I just ordered everything I needed off of Amazon! There aren't many dishes you can order off of Amazon! Of course, having ADHD means I spend a lot of money buying a lot of weird shit on Amazon. I just received seven tins of green chopped chilli in a box and also 500 flat red and white boxes that you fold together and it makes the kind of plate one might use at a carnival to hold a hot dog. Why? Shit like this turns up all the time. I have a long history of ordering things that turn up in huge amounts or on a truck.

When I was 18, I found myself living in the very north of Israel. I loved it so much I stayed, on and off for the best part of two years. The bit I hated though was the food. For me, at that time, it was absolutely shit. If you liked fruit and vegetables and rice and pulses and really good food, then you'd have loved it. If, like me, you were used to eating shit, you were fucked. And since at this age I was still very much in my not-eating-veg stage of my life, it meant the kibbutz was tricky for me when it came to food.

After being there a while, you can work out all the scams, which means you can wheel and deal and in the end feed yourself pretty well. In the morning I'd start work at 6:30am. After a quick coffee, eight fags and a couple of hard biscuits, I'd work until about 8:30am, at which point the factory conveyor would judder to a halt and then it was every man for themselves ... The aim was to get to the front of the line for breakfast, that way you had more choice of the hot breakfast items.

I'd run out of the door and run all the way up a massive hill and straight up the stairs that led to the massive dining room. I wouldn't even break a fucking sweat. It makes me sad I'm not like that any more. It makes me sad I don't have that energy, that verve. I'm ashamed to say that sometimes my knees hurt so bad, it takes me five minutes to walk to the toilet in the night. It sounds like a fisher-man crashing through dry sticks at night.

I think that 18-year-old kid would be absolutely livid if he could see what I did to his exterior. At the start of my time on the kibbutz, I'd notice old-timers with like, ten eggs on their plate. (*heave) That's a lot of fucking eggs. I soon found out why though. Mass cooking thousands of eggs every day meant it was very hit-and-miss when it came to how cooked they'd be. Some were hard and grey like the boiled eyes of a huge dead halibut, while most were a soup of runny yellow liquid with jelly and beaks. (*heave) I learned soon enough, you take ten eggs and maybe you found one or two that were edible. I'd put them in a bowl with mayo and pepper and mash them up, putting it on toast. Lovely. That and hot coffee and some fruit. That was my breakfast every day. Usually.

Hating all/most of the food turned out pretty good for me, for a while. Not eating much and doing hours of manual labour in eye-melting heat and then playing sport and running around all afternoon meant in ten months I lost over nine stone. I looked completely different.

The first time I went home between stays in Palestine, at Heathrow, my mum literally looked right through me. She looked around me, craning her neck to see past this thin, dusty hippy standing in front of her. When she finally focused her eyes on me, she burst into tears.

'What have they done to you?!!'

Again, thinking about that boy, I can't help feeling like I've let him down. I put all that weight back on. I ate a lot of shit. A lot of tasty, tasty, shit. I'd also say that young man had undiagnosed issues that meant he couldn't help himself when it came to eating. An undiagnosed PTSD and a severe undiagnosed ADHD and a ton of anxiety and lifetime of depression meant the tiny plips of joy I got from eating a whole box of Mr Kipling Cherry Bakewells was a kind of validation I needed. It was the dopamine hit I'd later turn to drink and drugs and shitty sexual liaisons to find. So, to that young man, I'd say I'm so sorry but it has a happy ending. I saved us. So far.

Towards the end of my time on the kibbutz, I'd kind of stopped eating. Trying to think about it now, I feel like what I'm writing about was a big thing, but I don't remember it like that. I'm confused. All I can remember eating are bowls of white rice and soy sauce. I'm seeing a red flag waving in my mind as I write this.

Maybe I'd become addicted to the pain and focus not eating brought me. There was definitely a vibe that people were worried about me. People were starting to notice. I guess if you have an eating disorder, the best way to hide it is inside the centre of a drink problem. No one looks past the dirty, dusty shorts with the piss-wet crotch.

I have a memory of a friend I had at the time, Offir, an Israeli, coming to my room with a tray of food and making me eat. We had a definite showdown, he told me the community was worried about me and he'd been sent to watch me and make me eat. I was not happy. 'I'm fine. Seriously. Leave the food and I'll eat it later.' (I won't.)

Offir hated the smell of matches being struck. I'd say it was a phobia, there were rumours floating around that Offir had been captured by Hezbollah and tortured with lit matches. It's got to be bullshit, right? Anyway, I was so pissed off by Offir sat in my room waiting and pressuring me to eat, I took a box of matches, lit one, stuck it back in the box amongst the unlit match heads and tossed it at him. It genied up as they all lit together. I ran off. What a cunty thing to do. When Offir found me later, I totally got a massive and well-deserved dead arm.

The closest town to where my home was in Israel was an ancient place called Safed. This was the place where we, the volunteers, would go to get booze if we were having a party. Usually, three of us would go with a pocket of shekels and a list of stuff to get. Chocolate and shampoo were the winners, and vodka, litres and litres of cheap vodka.

It was an absolute ballache to do the vodka run, but if you could do it quick enough it meant you had about 15 minutes before the bus went back to eat a hot fresh falafel. It was bliss. I'd fallen for falafel months before when I was in Tel Aviv and absolutely broke. I met an English girl who told me there was a falafel stand in the old bus garage that, provided you kept your pitta intact, you could keep going back to fill the soggy pocket with crispy, brown on the outside, green on the inside goodness, all for four shekels.

I also found a place in Safed that did pizza by the slice. I still think about that pizza today, it was amazing. It was exactly like the slices of crispy, buttery cheese pizza you can find in NYC and that I'd eaten years before at Auntie Melanie's house. It was so good. A couple of slices of that and a large, cold Maccabi (beer) hit the fucking spot. It tasted like NYC pizza because the owner was an American from Brooklyn, who also happened to be a fierce Zionist. He still holds the record for the amount of hand guns I've seen strapped to a person. (Six.) He had decided the protection of Israel and its people was more important than a life in the States. He still wanted to eat good pizza though, so he opened his own place, and I'm glad he did.

Sometimes, not often because we always had fuck all money, me and a couple of the others would take a day off work and head into Safed to be a tourist, but mostly to sit and drink cold beer during the day and eat a slice of pizza every 45 minutes or so. It was amazing. I had fallen totally in love with a lovely girl called Claire. I say fallen in love, I thought it was, it felt like it, still does, but knowing me now as I do, the love thing was probably more like me desperately wanting someone to look after me. Please don't leave me!

That felt like my thing, I did it a lot as I got older. I fell in love really quickly and with all of my heart and when they (rightly so) somewhere down the line left me, it enabled the traumatised Sorrow Sucker that lived, that lives, inside me to drop to its knees, tears rolling down its bloated face, waving his fist into the sky screaming, 'WHY!!!!!!!'

Of course, now I know why. Then I didn't. Then it gave me the opportunity to grieve and sob and say, 'Poor old me ...' (Again, very unfuckable by the way.) Me and my friend Richard had taken a day off work that coincided with Claire and her friend leaving the kibbutz. I couldn't work. I wanted to sit in my emotions and feel sorry for myself, so that's what I did. She left and it broke my heart. Poor cunt.

Embarrassingly, after Claire left I probably cried like a grieving African widow for about 50 minutes. Certainly, for most of the bus ride into Safed. I managed to get myself together and we ordered huge beers and slice upon slice of crispy, buttery pizza. I remember sitting there, it was hot and the radio was on. No word of a lie, the first song that came on was by Gilbert O'Sullivan, the name of the track ... 'Clair'! More tears. It was a sign. I should go. I didn't, I rallied and drank and ate pizza. It was nice.

The other nice memory from the kibbutz was sitting in the heavily fortified guardhouse at the main gate of the commune. After Friday night disco had finished, I'd secretly slope off and walk to the guardhouse. They were always nice to me and welcoming, usually around 1am they'd make chips. Amazing chips. The only other time we got chips on the kibbutz was when it snowed. Unless, that is, you were friends with the soldiers.

Here's why those chips were so nice. a) I was completely fuck drunk. b) It was a super-secret sneaky food. Only a couple of the others knew. Obviously, like the film *Cocoon*, eventually too many people found out and fucked it for all of us. c) Onions.

The soldiers had an old-fashioned, plugged-in, filled to the brim with volcanic lard, deep-fat fryer. They even had a little fry basket. Here's the onion bit ... The soldier would take a big white onion and quarter it and drop it in the hot oil to fry and simmer, then they'd put the hand-cut chips into the onion oil. It made the best chips, like if a roast potato and a shallot were killed while fucking in a motorbike accident. Imagine that flavour. I can still taste it in my mouth 30 years on. If the soldiers liked you, they'd drive you back in their armoured jeep after you'd eaten.

Not So Sweet

Favourite kinds of cake:

1) Christmas
2) Wedding
3) Victoria Sponge
4) Lemon Drizzle (but any kind of lemon cake actually)
5) Any other cake that has icing on it

I thought long and hard about adding a Victoria Sponge to the book but, honestly, I don't really bake many cakes. I can, but I don't. I love a decent Victoria Sponge with a cup of tea, it HAS to be heavy with a weight of buttercream. And raspberry jam.

We love finding a family-friendly franchise of garden centres (Squires, etc.) for a Sunday brunch adventure. Head in for a nine-item breakfast and leave with a pretty good homemade Victoria Sponge. And a big tree fern.

If you want to hear my tuppence worth about a cake like the Victoria Sponge, here it is ... Wait around outside some kind of 'centre' which is heavily used by the elderly. Sit in your car and watch for the old ladies coming in and out.

Here's a tip ... If you see them coming out of the toilet covered in white powder, that's not cocaine, it's flour! If they have flour on their clothes, bingo ... Cake makers. They're the ones you want. Once they leave the centre (usually filled to the brim with Drambuie), follow them home and gradually befriend them. Take your time, it'll be worth it. Trust me.

Choose one with thick glasses. Their shortsighted-ness will make it easier to slip, seamlessly, into her life. If you introduce yourself loudly and confidently as someone she *should* know from her life, the aged one, unsure at first, will completely accept you. Once inside her home, make an excuse to go to her toilet, find her dirty washing and, go with me on this, roll in it. Like a terrier in a fox shit, roll in it ... The smell of her old drawers on your clothes is essentially a nasal green light for you, you'll just be accepted. She subconsciously smells another old person and will completely relax around you. It will enable you to enter the nest as and when you choose.

At some point, she will eventually reach into her huge bag looking for a mint. If you're lucky, you'll see it sat there inside, glinting, the book that holds all of her cake recipes! The Holy Grail. Written down long before the age of the cataract took over. The book is creased and heavy with every recipe to every cake known to humans. It's beautiful.

You watch as she clumsily uses her butter claw to finger the book out of her handbag as she finally 100 per cent accepts you into her brood. She offers to make you her trademark, award-winning, buttercream-heavy Victoria Sponge. You did it. It bloody worked.

You sit in her boiling-hot parlour room, just the two of you, eating slice after slice of rich, buttery sponge. At one point, her swollen and flabby ovipositor jabs at the side of my mouth. I'm nervous at first but it jabs again, this time more insistently. I reluctantly open up and the greasy tube slides inside. I'm nervous for a moment until Eileen begins pumping litres of buttercream directly into my mouth. It's incredible. So sweet yet oddly umami.

Eileen squawks about disrespectful Asian teens, swearing or the pointless expense of space exploration, or any other number of mildly racist opinions. This is just part of the buttercream making process. Still, I use my tiny in-ear noiseless buds so I don't hear any of her racism or how lonely she was before she met me. I just want the cake and the warm, fresh buttercream.

I can't imagine how Hayley would react if she could see me gobbling down fresh icing direct from this old woman's musty butter-prong. I can't imagine she'd be happy, so I tell her I'm in a meeting. Which isn't a massive lie.

My greed and hunger has kind of fucked me though. It often does. I promised Eileen I'd attend a Macmillan coffee event with her next month. It was only after I said 'Of course!!!' and she had burst into tears, saying something about, 'No friends and a dropship bombing her family's egg hatchery from orbit' (I couldn't really hear her to be honest, these in-ear buds are great!), that she revealed the event was in Swansea.

Fortunately for me I shot a movie in Swansea recently, so I guess I'll tell the family they need me to shoot more stuff. That works as a cover. FUCK! How do I get out of this? Why does this keep happening? Eileen always insists on a twin room in case she falls and needs help. Why can't I say no? How do I get out of this? All this for fucking cake.

One afternoon, Eileen and I have a lovely lunch in a restaurant in Chiswick. It really is worthy of its star. The food is wonderful. Eileen doesn't really eat food any more but she's paying, so I take the piss a bit. I keep goading her on to drink more and more Drambuie. This makes her super flirty (bleurgh) and while the waiters aren't looking, she keeps dabbing blobs of buttercream down my throat and laughing uncontrollably. Her laughter is so loud it shatters one of the large front windows.

We all watch and laugh as a homeless guy's German Shepherd-cross leans through the broken window and pinches the colonel's turbot straight off his plate. The colonel is fucking LIVID. Eileen, now hammered, slips her flexible gland into his mouth and gives him a dollop of instant chill out. He sits there, dumb smile on his face, dribbling. No one saw and everyone thinks he's broken his brain. Before the ambulance arrives, I hustle Eileen out of there.

We leave and jump into a big Uber en route to Hammersmith, the Lyric Theatre to be precise. Eileen got tickets for a matinee performance of *Charlie and the Chocolate Factory.* There's hardly anyone there and, full of Drambuie, she quickly falls asleep. I shouldn't tell you this but I'm going to ... While Eileen went to the loo in the restaurant, I crushed half a Quetiapine into her Drambuie. The Quietiapine quietens down my psychopaths. It also aids restful sleep. It's working.

Eileen's head slumps back and her thick armoured tail lolls into the aisle behind ours and there it is. I see it, her bag, and inside glinting is her book. The cake book. The book with every cake recipe known to humankind. I'm at my wits' end, I need to get out of this. Yes I love Eileen's tender, icing-filled ovipositor but I'm fucking married! I have three kids. (That I know of.) I can't do this any more. I shouldn't do this any more.

I lean over and, resting on her leathery egg sack, I pull the book out of the bag. It's mine. I stand and wait a second to see if she wakes. From where I am it would be easy for me to toss the book back in the bag and sit down again real quick. She does not re-emerge into this realm. I back out. I'm now in the aisle. I could actually do this. Do it. Run. You never have to see her again. But the buttercream ... Nick ... RUN!!!

As I turn to go, there's a very loud hum and POP as Augustus Gloop is pulled through and out of the chocolate pipe. It rouses Eileen. She instantly feels

I'm missing, opens an eye, sniffs my empty seat. She looks down and her tongue flicks across the open bag. I'm stiff with fear. Her tongue stops flicking and retracts back into her head. She knows.

Eileen turns her head so quickly and sees me, smells me and knows that I have the 'Tome du Gateaux'. I will never forget the sound she produced. I can only describe it as the noise of a Yeti bumming a Frankenstein being caught by the Frankenstein's husband, who happens to be the Loch Ness Monster.

I turn to run as Eileen lumbers up and into the aisle. She lashes her ebony-hard tail out and it cuts an Oompa Loompa in half, poor prick. Now she's after me ... 'WHYYYYYYYYYY!!!!!!!' she howls.

I tear into the foyer and head out on to the street, the doors behind me explode as Eileen hurtles into the sunlight. Blinking and blinded by the sun, she stumbles into the road, is struck and killed by a number 267. Her ancient, crusty carapace literally explodes as the bus ploughs into her. Good.

That night, while watching the news, we hear the report about Eileen's death. Hayley says, 'A poor old alien lady got killed by a bus in Hammersmith this afternoon, that's so sad. Weren't you in Hammersmith today? Did you see anything?'

'Nope.'

I stuff another piece of incredible Victoria Sponge into my mouth and wash it down with hot, strong, yet milky tea. Poor Eileen. She would've loved this.

CRUMBLES

You have to learn how to make a very good crumble topping. Trial and error and years of making them comes in handy here. Or find a great recipe. I never put any nuts or dried fruit in my crumble topping. It's traditional and old-fashioned, and for the one I do it's three ingredients: flour, sugar, cold butter. That's it. I have no idea what's the best flour to use. I grab whatever sugar I can. I generally use caster, but I've used brown and golden caster before, as well as white, and they've all worked great. There's a slight difference in end colour and taste but they were all yummy. Lastly, cold butter you've got directly from the fridge. Unsalted.

Get your big bowl and shake into it 400g flour. (I'm making this up by the way, there's no recipe, I just feel it.) Then your sugar, 200g? Somewhere in that ballpark. And then usually three-quarters of a stick of cold, unsalted butter. Use your knife and chop into small chunks. I like this next bit: make sure your hands are clean and dry and then, what would one call it, flake all those ingredients together. I think technically the technique is rubbing it in.

You need to do it quickly too, before the heat from your hands warms the butter too much. What you need at the end is like crumbs, breadcrumbs. I know I'm there if I can squeeze a handful together and it stays in a hand-shaped clump, which then falls apart when prodded. It becomes like the texture of wet sand. Also, taste it. It should be crunchy and delicious. The boys love eating raw crumble mix. Naughty gibbons.

Now, take that lovely big bowl of crumble mix and

decant it into a big Ziplock bag. The measurements of mine are very hit-and-miss but it should be able to easily cover a dish big enough for six greedy pigs. Take that Ziplock bag and keep it in the fridge. Don't put it on your fruit base now. I've done this before and the liquid from the apples made the crumble damp and horrible. Keep the fruit base and crumble topping apart for as long as possible.

In terms of the fruit base for this one, and it's one I did on Sunday and it worked a charm. Everyone went quiet for two minutes. Everyone had seconds. Dessert is also the thing the kids will join us at the table for. Roast meat isn't all the kids' favourite, but they'll defo sit still for five minutes to have some crumble and ice cream. This is one of those things I like to sit and watch my three-year-old come up with more and more crazy excuses to get another portion. His last being simply the word 'Poo'.

Apples, there are 7,000 different kinds of apple. Wow. That's a lot. I've made crumbles with two of those. Three maybe, at a push. There's only one person I can find who has used every different breed of apple to make crumble with. Dr Sheila Bailey set out in the autumn of 1955 to make apple crumble using all 6,600 types of apple. (Four hundred breeds of apple would be discovered during her crumble mission.) She made nine crumbles a week for 60 years before sadly choking on the last crumble she ever made, number 7,000. She was 85 years old. In 2020, they found the 7,001st apple, in honour of the doctor, they named it the Bailey Choker. It has been described as a pleasantly coloured apple, juicy, sweet, suitable for cooking, but sadly with incredibly thin skin it has a tendency to succumb to worm. A bit like Dr Bailey herself. What a wonderful story.

Obviously, an apple crumble means muggins here has to peel a shitload of apples. I remember peeling apples and potatoes for my mum and having to do it without moaning or I got hit with a brush! On my fucking head! My 11-year-old probably gets through peeling half an apple before he lays on the floor and suggests what I'm putting him through is an assault. I resist the temptation to assault him with a brush. I have to do it. I peel the apples, then I quarter them and then I cut the cores out. You could just peel and core and then cut into quarters. Whatever. Once I have a load of peeled apples, I take a big knob of butter and heat it in a frying pan. I then take a handful of caster sugar and add that to the butter. Shaking the pan, I watch the sugar and the butter turn into a caramel. I then add some good vanilla seeds. (Don't add the pods, also YouTube it. You take a vanilla pod, cut it in half and then drag a blade down the pod so you're left with a lot of little black, heavily scented vanilla seeds, add these to the caramel.) Now toss all the apples in the caramel and squeeze in half a lemon.

Add 150ml water and shake gently at a low temperature to cover the apples with the caramel and cook them until you can easily push the point of a knife through them. Now either put them into the ovenproof dish you're going to cook them in or keep them in a bowl in the fridge covered in clingfilm. If you want to add cinnamon to the caramel, you've then got apple pie crumble. I've done Apple & Raspberry before. Apple & Blackberry. Apple & Pear, Apple & Blueberry, Summer Berries, Peach Crumble,

Nectarine, blah, blah, blah ... If you can cook the fruit, it can be crumbled. I think. I may be wrong, as I said, I'm not a professional.

One of the things I've banged on about throughout this book is learn techniques. This is that but with puddings! Once everyone is ready for dessert, get your apples out and leave for a while to come up to room temperature. Then add a few spoonfuls of water to the base of the apples. It adds a little juice for the apples to sleep in and when they come out, it makes a sweet, lovely, vanilla/caramelly apple gravy.

Take your bag of crumble sand and, using your hands, quickly cover the apples with the mixture. Don't skimp here. I'd love the crumble to be at least one inch deep over the entire dish, some would say I had lost my mind at this point. I laugh at them. 'I'm coming Sheila!!!' I wave my fist at the sky. I catch my 11-year-old looking at me.

'What?'

'Are you okay Daddy?'

'Yeah, I'm fine.'

'Who's Sheila?'

'The Crumble. The Crumble is called Sheila. Go and sit down.'

'Yes, Daddy.'

He's a fucking angel. I grab the crumble (sometimes for fun it's pronounced cruum-blay) and slam it into the oven. Maybe 45 minutes at 180°C? Here or there. When it's ready, the crumble top should be a little brown and bubbles of volcanic apple juice should blob and plip from the odd vent dotted across the surface. This is hot as fuck.

Tell the kids to move and, with tea towels and oven gloves, pop it down on the table and let it sit for five to ten minutes until the plipping slows and then, finally, ceases. Serve a big helping of hot apple crumble and a huge ball of vanilla ice cream on top. You get that lovely bit towards the end when the ice cream has melted a bit and it's all now just sweet liquid ice cream and caramel and succulent little pieces of apple and a super-crispy crumble layer. Get it inside your mouth. It may be awful for diets but your soul will thank you. Trust me, everyone has a fat soul. Heaven is full of fatties. We all die. Not all of us choose to eat crumble and fuck the consequences.

TARTE TATIN

Something else with apples I love, I love eating and I also love looking at pictures of is Tarte Tatin. It's just so beautiful, the way the caramel turns the apples into chubby amber gemstones is so nice inside my brain. Plus, there's always great joy in a dish that needs to be turned out, turning out good. I've done it before a few times when it burned slightly and only four bits of apple plopped out. It happens. Tarte Tatin itself was the result of a mistake, apparently. The two Tatin sisters owned a restaurant and one day struggled to get an apple pie into the oven. In their haste, they dropped the pie.

One of the sisters just picked it all up and put it all in the dish and then to try and save the situation, stuck the pastry back on top. When it was cooked, they got it out and turned it over, discovering there was no pastry bottom but the apples were amber-coloured, crystalline and chubby as fuck. It was dripping with caramel and sitting on top of a crisp base of pastry. They served it and et voilà! ... Tarte Tatin. What a tasty mistake.

It's not easy at first but, like oral sex, you get better at it the more you do it. Of course, it means me peeling loads of fucking apples again. Whatever. It's completely worth it. Again, the Tatin is something you can adapt and adjust and do with different fruit, not just fruit either, you can make nice savoury Tatins using sweet baby carrots or shallots or beetroot and goat's cheese. Yum. Perfect for a ladies' lunch with a bag of crispy salad and a vat of cold rosé.

I have made apple Tatin, I've done one with big, juicy, ripe plums, pineapple, banana is lovely, also pear is delicious, too. Don't ask me for measurements. As usual, Brain knows best. Trust Brain. Also ... you know I bought a proper Tatin dish off eBay (or three). I can't help it. It's lovely. It's made for apples, so let's focus on that one.

I've found lots of different ways to group the apples. Sliced in half or quartered and just pushed in. Or, and this is my favourite: halved and cored but then you squeeze them into the dish standing up. It looks so fucking Français. I'm getting ahead of myself. Put the Tatin dish on top of the hob and turn up the gas. Then put 150g golden caster sugar and maybe 100g unsalted butter into your dish. Cook together until you have a lovely caramel. Don't overcook too much at this point. Remember that you're going to cook this in the oven as well, that means the caramel too.

Once it's blonde and bubbly, it's time to squeeze in the apples. Here's a warning ... That caramel is going to

be so frigging hot. Be careful. Dry your apples. If you've washed them or they're super juicy, the caramel will spit when you site them. But site them you must. Get as many of those peeled/cored apple halves in there as you can, really shove them in. I find that I cut a few spare little quarters and slices to shove in between the pretty halves. I then turn the heat down slightly and cook the apples and sugar on the hob for about 15 minutes or so, then ...

And you could've done this earlier ... take a sheet of puff pastry, measure out the size of the dish you're using for the apples plus an inch over. The inch over is so we can push it between the apples and the rim of the dish. We want essentially a puff pastry bowl holding all those lovely apples. Push it right down the side.

Put your oven on at about 180°C and get it nice and hot. Take your apples off the hob and lay the pastry on top, tuck that puff pastry disc right in. I use the handle of a spoon to make sure I get it exactly where I want it. When this is done, oven please. For about 35 minutes. Every ten minutes, open the oven and, using a wooden spoon or a fat spatula or something the shape of a beaver's tail, push down the pastry base. It's puff pastry, so it wants to rise, but don't let it. This method makes a really nice, fragile, crispy base.

After 35 minutes (more or less), the pastry should be crisp and brown. Turn the oven off and take the tart out. Let it sit for a couple of minutes. Not too long though, you need to turn it out while the caramel is still super liquid. Ideally you'd have a plate that was flat enough to leave no gaps between the plate and the Tatin dish. Lay the plate on top and, using a good tea towel, flip the tart and the plate over as quickly and efficiently as is possible. This is not the time to fuck around. It's so hot. Flip it and leave it. If you're skilled/lucky, you'll feel the tart drop out of the pan and when you lift the dish off, you'll be met with a wonderful sight. A Tarte Tatin. All the apples will be, what I'm calling, jewelled and faceted, as they snuggle together covered in caramel. The pastry, crisp, buttery and holding all those sweet apples. (Be careful flipping around hot caramel. It can be super dangerous. Be mindful.)

Sometimes when I turn out a Tarte Tatin there'll be a couple of gaps where apples stick and stay inside the dish. If this happens, don't panic. Scrape them out and stick them back into the spaces where they should sit. Half the time you'd never know. Punters won't, look at them laughing and spitting and betting on the lizard races. Disgusting.

I find the Tatin to be a wonderful slicer. The pastry remains crisp, and the soft apples and caramel snuggle up top. Vanilla ice cream for me, please. Or cream, a little single cream might be fun. It also looks great. This is a dish where normal people who don't cook end up thinking you're some kind of fucking wizard. Once you get the hang of it and understand, technically, chemically and physically what's going on, it just gets easier and easier. You'll be confident enough to try more things. Again, this is part of being able to cook that I love. How often do you have dinner with mates and someone brings an incredible-looking Tarte Tatin to the table? Hell, even a shit-looking one? It must be 15 years for me. Cooking is a gift and it's all free. (Apart from obviously the food cost, which can be absolutely crippling, especially if you're cooking using eagle's eggs and elephant ham. I've never used elephant ham.)

PEAR & ALMOND TART

Another sweet treat we love is Pear & Almond Tart. This is another one that takes a while and needs you to use a few different techniques. If you don't fancy it, buy one. There is no shame. Or just poach some pears in a little water and vanilla and sugar and lemon zest and serve that as a pudding, with some ice cream. That syrup will be amazing. Delish. You could also do that with peaches and nectarines. Lovely.

I'm going to prepare my pears first. To a nice big sauce-pan, add water, caster sugar, vanilla pod (split and scraped), lemon juice and the zest from the lemon. I'd suggest peeling it like a spud and dropping the peel in like that, it's super removable that way. Also, sometimes I've dropped in a star anise but recently I've decided I hate the taste of star anise. Stick it in the bin along with all the fennel you can find.

Bring this liquid to a simmer, let's reduce it slightly and make it sweeter and a bit thicker, this is our poaching liquor. Peel the pears, use the coring tool (I got three from Amazon) to core the pears and then slice in half. Poach them in the sweet syrup for ten minutes, a real gentle simmer. Keep trying to push a knife into it, it should go through but with a little pressure pushing back. Remember this will cook more in the oven. When the pears are done, pull them out of the liquor and leave them in the fridge.

What I usually do now to get super flavour in the finished tart is simmer the liquor down until only a dense sticky, sweet liquid remains. I'll use a little brush at the end and paint this on to the finished pears for some extra shine. Careful not to wet the frangipane around the pears, I've found the liquid takes the crispness away.

For the frangipane

200g soft unsalted butter

200g caster sugar

160g ground almonds

100g self-raising flour

2 eggs, plus 1 yolk

I have a nice little hand mixer I bought from Amazon. This is deployed during times of frangipane. Nice big bowl and whisk all the ingredients together apart from the eggs. Put the eggs in one at a time and at the end. Make sure they're mixed in well. If the mixture splits slightly, add a little more flour, about a tablespoon. Lastly, add the remaining egg yolk. Now taste it. It has raw eggs, so don't be preggers, but it should be lovely and sweet and almondy.

I take a big spoon or a big spatula and I empty all the

mixture into a big Ziplock bag. Note of forthcoming fun ... We're going to cut the corners off this bag later and use it like a piping sack. So fun. For now, leave it in the fridge. You can also make loads and freeze it. I do this at Christmas as I'm never sure when I'm going to need a little Christmas Frangipane!

Tart casing ... Obviously mine is a block of ready-made shortcrust pastry or sweet pastry that I will remove from the fridge to bring to a little higher temp, and then quickly roll and line a fluted tart tin with a removable bottom. I would now stick that in the fridge for five minutes to re-cool slightly. While that is happening, I pull out a piece of greaseproof paper that is big enough to line the pastry tin and go way over the sides too.

Pull the chilled tin with pastry out of the fridge and scrunch that paper up as tight you might. Then unscrunch and lay in the bottom of the pastry. I have a really nice jar of ceramic baking beads, about 1kg. I got them from a place online called Amazon, I don't know if anyone else has seen the website, it's pretty great. Empty the ceramic beads into the paper-lined pastry case. It should line the base completely. The whole point of this section of the recipe is to 'blind bake' this tart base so it's crisp and hard and ready to take all the filling later. It's going to be a pastry shell. Throw this weird paper/dough/bead monstrosity into a hot-ish oven at 180° C for 15 minutes.

After this time, it should kind of be cooked and firm. Remove the paper and the beads and put the case back in for another ten minutes. Don't overcook it, this is going back in the oven later, once it's loaded. That's all the prep done. Wait ... Once the tart is cooler, take a long sharp knife and trim all the excess pastry off from around the rim. Now all the prep's done.

Put the kettle on and have a nice cup of tea. Just sit there and don't look at your phone, just sit and drink a cup of tea, take that time for yourself. That's yours. Finished? Ready? Okay. Let's do it. Take your frangipane and squeeze it all into one corner of your Ziplock bag. Take scissors and cut the corner off. Pipe a thin layer of the almond paste all over the bottom of the now-cooled tart. Then push the cooked pears into this thin layer of frangipane. I tend to arrange the fat bottoms facing the edges of the tart and the tapered tops funnelling towards the centre of the tart.

If I've done it right, I can get six halves of pear going around the tart. I want everyone to have a whole half a pear. If there's more people, bake a bigger tart, or people just get less than a whole half of pear. Simple. Put the pears core-side down. I want the big, white, shiny dome of the peeled and glossy pear facing upwards.

Take the rest of your frangipane and go around the whole tart, filling in the gaps around all the pears. It does not have to be very deep. If the pears are covered up to their shoulders, that's fine. This frangipane will rise a lot in the oven. But YouTube this, don't read my basic waffling and ever feel like you know what you're doing. It's an easy technique to get when you watch it but it takes pages to write, clearly, how a human might do it. Also, don't ever feel like you have to use all the frangipane. I want you to be able to see pears, they look sexy, like big white arses poking out of a bubble bath.

Bake this in a hot oven, at 180°C for 35–45 minutes. Signs it is done: it's risen and almost consumed the pears. The almond batter is now firm and nicely browned. It's done. Take it out, pop it on a bread board, don't fiddle with it and just look and listen to it and smell it. It's a real thing, not just of beauty, but something you should be super proud of. You've made this thing come into existence. You made this happen.

After your blood pressure has got back to normal, take the tart out of the tart tin (google it). I guarantee you'll be using a short stout beaker or a tin of syrup to push the tart through and out the top of the removable ring. Don't feel you have to get the metal tray from out the bottom. If you can, do. If not, serve it with the disc still in place. It'll make cutting it easy anyway.

Guys, you just made a fucking pear and almond tart! Look at it. It's amazing. You're like some kind of French pâtissier. What an achievement. Something to look out for as it cools: as the tart cools my pears have tended to shrink down a bit and it means there's a little space between the fruit and the frangipane. It's not always like this, and it still tastes amazing. Frangipane is pretty amazing, actually. I may contact the Pope and see if we can do anything about canonising frangipane. St Frangipane as she'll be known going forward.

The Pear & Almond Tart is an absolute staple in my house. In terms of you, dear reader, and the techniques, you can now make an incredible tart. The blind baking of a pastry-lined tart case is a technique you'd use to bake a load of amazing tarts. Tart au Citron. Delish. Chocolate Tart. Bosh. Bakewell Tart. Yesss! Once you've learned how to blind bake, it's something you'll have in your brain forever. For me personally, it's so nice to be able to treat friends for a dinner thing or staying with someone and giving them a homemade tart as a thank you. People really appreciate it. This technique is also the basis for quiche.

CHRISTMAS BAKEWELL

This Christmas I had a flash of genius. 'Let's make a Christmas Bakewell.'

'What? Who the fuck said that?'

'Anne, Sir.'

'Say it again, Anne.'

'Sir, umm, uhhh. We should make a Christmas Bakewell.'

'Go on, Anne ...'

'Instead of raspberry jam, Sir, I thought we could use ...'

'Use what?'

'I don't want to say, Sir ...'

'SAY IT ANNE!!!!' He slams his hand on the desk. The kids squeal and jump.

'In ... In ... Instead of jam we could use mincemeat, Sir.'

It seems the whole class is now holding its breath. Sir stands. His face and body turned away from us towards the board. He's muttering something the children can't hear. This isn't good. Anne knows it. She drops her head on to the desk wishing Lord Hadron would open the earth around her and swallow her up like he did her mother, eight years before. Then Sir speaks, whispering at first.

'Instead of jam we could use mincemeat. Crisp tart shell, mincemeat and Saint Frangipane atop her heavenly throne above.'

Sir spins around, his eyes joyous and frantic. He jumps into the air clicking his heels together. He runs to Anne's desk and leaps upon it, he performs a little jig. 'You've bloody done it Anne!!!'

'What have I done, Sir?'

'You've only gone and broken Einstein's Bakewell Code!'

'I have?'

'You have!'

Everyone is thrilled and they've gotten out of their seats and they're whooping and cheering. Something incredible has happened. Sir leaps across from Anne's desk on to another which is covered with papers. They slide out from beneath him as he lands. His legs are cast into the sky, Sir takes flight. The class gasp. Sir is now horizontal but 6 feet above the floor of the classroom. Everyone is spellbound as he seems to just hang there a moment.

Then gravity takes charge and as he falls back to Earth, he tries to spin like a falling Maine Coon but he can't. His big head strikes the desk. A large rectangular section of jagged skull breaks loose inside his head and pushes into his soft brain. It triggers his last living memory, seeing a large, black labrador run on to the pitch during a cricket match and lay a massive stool right on the wicket. He was ten. Fin.

Sir's head is jammed under the desk, his heavy body falls the other way. The crunching sound of vertebrae shattering is unforgettable. The children scream. Sir's body crumples in a heap. Letting out a loud, gwelpy death guff, he lays bent on the floor, massively dead.

The kids flee the class, except for Anne. She sits down. Choked, terrified, smiling?

'Goodbye Sir. Have a nice trip.'

Fuck! It was Anne all along. RUN!!!

So, for the Christmas Bakewell, I didn't use a round tart tin, I used a long rectangular one. It's about 4 inches wide by 12–15 inches long. It still has a removable base and obviously the tricky element with this is trying to get your pastry to fit a non-round tin, but you're smart, you'll figure it out. I know it. Only smart people will buy this book. You can make it work. Or buy a huge Dairy Milk and eat it in bed with a hot cup of tea.

Cook exactly as you would a round one: crumpled paper, baking beads, remove, finish the case empty until pleasantly biscuit coloured. Remove. Trim. Cup of tea. You want the case cool, then ... A jar of Christmassy mincemeat. Spread it nicely to fill the base of the tart case. I'll assume that you already have a nice bag of Saint Frangipane's body ready to deploy. Squeeze it across the mincemeat and then bake until the almond paste is not wet wobbly when you shake it. It should be nice and brown. Get it out and let it cool a bit. Remove from tart case, again don't worry about the bottom bit. Leave this to cool and then, make it snow. Nope, I'm not suggesting you cover the dish in coke, I'm suggesting you cover the tart with a layer of icing sugar. Like snow, at Christmas. Enjoy. I was thrilled when I posted pics on Insta and some actual chefs said things like 'What an amazing idea ...' (Yeah, I guess. Thanks Anne. Wink.)

TARTE AU CITRON

Another one of my favourites is Tart au Citron. Lemon tart. This is so nice and I always serve it with berries and perhaps a little fruit sauce made from other berries. Chaps, make and blind-bake a tart case. Easy. Also, thinking about what you can now do, it makes looking at recipes online or in books so much easier because you're tuned into the language and it's not frightening any more.

Get a medium saucepan and half-fill it with water. This is going to be used to melt the 275g caster sugar I haven't yet told you about. It's going to be a bain-marie, a water bath. The energy the water produces by going from a liquid state to a gaseous one will melt the sugar that sits in a bowl above it. Finely zest five lemons on to the sugar using a Microplane. (Amazon have thousands in stock. Also coming all the way from South America you'd think you'd have to wait ages for the stuff you buy online but you don't. It's here sometimes the same day!) Slice the lemons in half and squeeze four of them into the sugar/ zest chalice. Take out pippys.

Crack four eggs into a jug and whisk gently. Pour these whisked eggs into the sugar and lemon bowl, then set it over, but NOT TOUCHING, the simmering water. Heat gently, stirring all the while. Listen up fucksickles, chemistry is about to happen. The mix will thicken to the consistency of lemon curd, which should take about 20 minutes. Lift off the bowl, leave the filling to cool for ten minutes, then whisk in the 300g cold unsalted butter. Cut this into cubes first and plop them in a few at a time.

If you're concerned you may have curdled the egg a bit or you want it to be super-smooth, unload the mixture through a fine sieve and rub it through with a spatula. It'll catch any filth or lies that may have fallen in. Pour this wobbly lemon mixture into your pastry case. Right to the top. Because this may be a little more runny than other stuff we've done, I'd say place your pastry case on a baking sheet first and then slide the lot into the oven for, at a guess, about 40 minutes at 180°C. When I open the oven, I very gently wobble the lemon yellow jelly. You should get a vibe from it that it's kind of done or not. If it's super wobble, give it another five minutes, but if it looks fine, let's get it out.

Look at that. Look what you just made! Again! Fuck! You're amazing. Leave this somewhere cool, like Copenhagen, for at least one hour. This tart will firm up and set so nice. When you cut a slice sometimes you can kind of see through the gelatinous lemon filling a bit and get the feeling you're staring through a wobbly shard of frozen piss. Delish.

I mostly serve this with big, sweet raspberries and a raspberry compote. It's completely unimaginative and because I like the taste and the colours go nicely together, I rarely do anything else to be honest. Again, not a chef ... But blackcurrants would work. Blueberries would work. Blackberries, the jewels of the hedgerows, would work great. You could even do a sweet Berry Medley, use them all, use every berry.

Let's focus on juicy raspberries. I'd get two different kinds. Shitty cheaper ones for the sauce. And big, ripe, sweet, medal-winning rasps to sit atop the slice. Feed the eyes, yeah?

I know we've used a lot of sugar for the tart but we need a little more for the compote. By the way, I've no idea if this is a trad compote. It's just the way I've always done these fruit sauces and it's easy and the end product is delicious, so I've never questioned the technique. Also, this feels like if you wanted to you could stamp on a raspberry and that would be fine. Just find a way to suit not only what you like, but your kitchen, your 'can't be arsed level' and your budget. People care that you've given a shit and produced magic. They don't care whether your method is that which is written up in Escoffier's – a guide to modern cooking. No one gives a fig. (Which is also a recipe in Escoffier's master work ironically.)

Take all the shitty little bent raspberries and place them in a pan on the gas. Now add perhaps 250ml water, one tiny squeeze of lemon juice and about two large tablespoons of icing sugar. (Or honey.) Gently let this start to simmer. Be really gentle with it. Imagine it's your chubby one-year-old daughter and she's just fallen off a high bed on holiday in Crete. Lift her up. Kiss her. Give her a little Mini Milk.

Stir your raspberry mixture until all the red jewels have popped and it's just essentially liquid. Turn the gas off. Let it sit a while. Taste it. Lovely. It may need a bit more sugar but we'll discuss that in a second. The texture has also changed a bit too. It might be a little more 'jammy' now.

Get a small, clean saucepan. In its mouth, lay a fine mesh sieve, into the sieve pour the jammy rasps and then, with the back of a spoon, push all the liquid through into the clean pan below. Get it all out and make sure to get it all off the sieve too.

It's done. That's how I make a compote. Now I may even

add a little water to this if I wanted to make it a little more 'sauce-like'. You should definitely taste this, a lot. Is it sweet enough? Raspberries should be a little tart I think. Weigh up adding another spoonful of icing sugar at this point. The tart is sweet and the point of the sauce is to cut through that sweetness with something fresh and fruity. Feel it out. Make a choice, own it.

Cut a slice of this tart. Set it upon a nice white plate. Add some of the big, fancy raspberries on top and all around, and you can either pass the sauce around in a gravy boat or, as I like to do, put a little splash on the plate and then sit the slice on top and the raspberry all over. It's a very good thing you've just done.

I love that bit in the first *Matrix* movie when Neo says, 'I know Kung Fu.' You can now do that with Tart au Citron – 'I know Tart au Citron.' Oh my God! What an amazing movie that would be. And instead of John Wick, it's a young Mary Berry that says it. And Mary Berry is played by Amelia Jones. This idea is great. I'm going to DM Amelia. If I can get her to attach, this may have traction. The problem we've had with the Mary Berry biopic is she insists the whole script be written in Alphabetti Spaghetti on sheets of fresh lasagne. a) It costs a fortune and b) although tasty, it's essentially unreadable by the time it's been posted out to producers/actors/agents etc. Also, a lot of actors won't even look at a script if it isn't gluten-free. It's a shame because it's an incredible story. A mix between *Inglourious Basterds* and *Mad Max* but set in a service station near Maidstone. There's a whole incredible set piece where she drives a huge sausage roll through a cathedral. Pastry and myrrh everywhere, Mary rides atop like a horny Valkyrie!

I can't get anyone to read it. Mary keeps saying, 'Get them to eat the script, dear.' Mary believes that somehow their brains will, via osmosis, just have the script pop into their minds. That wouldn't work. Would it?

LEMON DRIZZLE

I was watching a health guy on YouTube a while ago and his whole bit was this: you can eat all the pies and buns and cakes you want, but you have to make them from scratch. That's cool. I cooked a Lemon Drizzle cake that afternoon. Me and Hayley sat in bed and ate big slices with hot cups of tea. It was totally worth it. Just that slice of lemony, spongey, sugary cake gave us a moment. We loved each other and had a kiss and watched four episodes of *Below Deck Down Under*.

Food is not something that resides completely on the physical plane alone. That piece of cake took time and passion and care to make. It was presented as a secret naughtiness that the kids couldn't see, that was just for us. It actually connected us as people. It briefly made us one. We sat in silence, our connection deeper than words, we shared an experience together, and it bought us closer and for a second we forgot the kids and finding work and paying the mortgage and then we kissed and laughed.

Fuck dude, that was just lemon zest and eggs and sugar and flour, and it did that! That's what food is for me. It can induce kisses. It can also induce anger. And passion, intense joy, silence, tears in some cases, laughter in others. It can disgust and it can astonish. It has the power to heal and it can dredge up long-dead memories and it can re-unite the dead with the living. What a fucking thing. Here's the recipe for the Lemon Drizzle cake that brought us a tiny bit closer that night, even if only for those four episodes.

You need ...

3 eggs

175g self-raising flour

175g caster sugar

200g soft unsalted butter

2 teaspoons baking powder

1 big lemon, zested using a fun Microplane (Don't throw the lemon away, you'll need its blood later)

100g granulated sugar

Put the oven on to 180°C. And here's something we haven't mentioned for five pages: a lovely big mixing bowl. A cloth, folded neath the chrome eye that dost prevent slippage!

I have a hand mixer, I also have a stand mixer but it's big and lives up above the fridge in a cupboard that's so full of culinary booby traps I daren't even open it for fear of losing my front teeth. I'll use the hand mixer ... Beat the eggs, flour, sugar, butter, baking powder and lemon zest together until smooth. Easy. I have a nice, very well-used, cake tin for this. Not round, rectangular, nice steep, high sides, coated in Teflon, slidey as heck, this is perfect for LDC. It's about 15 inches long and 3 inches high, that kind of size. Even though I'm 99 per cent sure it won't stick, I can't be 100 per cent sure. So, we're going to line the tin.

I use butter and greaseproof paper and some decent scissors. This is definitely something you get better at the more you do it. I'd absolutely suggest watching how to do it on YouTube. I can essentially cut out from memory the template for the liner I'll need. Wipe the inside of the tin with the butter and then line the tin. If you're clever, you can include a little foil or paper handle which makes getting the cake out child's play. You simply lift it out like a brick in a bra. Also, if push comes to shove, you basically cut out five rectangles of greaseproof paper and install them in the cake tin as individual facets. Would totally work.

Pour your mixture into the tin and bake for 40 minutes. Visual cues the cake may be ready: it shrinks from the sides and when you push a skewer in it comes out clean. It's springy, so springy that a family of Jewish mice could use it as a trampoline at a mouse bat mitzvah. Cute image.

Add the juice from the big lemon you used earlier to 100g granulated, bog standard sugar. Stir until it's dissolved. Take a skewer and shank the cake 21 times. Laugh and walk off quickly, remember to lose the shank as you flee. The prison guards will never know it's you. Pour in the lemon and sugar mixture and leave the cake to cool.

Once it has cooled, lift the cake out, peel the paper off and enjoy the first look at your lovely cake. Well done. Put the kettle on. You should have tea to go with this.

This cake, like lots of cake before it, fills my house up with the most wonderful smell. What I also like about this cake is if you've used nice, decent, Burford Brown-style eggs, the ones with great orange yolks, the colours are amazing. The sugar in the cake has caramelised as you bake it and the outside is a lovely tanned colour, while the inside is a bright yellowy orange from the eggs. It's what I call a three-sense cake. (Never called it that before.)

CHOCOLATE TART

Last tart ... My mate Mark (Boney) loves chocolate. If him and Louisa and their boys come over, I'll always make him this. Our children really love each other and have been friends from birth, but they're also a little crazy and I find the shit (mess) the kids produce and leave around the house makes my eye twitch a bit, I can feel an episode arriving.

Louisa has learned the signs and will often place a loving hand on my arm and say something soothing like, 'We'll sort it all out before we go.' She's an angel. It's nice having those mates that all had kids at the same time and you're close enough to say stuff like 'My kid's a fucking dickhead at the moment' or quietly through gritted teeth, 'I couldn't hate them more right now.' And it not be a problem. What's tougher is when you don't know the people you're with and you end up saying something to one of the kids like 'Eat a shit you little helmet.' A lot of the younger mums take offence at language like this at Snakes and Ladders.

The first time I met Louisa it was a little dinner party at mine for four people. I was nervous and wanted to impress, so I cooked my heart out. We ate and laughed and it was going great. After dinner I proudly brought in the dessert, which I had really put a lot of effort into, a baked NYC-style cheesecake. It looked so beautiful. I'd perfected the recipe so the top did not crack. Sweet. I came and dropped it at the table and went back into the kitchen to get the coulis. When I returned I found my beautiful, uncracked cheesecake now had a big smiley face on top of it. Louisa, drunk and smiling, licking the cheesecake off her fingers, clearly guilty.

Why the fuck would someone do that?! It's crazy. I know she thought I'd bought it, so didn't realise the pain she'd caused. She was fairly mortified next day when she was sober. But I didn't care. I thought it was amazing. I fell for her a little that day. To this day our WhatsApp group is still known as Cheesecake Destroyer.

Me and my ex-wife went on holiday once to the south of France for maybe four nights, just a little getaway before we had our son. We had a great suite and the hotel had a lovely pool, good food. We were sat poolside one morning and a rich British-Persian family we'd spent a lot of time watching through sunglasses came down after breakfast to use the pool. Great. The dad was a big fat beachball with no hair. He was like the cartoon baddie, Kingpin. None of the family really liked each other and the strain of having two kids under three years old meant that Mum and Dad bickered constantly. It was wonderful to watch while pretending to be asleep in the warm sun.

At one point Dad was in the pool throwing the three-year-old up in the sky and every time he caught the child, quite loudly he'd say, 'I don't like you!' Throw innocent child up into sky. Catch.

'I don't like you.' I know it's desperately sad and, yes, I feel sorry for the kids, but fuck, we laughed. What kind of dad says that?!

Anyhoo, let's make a nice chocolate tart for Boney and Lou and our kids and the mess they cause and nice friends who make the world a better place.

Make a tart case … Here's a slight difference, because the mixture you're going to put in this case is liquid, I need you to do a little something different. Take the baking beads and paper out as normal, bake for another however many minutes and then take it out. Set aside. Crack an egg into a cup and whisk vigorously. Then paint the bottom of the tart case all over with the beaten egg and send it back into the oven for a further two to three minutes. This bakes the layer of liquid egg hard and essentially seals the case, ready to accept my hot liquid.

I've done tarts before where the pastry cracks when the weight of the filling presses into it, and when you get the tart out, there's filling everywhere. Barely any left in the tart. It's funny but sad too. Like when they execute a stand-up comedian.

Let's talk about filling …

320ml(ish) double cream

250g caster sugar

pinch of sea salt flakes

125g soft unsalted butter

450g good cooking chocolate (75 per cent or darker)

125ml whole milk

Pour your DC (double cream, cool people are calling it DC right now. It's back, as predicted by moi) into a nice saucepan with your sugar and a little pinch of salt and bring to a gentle, rolling boil.

The moment it boils, turn out your flame. Add your butter and that nice chocolate. If you have to spend a bit more on good dark chocolate, you should do it if you can. It's a chocolate tart. The chocolate should be good. Gently, and even a little erotically, stir the fluid. As it cools, add in the milk between stirs and you should notice this becoming shiny and smooth. Allow to cool a bit. Pour this amazing liquid into a jug. Now pour it into the tart case. Shake a bit to even out the surface and take this tart to Stockholm to cool down and set completely.

It's a super-rich tart, so you don't need much. (Unless you're Boney.) They always get about half the tart to go home with, while I silently rail against it with Hayley. She's like, 'Take it all home guys.' I'm livid. I want the kids in bed and me and Hayley eating some tart with hot tea in peace.

GATEAU BASQUE AND NYC

Obviously these cheesecakes are different. One is from New York, the other is from the Basque region. It's in Spain. If you can make one, you can make the other. The only difference in my eyes is the biscuit base. You'd take a load of digestives, smash 'em to fuck. Take a load of butter and melt it until it's a liquid, tip the biscuits in. The butter should act as a kind of mortar. You'd put greaseproof paper in the bottom of a loose-bottomed tin and then tip the biscuits in. Tamp down with the back of a spoon and also draw the biscuit up the side a bit, so it kind of makes a bit of a biscuit bowl. Bake in the oven at 180°C for 18 minutes so that it bakes a bit hard. Leave this to one side to cool. I'm now going to drift off and make the Basque cheesecake but there'll be a point in another universe where we'll intertwine and NYC and Basque will become one ... We RIDE!!!

This is one of those desserts (this phrase probably crops up in every cookbook written since 1987) that is a) fucking easy, b) looks complex as hell and is c) tasty. Tasty, very, very tasty. It's also one of the only dishes that I'm happy burning. All that sugar in the mixture makes the top layer burn in the hot oven. Don't panic though, it's meant to.

Somehow gather these items ...

butter

900g cream cheese

300g sugar

6 large eggs

500ml double cream

1 teaspoon vanilla extract

45g plain flour

Springform tin. Cover with butter and then take a large square of greaseproof and crumple it up, then lower the bottom disc into it and close the springform. The paper should be crumpled into the sides and up out the top. Trim if it's mega long out the top. I know writing this confuses me, so let me simplify this. When it's cooked, you want to be able to release the springform and the cheesecake and the paper come out together. With the burnt cake nestled in the paper. Right? (Call the Basque Home Office if confusion continues.)

Put this on a baking sheet in case you fuck it up. I'd rather clean a baking sheet than, oh my God, I can hardly write this ... Boiling hot oven, misplaced greaseproof, half a gallon of eggy, sugary liquid flooding out of the springform and on to the boiling floor of the oven beneath. Steam, smoke, lava, tears.

Beat the cream cheese and sugar together in a big stainless-steel bowl. Mmmmm, steel. Cold, Welsh steel. Yummo. Don't use a spoon. Use a hand mixer or a stand mixer. If it's measured as a 1–10, set the speed to 3. Every couple of minutes, scrape all the cream cheese and sugar off the sides and back into the centre of the bowl. This initial mix should only be three to four minutes. We want the sugar dissolved and the cheese smooth like Billy Ocean. Turn up the blending speed to 5 and gently add the eggs, one at a time, blending softly between eggys. Every now and then scrape down the sides to ensure complete mixing. Now turn the blender down – to 3.5 – and add the cream and the vanilla. Turn off the machine and then add the flour; use a hand tool now in a nice figure-of-eight action. The cake will thank you later.

The final mixture should be glossy and rich and smooth and sexy. As. Fuck. You could pour this on yourself and wear it to the Met Gala. Which is actually in NYC, which is where our next segue is from. If you wanted to do the NYC version, now would be the time you poured the batter into the biccie bowl you made. If the Basque region is where you want to be, pour the mixture into your specially prepared, paper-lined springform tin.

Let's talk about the oven ... For Basque you need it hot, very hot at first, 220°C for at least 45 minutes. Keep eyeing it though. You can always have a tinker if yours looks too burnt – after all, you want to eat it, not sprinkle if over a piece of privately owned woodland in Sussex like we did with Nan.

For the NYC, you'd put it in a cooler oven for a similar time – 45–50 minutes. Remember, Basque, you want to be burnt (caramelised) and sweet and brown. NYC, you want smooth and white/yellow like camel's teeth. Both the cheesecakes need to be removed and cooled for at least five to six hours. The Basque will fall and contract and look like a dark brown cheese sat in its paper shroud. Pull it out and leave it in the paper and let it cool. Serve at the table in the paper. It looks great. Compote, anyone?

EASY LOLLIES

Surely you could just buy the kids lollies? Of course I could, and we do, but I can also make them and get the kids to help me make them. Once they're invested in a process, you've got them. They're in! Generally, I'll wait until they're out at the park before I make lollies. I do it this way so they don't fuck it up. Sometimes, though, their assistance is, sadly, unavoidable.

The first lollies I made came about because ADHD had ordered 4kg tangerines from somewhere in Northern Tunisia.

I didn't want them to go to waste, so I peeled what we hadn't eaten, roughly 3.5kg tangerines. I placed them in a big vat/container/bowl and, using my hand blender, blitzed them down, literally to a pulp. They smelled amazing. Having matured in the lush, subtropical forests of Pépinière, I knew these tangerines would make wonderful frozen treats for my spoiled, middle-class children.

I poured all the pulp, in batches, through a fine sieve. Using the back of the ladle, I made sure as much juice as possible had been harvested. I then took a knife and cleaned the sieve so I had all the juice. Sadly, I then binned the pulp. I bet there's a recipe somewhere for a Tunisian tangerine cake that calls for this pulp. Find it out. You make it! Lollies and cake from one fruit. Wow. Maybe there is a god?

I used a spoon and tasted the juice. Boy, oh boy ... It was amazing. I could taste the warmth of Tunisia itself. I could taste the hope of the blind fisherman. I could taste a tangerine, a nice tangerine. I poured the juice into the lolly moulds and shoved them in the freezer. When they came out and we all had one after dinner, it was amazing. We all sat outside and silently enjoyed those lollies. What a simple thing. Frozen fruit juice.

Other things I have lollified ... Strawberries. Take loads of strawberries, blitz them up, ladle and lolly mould, freeze, eat. Raspberries and then there was a general berry mayhem. Black and blue (berries), black (currants), etc. Again, lovely. Here's what's next ... pineapple. And maybe mango. I may need a lot of pineapple as it's a really fibrous fruit. To get lots of juice, I may need a lot of base.

The lollies are so nice I have made the decision that if I ever open some kind of eatery that does pies and mash and chips and other nice things, this would be the free mouth cleanser everyone would get at the end. This would be your last thought and memory of Cafe Friedgold. They're so good. Healthy, fresh and tasty as fuck. Also, it's just blitzed-up old fruit you freeze. It's easy.

Tastes good. Check

Easy to make. Check

Fruit blitzed and frozen. Check

Relatively cheap. Check

Kids love making it. Check

That's it. The five criteria have been checked. Go to it ...

ETON MESS

One of my, and there aren't many, go-to desserts is a kind of Eton Mess. Once you can do an amazing meringue, and a vanilla whipped cream, you can stick whatever you like on top. As I've said loads of times, there's no wrong answer in your kitchen, unless you put say, turkey vindaloo atop the meringue. That would be a wrong answer, that would be a really wrong answer.

Let's do the berries first. Again, you can work out amounts in your own time. You know what we should do first? Have a wee. Wash your hands slow and warm and then cold and soft. Grab a large stainless-steel bowl. Into this add two punnets of blackberries, grab a large punnet of bright, ripe strawberries. What I'd also say is I'm not Noma. Believe it or not. I'm not the Fat Duck, I'm a Fat Fuck. Do I care about using food in season, absolutely I do. Does that mean I can only eat fresh strawberries in June? Yes?! Then eat a dick.

This is the twenty-first century and I can eat strawberries in February if I want. Take a small, very sharp
paring knife and a small chopping board and process
these nice strawberries. Chop in half. Maybe half again?
Depending how big. Add to the blackberries. Now add two
punnets of raspberries. Be gentle, they're ever so soft and
naive, raspberries are not 'big city' fruit, they're afraid of
it, compelled by it, but these are simple hedgerow berries
not used to the complexity and speed of big city life. Sure,
they come with bright pips and a bag full of juice, but soon
they leave macerated and beaten, the bright light dimmed
by a filthy contretemps with a soggy old marrow in an alley
behind a tattoo parlour.

Into the bowl, first zest and then squeeze a lemon. Add
a small spoon of good vanilla extract and two tablespoons
of icing sugar, don't go bonkers, into the berry bowl.
Stir gently and cover with foil and stick it in the fridge.
This can be left in the fridge all day. The berries will sit
and stew and leach out loads of juice and sweetness.
It's incredible.

In terms of making things that can be used in other
things, this is one of those things. You could use this berry
mix on ice cream, on porridge, on cheesecake, as a lolly, in
pancakes. You get the gist.

The other aspect of my Eton Mess, apart from the
meringue and the berries, is the cream the berries lay
upon. It's easy and again something once learned can be
turned to use on lots of other things.

Grab a large tub of whipping cream. It's not the cans of
whipped cream. It's cream that when whipped goes from

a lovely, creamy, liquidy consistency to a nice firm, silky, puffy, rich consistency.

I've used a hand whisk to do this a few times. It takes ages. Balls to that. Use a hand or a stand mixer but watch the cream. It can go from perfect to a buttery-style clod-fest in a very short space of time. So, add a little golden caster sugar and get whisking. It needs to transform from liquid to a nice solid that will, along with the meringue, gently cradle that lovely berry mix. Once it is where you think it should be, taste it. It should be lovely. It shouldn't be super sweet, the berries will be sweet and the meringue, so the cream can be the less-sweet element. It's always easy to add more sugar or lemon zest or orange zest or lime zest or pomelo zest or hell, any zest. I've also flavoured it with vanilla extract. It was lovely. Put your cream in the fridge. Don't leave it for ages though, I prefer the cream to be a little fresh.

Now ... meringue ... I know there are many different kinds, French, Italian, Swiss, and I honestly don't know which one it is I can make. It's the one with eggs and sugar and a drop of lemon juice and you whip it and then cook it in a cool oven for 11 years. Let's do it. Huh? Who's with me!!! HUH??!! LET'S GOOOO! (He grabs a British flag and turns, running blindly into a passing threshing machine.)

Things to remember: everything you use to make the meringue needs to be squeaky clean and free of any grime or grease. I make a point of washing and drying everything I'm going to use. The other thing I need to tell you is this: the egg whites you use have to be COMPLETELY free of ANY yolk.

I ended up losing my shit once and smashed maybe a dozen eggs in fury and spite when the first four or five eggs bled their yolk into the whites. The angrier I got, the worse my egg-cracking got. Worra dick. Luckily, one can now buy just egg whites or just egg yolks at a supermarket. I've never used them though.

One could probably fill up pages and pages of a book trying to explain how to crack eggs and successfully separate the yolks. I generally crack into my hand and let the white glob through my fingers into a dish beneath. This works, here's a further tip ... If you're using six eggs, use a bowl for every egg. That way if you fuck one up, you don't fuck them all up. Yes it's annoying and triggering to use a lot of bowls that need to be immediately washed up but it is definitely easier this way.

The other way I've used is cracking all the eggs into a bowl and then reaching in and pulling all the yolks out. Whatever method you use make sure your eggs are CLOACA FRESH. It makes them easier to separate and they tend to keep their size and air once they've been whisked.

Set the oven low, about 120°C.

6 large egg whites

250g caster sugar

*the hat of a lemon, squeezed so 3 drops of
lemon juice release*

Put your clean, fresh egg whites into clean mixing bowl and turn on and whisk until your whites form beautifully firm, glossy, shiny peaks. Then slowly add the sugar to the mixing bowl, which you've turned to low, one spoonful at a time. Take the lemon hat and squeeze. That's all you need. Once the sugar has dissolved, stop whisking.

Grab a baking tray and line it with greaseproof paper. There's a cool little hack where you use four blobs of the meringue to glue the paper to the baking tray. I like it.

Grab a metal spoon and take big pillowy dollops of the mixture and place them on your baking tray. I aim to give everyone one meringue, they're fairly big. With my spoon I create a dip in the middle of the meringue. This becomes a great bowl to take the cream and the berries later. Put into the oven and cook for 1½ hours. Then turn the oven off and open the door. (I'm getting bored of writing meringue to be honest, so from this point on they'll be called sugar clouds.) Leave the sugar clouds in the now-chilling oven for at least four hours.

Remove your perfect, white, crisp, soft, flaky sugar clouds from the oven and sit them on a wire rack. Edgar and his missus are coming over this Sunday for lunch. I'm going to make Eton Mess as a pud. My time is tight this weekend, so I'm making the sugar clouds on Saturday afternoon. I'll then gently wrap them in greaseproof and store them in an airtight container. They'll be fine.

The first time I tried this dessert I stupidly put the toppings on the sugar clouds and left them in the fridge. By the time I served dessert, the clouds had taken up all the moisture from the cream and the berries and they'd essentially dissolved. Don't make the same mistake I did. Please, I love you too much, babe.

Let's eat. Take your wonderful, crispy, sweet cloud and place it on the plate. Into the middle add a generous dollop of your lovely, whipped cream. On to that, a large spoonful of your berry salad. I like it when it all drips down the outside of the meringue. It looks amazing, it tastes amazing. It was egg whites and sugar, that's it. Try it.

TONY'S

I often hide a Tony's Chocolonely under the frying pans and when I hear Hayley packing up to go to bed, 'Are you off up, darling?' I casually enquire.

'Fuck off Nick!' (She's kidding?)

'Okay darling, see you soon. Be up in a minute, love.'

I listen to the stairgate close behind her and once she's gone, I'm up like a rat up a drainpipe. My ears twitch, seeing if I can hear her coming down for the charger she forgot. I do not want to be caught with a Chocolonely milk caramel and sea salt bar hanging out of my mouth. One of the ADHDs, it's a male voice, so it's either David or Dean says, 'Go into the toilet just in case and turn the taps on so she won't hear the wrapper.' Fuck he's cunning. He's also correct.

I hammer in, lock the door and turn the taps on. I open the bar and I begin to eat it. Greedily, ashamedly. My spirit lifts out of my body slightly.

'What are you fucking doing?', he says. 'Why have you taken your pants and shorts down? You're not even shitting.'

'I just wanted to sell it. You know?'

'No, I don't fucking know. Why are you doing this? You've worked really hard the last few weeks to shift that stone.'

Helen answers, another one of the ADHDs. 'We'ze doing it because without drinks, or drugs or ciggies, or driving fast or flirting or sex, we'ze neeeeeed that dopamine hit somehow.'

I nod. She's right. She is right. Floating me is very disappointed. I release a high-pitched toot of gas. I'm thrilled. It adds to the subterfuge, which also gives us some sweet, sweet dopamine. Floating me is fuming and confused, and rightly so, and can see his side of this.

'You're not even shitting. You're in a toilet eating a massive bar of chocolate, pretending to have diarrhoea so you can stuff your face with chocolate.'

I nod. 'Yes.'

'Why did you fart?'

'Covering my tracks.'

Floating me lols.

'She's up in bed, she's not coming back down, Dickhead, she doesn't give a fuck.'

I shrug, 'I'm a character actor.'

Floating me comes back inside, 'You're a dick.'

All the dopamine has left me, replaced by shame and guilt. Fuck.

Me's liked that feeling. What shall I do now? I hear Anne pipe up, 'Wank into the toilet!' I shouldn't but I do.

This conversation isn't new to my mind. I've probably had it, at points, 50 times a day, about one thing or another. Let me tell you, this shit is tiring and it's deadly and I'm ashamed of it and I know that one day it could totally kill me. Take something which, if abused, can be deadly, in this case food, but it could also be fags, or drinking or raving and getting nutted, or addiction of any kind, and secretly do it because your brain likes it until you die. Who said, 'Find something that you love and let it kill you?' I understand that sentiment so badly. I'm thrilled by the poetic notion of it.

Coming from a family who essentially drank itself to extinction, I get it. Me now, however, will spend each day railing against that, but for years I often heard 'But he was happy ...' Dead but happy. Fuck. A compulsion, an uncontrollable urge killed those people. Killed my mum. The thing about food too is it's super forward facing. It's acceptable. 'He's got such a sweet tooth hasn't he?' Yeah. He also weighs 25 stone and sits in a toilet farting while cramming Snickers into his chubby hole.

Food and I guess one might call it an eating disorder (hooray, another disorder), should be talked a bit more often. It's so com-plicated a thing, it's so triggering. Perhaps then I'll talk about myself, and you can look for the similarities and not the differences.

'Hey, Dickhead ...'

'Hey, be nice.'

'Sorry, Nick?'

'Thanks. Yes, Nick?'

'When you were a little boy, what was it like?'

'Wow. Big question! Honestly, I loved my mum and dad soooooooo muchhhhh. I felt encouraged and protected and we laughed a lot ...'

'Ah, that's nice. I find ...'

'Hang on. I wasn't finished.'

'Sorry. Continue, please.'

'Thank you. We laughed a lot ... at first. Then things started to change, the older I got the less love I felt, the more fear. That felt so confusing to me, I didn't know who to trust any more. Even the love felt wrong, it felt forced, it was for her, not for me. It was a reassurance for her, reassurance that she was still loved by me. Not me by her. The more time they spent in the pub, the less safe I felt. Most Saturdays I was one of five or so kids who would sit under mountains of chairs in the unused banqueting suite of the Dr Johnson. We wouldn't really talk above a whisper. We were afraid of getting caught. If people came in, we'd scuttle ever deeper into the chair mine.'

'Sorry to interrupt, but this sounds terrible. Children shouldn't be brought up in this kind of environment.'

'You're completely right. They shouldn't. What was worse is that we had times that were amazing. Then Mum would drink ... I crawled deeper inside the mine. But I had things I used which made me happy, and I wasn't scared of them and I could not only depend upon them but trust them.'

'Oh, amazing. Friends?'

'Not really friends, no. Food. The only proper friends I had were sweeties and crisps and iced buns and chocolate and biscuits and Fanta and Lucozade. I grew to love these things that aren't parents. I trusted them, they made me happy, they were consistent, fair, we laughed. They also gave my young, undiagnosed brain something called dopamine. I LOVED it. If you can't love me properly, then I'll get what I need emotionally from these four iced buns. I'll be parented by Iced Buns. This worked fine until I needed buns to sign a consent form allowing me to go to France with the fifth year.'

'Man, that's pretty sad. Kids are supposed to look to and trust their parents for guidance, love and support while growing up.'

'Yep. When I look at pictures of myself as a little boy do you know what happens?'

'No.'

'I cry. Pictures of me as a child make me cry. They don't make me happy or long for those times when we spent long hot summers laughing and running in the sea. They make me cry.'

'Why?'

'Because I look at that innocent little boy and I'm sad and ashamed that I couldn't stop him from experiencing all that pain. His innocent smile and eyes that begged to be loved would eventually dull and the joy inside of him would leach out and gather unseen like a puddle of melted lolly on a boiling floor. (But that would take 47 years.) Imagine allowing a child to go through that.'

I did that. Even though it took me a whole life to understand what had happened/what was happening to me, I did it, I made a change, and I did it just in time. I'm now strong and brave and honest with myself. (MOST OF THE TIME.) Life is about trying to be happy, I think. Trying to accept who I am and looking in a mirror and believing that I'm pretty fucking cool and nice and good and talented, and a person people want to be with and love. I'm worthy of that love. I am. So fucking worthy. This is a truth I have to believe. Every day I have to believe it. It's fucking difficult.

Sometimes, most days, my self-hatred and lack of self-esteem wants to hide and eat four Snickers. Sometimes I allow it. I shouldn't, but I do. I have no choice sometimes. This is the last vestige of that frightened child who huddled in that dark, stifling chair mine with those other children of alcoholics and addicts, themselves fragile and broken as fuck. Not just the kids, but the parents we hid from.

But on the whole, and eventually, I have been saved! I now

have a chance to try and break that long, long, long chain. The chain of fear and misery and drink and drugs and violence and death. When I look at pictures of my children, I don't see shame and pain and fear. I see laughter, and pride and hope, and probably for the first time in my life I allow myself to be happy and to be proud and to be hopeful.

After 50 years of trying, I've finally made amends to that frightened, awkward little boy. I hold out my arms and he runs to me, smiling. Innocence and trust restored. I hold him so tightly and I can smell my mum and dad on his cardigan. I cry. Why did I have to lose everything to get here? Surely there's a better, easier way? When I look at that little boy though, I don't see fear any more, it's gone. It's been replaced by hope, and it's then I know, that finally, his story will have a happy ending!